HARRAP

FRENCH
OFFICE I.T.
DICTIONARY

HARRAP

FRENCH OFFICE I.T. DICTIONARY

English-French
French-English

HARRAP

First published in Great Britain in 1999
by Chambers Harrap Publishers Ltd
7 Hopetoun Crescent
Edinburgh EH7 4AY

ISBN 0245 606653 (UK)
ISBN 0245 503870 (France)

Graphics produced using Corel Draw clip art

Dépôt légal : juillet 1999

Designed and typeset by Chambers Harrap Publishers Ltd, Edinburgh
Printed and bound in France by IFC

Editor/Rédacteur
José A. Gálvez

with/avec
Rose Rociola
Georges Pilard

Publishing manager/Direction éditoriale
Patrick White

Specialist consultants/Consultants spécialistes

Bob Norton
Head of Information Services,
Institute of Management, Corby, UK

Cathy Smith
Systems Controller,
Institute of Management, Corby, UK

Trademarks

Marques déposées

Contents

Table des Matières

Preface

Computers have come to dominate both business and everyday life. This new dictionary, developed and expanded from the databases used for the **Harrap French Business Dictionary**, covers the whole range of IT terminology, from business and personal computing to the Internet, desktop publishing (DTP), and telecommunications.

The Internet is becoming more and more a part of modern business life, as e-commerce revolutionizes the way business is conducted at the end of the 20th and beginning of the 21st century. Users of this dictionary will find the key terms in the dictionary itself, and will also find practical help in a guide to the business implications of the Internet in the supplement. This section also includes advice on writing e-mails.

Although English is the dominant language of IT, as it is in the business world itself, new laws in France have sought to introduce official French terms for certain anglicisms. While in practice they are not widely used, we have included these terms in this book with the label JO to indicate that they are attested in the Journal Officiel (a government publication listing new laws).

Because so many new terms are being invented in this area, it is difficult to know with certainty which terms and which usages will become accepted. Advice on usage is given in panels, with the heading FAQ, at certain entries.

Illustrative panels have been included throughout the text on: the journey of an e-mail, printers, the Internet, networks, a multimedia computer, the French and English keyboards and the Windows and Macintosh desktops, in order to give the reader further context.

Préface

Les ordinateurs sont désormais omniprésents dans notre environnement quotidien ainsi que dans le monde des affaires. Ce nouvel ouvrage, conçu à partir des bases de données utilisées lors de l'élaboration du **Harrap's Business**, couvre toute la terminologie informatique depuis l'informatique individuelle et l'informatique de gestion jusqu'à l'Internet, la microédition et les télécommunications.

Aujourd'hui, l'Internet tient une place de plus en plus importante dans le monde des affaires, avec notamment l'avènement de l'ère du commerce électronique. Les principaux termes liés à l'Internet figurent dans le corps de cet ouvrage. Dans un supplément pratique l'utilisateur trouvera de nombreuses informations sur les conséquences du développement du commerce électronique sur le monde des affaires. Ce supplément comprend également des conseils pour la rédaction de courriers électroniques.

Bien que l'anglais soit la langue dominante dans le secteur de l'informatique ainsi que dans le monde des affaires, les pouvoirs publics français tentent de promouvoir l'usage de termes français. Bien que certains de ces termes français ne soient pas toujours employés fréquemment, nous avons décidé de les faire figurer dans cet ouvrage accompagnés de l'étiquette JO de façon à indiquer qu'ils ont été adoptés par le Journal Officiel.

L'informatique génère de très nombreux néologismes et il est impossible de savoir avec certitude quels termes et expressions subsisteront à long terme. Dans ce dictionnaire, certaines entrées sont accompagnées d'encadrés précédés de la mention FAQ, où figurent des conseils d'usage.

De façon à donner de plus amples informations à l'utilisateur, des tableaux illustrés sur les sujets suivants ont été intégrés au texte: le trajet d'un courrier électronique, les imprimantes, l'Internet, les réseaux, l'ordinateur multimédia, les claviers français et anglais et les bureaux Windows et Mac.

Labels

Indications d'Usage

gloss [introduces an explanation]	=	glose [introduit une explication]
cultural equivalent [introduces a translation which has a roughly equivalent status in the target language]	≃	équivalent culturel [introduit une traduction dont les connotations dans la langue cible sont comparables]
abbreviation	*abbr, abrév*	abréviation
adjective	*adj*	adjectif
adverb	*adv*	adverbe
North American English	*Am*	anglais américain
British English	*Br*	anglais britannique
Canadian French	*Can*	canadianisme
desktop publishing	*DTP*	publication assistée par ordinateur
feminine	*f*	féminin
familiar	*Fam*	familier
Internet-related term	*Internet*	vocabulaire de l'Internet
official French term [recorded in the Journal Officiel]	JO	terme figurant dans le Journal Officiel
masculine and feminine noun [same form for both genders, eg **keyboarder** claviste *mf*]	*mf*	nom masculin ou féminin [formes identiques]
masculine and feminine noun [different form in the feminine, eg **user** utilisateur(trice) *m,f*]	*m,f*	nom masculin ou féminin [formes différentes]
noun	*n*	nom
feminine noun	*nf*	nom féminin

feminine plural noun	*nfpl*	nom féminin pluriel
masculine noun	*nm*	nom masculin
masculine and feminine noun [same form for both genders, eg **analyste** *nmf*]	*nmf*	nom masculin ou féminin [formes identiques]
masculine and feminine noun [different form in the feminine, eg **technicien, -enne** *nm,f*]	*nm,f*	nom masculin ou féminin [formes différentes]
masculine plural noun	*nmpl*	nom masculin pluriel
desktop publishing	*PAO*	publication assistée par ordinateur
plural	*pl*	pluriel
telecommunications	*Tel, Tél*	télécommunications
intransitive verb	*vi*	verbe intransitif
reflexive verb	*vpr*	verbe pronominal
transitive verb	*vt*	verbe transitif
inseparable transitive verb [phrasal verb where the verb and the adverb or preposition cannot be separated, eg **go into**; he **went into** the program]	*vt insep*	verbe transitif à particule inséparable [par exemple : **go into** (aller dans); he **went into the program** (il est allé dans le programme)]
separable transitive verb [phrasal verb where the verb and the adverb or preposition can be separated, eg **shut down**; he **shut** the computer **down** *or* he **shut down** the computer]	*vt sep*	verbe transitif à particule séparable [par exemple : **shut down** (éteindre); he **shut** the computer **down** *ou* he **shut down** the computer (il a éteint l'ordinateur)]

English-French
Anglais-Français

abandon vt (file, routine) abandonner

abort **1** n (of program) suspension f d'exécution, abandon m
2 vt (program) suspendre l'exécution de, abandonner

.ac Internet = abréviation désignant les universités et les sites éducatifs dans les adresses électroniques britanniques

accelerator n accélérateur m
◊ **accelerator board** carte f accélératrice
◊ **accelerator card** carte f accélératrice

accent n accent m

Acceptable Use Policy n Internet = code de conduite défini par un fournisseur d'accès à l'Internet

access **1** n accès m; Internet **up to 56K access** accès jusqu'à 56 Kbit/s; **access denied** (DOS message) accès refusé
2 vt (data) accéder à; **can you access last year's figures?** est-ce que tu as accès aux chiffres de l'année dernière?
◊ **access authorization** autorisation f d'accès

◊ **access code** code m d'accès
◊ **access control** contrôle m d'accès
◊ **access level** (in network) niveau m d'accès
◊ **access number** (to ISP) numéro m d'accès
◊ **access privileges** droits mpl d'accès
◊ Internet **access provider** fournisseur m d'accès
◊ **access speed** vitesse f d'accès
◊ **access time** temps m d'accès

account n (with Internet service provider) abonnement m (**with** auprès de); **to set up an account with sb** s'abonner auprès de qn

accounting program n logiciel m de comptabilité

acknowledgement n accusé m de réception

activate vt activer

active adj
◊ **active desktop** bureau m actif
◊ **active file** fichier m actif
◊ **active matrix screen** écran m à matrice active
◊ **active program** programme m en cours d'exécution

◇ *active window* fenêtre *f* active *ou* activée

acute accent *n* accent *m* aigu

adapter *n* adaptateur *m*

◇ *adapter card* carte-adaptateur *f*

add-on *n* produit *m* supplémentaire, extension *f*

address 1 *n* adresse *f* 2 *vt* adresser, accéder à

◇ *address book (in e-mail program)* carnet *m* d'adresses

◇ *address bus* bus *m* d'adresse

◇ *address file* fichier *m* d'adresses

ADP *n (abbr* **automatic data processing***)* traitement *m* automatique des données

advertising banner *n (on web page)* bandeau *m* publicitaire

agent *n (software)* logiciel *m* client

AI *n (abbr* **artificial intelligence***)* IA *f*

alert box *n* message *m* d'alerte

ALGOL *n (abbr* **Algorithmic Oriented Language***)* algol *m*

algorithm *n* algorithme *m*

alias *n* (a)*(in e-mail)* alias *m* (b) *(on desktop)* alias *m*

aliasing *n DTP* aliassage *m*, crénelage *m*

align *vt (characters, graphics)* aligner, cadrer

alignment *n (of characters, graphics)* alignement *m*, cadrage *m*

allocate *vt (memory)* attribuer

allocation *n (of memory)* attribution *f*

alphanumeric *adj* alphanumérique

◇ *alphanumeric characters* caractères *mpl* alphanumériques

◇ *alphanumeric code* code *m* alphanumérique

◇ *alphanumeric keypad* clavier *m* alphanumérique

alphasort 1 *n* tri *m* alphabétique; **to do an alphasort on sth** trier qch par ordre alphabétique 2 *vt* trier par ordre alphabétique

alpha version *n (of program)* version *f* alpha

alt *n* **e acute is alt 130** pour e accent aigu, il faut taper Alt 130

◇ *alt key* touche *f* Alt

.alt *Internet (abbr* **alternative***) (in newsgroups)* = abréviation désignant des forums de discussion qui peuvent porter sur toutes sortes de sujets

ALU *n (abbr* **Arithmetic Logic Unit***)* unité *f* arithmétique et logique

ampersand *n* esperluette *f*

analog *adj* analogique

anchor *n Internet* ancre *f*

AND *n* **AND circuit/element** circuit *m*/élément *m* ET

animate *vt* animer

animated GIF *n Internet* (fichier *m*) GIF *m* animé

animation n animation f

anonymous adj Internet
◊ **anonymous FTP** protocole m de transfert anonyme
◊ **anonymous remailer** service m de courrier électronique anonyme

ANSI n (abbr **American National Standards Institute**) = association f américaine de normalisation

answering adj
◊ **answering machine** répondeur m (téléphonique)
◊ **answering service** service m de répondeur téléphonique

answer mode n (of modem) mode m réponse

answerphone n Tel répondeur m (téléphonique)

anti-aliasing n DTP anti-aliassage m, anti-crénelage m

anti-glare adj
◊ **anti-glare filter** or **screen** écran m antireflet

antivirus n antivirus m
◊ **antivirus program** programme m antivirus
◊ **antivirus check** vérification f antivirale

apostrophe n apostrophe m

append vt (list, document) joindre (**to** à); (to database) ajouter; **to append a document to a file** annexer ou joindre un document à un dossier

Apple menu n menu m pomme

applet n Internet appelette f, ⌊JO⌋ appliquette f

application n application f
◊ **application program** programme m d'application
◊ **application software** logiciel m d'application

Archie n Internet Archie m

architecture n architecture f

archive 1 n archive f; **archive (copy)** copie f archivée **2** vt archiver
◊ Internet **archive site** site m FTP

area code n Am Tel indicatif m

array n matrice f, tableau m

arrow key n touche f fléchée, touche de direction

article n Internet (in newsgroups) article m

artificial intelligence n intelligence f artificielle

artwork n DTP illustrations fpl, iconographie f

ascending adj
◊ **ascending order** ordre m croissant
◊ **ascending sort** tri m en ordre croissant

ASCII n (abbr **American Standard Code for Information Interchange**) ASCII m
◊ **ASCII art** art m ASCII
◊ **ASCII code** code m ASCII
◊ **ASCII file** fichier m ASCII
◊ **ASCII text** texte m ASCII
◊ **ASCII value** valeur f ASCII

assembler n (program) assembleur m

assembly language n langage m assembleur ou d'assemblage; **assembly lan-**

guage program programme *m* en assembleur

assistant *n (program)* assistant *m*

asterisk *n* astérisque *m*

asynchronous *adj* asynchrone

◊ *asynchronous transfer mode* commutation *f* temporelle asynchrone

at *prep (in e-mail address)* arrobas, a commercial; **"gwilson at transex, dot, co, dot, uk"** "gwilson, arrobas, transex, point, co, point, uk"

◊ *at sign* arrobas *m*

ATM *n (abbr* **asynchronous transfer mode)** ATM *m*, commutation *f* temporelle asynchrone

attach *vt (file)* joindre (**to** à); **to attach a file to an e-mail message** joindre un fichier à un message électronique; **please find attached...** veuillez trouver ci-joint…

attachment *n (of e-mail)* fichier *m* joint

AUP *n Internet (abbr* **Acceptable Use Policy)** = code de conduite défini par un fournisseur d'accès à l'Internet

authentication *n* authentification *f*

authenticate *vt* authentifier

authoring *n*

◊ *authoring language* langage *m* auteur

◊ *authoring software* logiciel *m* auteur

◊ *authoring tool* outil *m* auteur

autocorrect *vt* corriger automatiquement

autoexec.bat *n* fichier *m* autoexec.bat

autoflow *n* passage *m* automatique à la ligne

automatic *adj* automatique

◊ *automatic data processing* traitement *m* automatique des données

◊ *automatic dialling* composition *f* automatique

◊ *automatic feed* avance *f* automatique

◊ *automatic pagination* séparation *f* automatique des pages

automation *n* automatisation *f*

autosave 1 *n* sauvegarde *f* automatique
2 *vt* sauvegarder automatiquement

autostart *n* démarrage *m* automatique

available *adj* disponible; **available on CD-ROM** existe en CD-ROM *ou* JO cédérom; **available on DVD, available in DVD format** existe en DVD; **available for the Mac/PC** disponible pour Mac/PC; **available to download from our web site** peut être téléchargé à partir de notre site web

◊ *available memory* mémoire *f* disponible

avatar *n Internet* avatar *m*

AZERTY keyboard *n* clavier *m* AZERTY

▸ **back up** 1 *vt sep (data, file)* sauvegarder
2 *vi* sauvegarder

backbone *n* Internet *(of network)* (épine *f*) dorsale *f*, réseau *m* national d'interconnexion

background *n* arrière-plan *m*; **the program works in the background** le programme est exécuté en arrière-plan

◇ *background job* tâche *f* de fond

◇ *background (mode) printing* impression *f* en arrière-plan

◇ *background task* tâche *f* d'arrière-plan

backlight *n (of screen)* rétro-éclairage *m*

backlit *adj (screen)* rétro-éclairé(e)

backslash *n* barre *f* oblique inversée

backspace *n* retour *m* arrière

◇ *backspace key* touche *f* de retour arrière

backup *n* (a) *(support)* soutien *m*, appui *m*

(b) *(of data)* sauvegarde *f*; **to do the backup** faire la sauvegarde; **the backup has failed** la sauvegarde a échoué

◇ *backup copy* copie *f* de sauvegarde

◇ *backup device* unité *f* de sauvegarde

◇ *backup file* fichier *m* de sauvegarde

◇ *backward search* recherche *f* arrière

◇ *backup service* service *m* après-vente

◇ *backup system (for doing the backup)* système *m* de sauvegarde; *(auxiliary system)* système de secours

backward-compatible *adj* compatible avec les versions antérieures

bad *adj (in error messages)*

◇ *bad command* commande *f* erronée

◇ *bad file name* nom *m* de fichier erroné

◇ *bad sector* secteur *m* endommagé;

bandwidth *n* largeur *f* de bande

banner *n (on web page)* bandeau *m*

bar *n (menu bar)* barre *f*

◇ *bar chart* graphique *m* en barres

◇ **bar code** code *m* à barres, code-barres *m*

baseline *n DTP* ligne *f* de base

BASIC *n* Basic *m*

batch *n*
◇ **batch file** fichier *m* séquentiel
◇ **batch processing** traitement *m* par lots

battery *n* pile *f*

baud *n* baud *m*; **at 28,800 baud** à (une vitesse de) 28 800 bauds
◇ **baud rate** débit *m* en bauds

bay *n (for disk drive)* baie *f*

BBS *n Internet (abbr* **bulletin board system)** BBS *m*, serveur *m* télématique, *Can* babillard *m*

Bcc *Internet (abbr* **blind carbon copy)** copie *f* cachée

benchmark *n* référence *f*

Bernoulli ® *n*
◇ **Bernoulli disk** cartouche *f* Bernoulli ®
◇ **Bernoulli drive** lecteur *m* Bernoulli ®

beta version *n (of program)* version *f* bêta

Bézier curve *n DTP* courbe *f* de Bézier

bidirectional *adj* bidirectionnel(elle)

Big Blue *n (IBM)* Big Blue *m*, = surnom de la société IBM

binary *adj* binaire
◇ **binary code** code *m* binaire
◇ **binary file** fichier *m* binaire
◇ **binary search** recherche *f* binaire *ou* dichotomique

BinHex *(abbr* **Binary Hexadecimal)** BinHex

BIOS *n (abbr* **Basic Input/ Output System)** BIOS *m*

bisync, bisynchronous *adj* bisynchrone

bit *n* bit *m*; **bits per second** bits par seconde
◇ **bit command** commande *f* binaire
◇ **bit rate** débit *m* binaire

bitmap **1** *n* bitmap *m*
2 *adj (image, font)* bitmap, en mode point

bit-mapped *adj (image, font)* bitmap, en mode point

blank *adj (disk, screen)* vide; *(unformatted)* vierge; **blank unformatted disk** disquette *f* vierge

bleed *n DTP* fond *m* perdu

blend *n DTP* dégradé *m*

blink rate *n (of cursor)* vitesse *f* de clignotement

block **1** *n (of text)* bloc *m*
2 *vt (text)* sélectionner; **to block text** sélectionner du texte
◇ **block copy** copie *f* de bloc

blocking software *n Internet* logiciel *m* de filtrage

board *n (in PC)* carte *f*; *(in mainframe)* panneau *m*; **on board** installé(e)

body *n (of letter, document, e-mail)* corps *m*

bold **1** *n* gras *m*; **in bold** en gras
2 *adj* gras; **bold face** *or* **type** caractères *mpl* gras

bookmark **1** *n (for web page)* signet *m*

2 *vt* créer un signet sur; **don't forget to bookmark this page** n'oublie pas de créer un signet sur cette page

◇ *bookmark list* liste *f* de signets

Boolean *adj* booléen

◇ *Boolean operator* opérateur *m* booléen

◇ *Boolean search* recherche *f* booléenne

boot *vt* (computer) amorcer, faire démarrer

◇ *boot disk* disquette *f* de démarrage

◇ *boot sector* secteur *m* d'initialisation

▸ **boot up 1** *vt sep* (computer) amorcer, faire démarrer
2 *vi* (of computer) s'amorcer, démarrer; (of person) démarrer

border *n* (of paragraph, cell) bordure *f*

bounce *Internet* **1** *n* **bounce(d) message** = message électronique non délivré revenu à l'expéditeur
2 *vi* revenir à l'expéditeur

box *n* (for graphic) cadre *m*

bpi *n* (abbr **bits per inch**) bpp

bps *n* (abbr **bits per second**) bps

bracket *n* (square) crochet *m*; (round) parenthèse *m*; (curly) accolade *f*; **angle brackets** signes *mpl* inférieur et supérieur, signes '‹' et '›'

branch *n* (of network) branchement *m*

break *n*

◇ *break character* caractère *m* d'interruption

◇ *break key* touche *f* d'interruption

bridge *n* (in network) pont *m*

briefcase *n* (in Windows) porte-documents *m*

broadcast message *n* message *m* système

browse 1 *vi* se promener
2 *vt* **to browse the Net/Web** naviguer sur l'Internet/le Web

◇ *browse mode* mode *m* survol

▸ **browse through** *vt insep* se promener dans, survoler

browser *n* Internet navigateur *m*, logiciel *m* de navigation

browsing *n* Internet navigation *f*; **fast/secure browsing** navigation rapide/sécurisée

bubble-jet printer *n* imprimante *f* à bulles

bubble memory *n* mémoire *f* à bulles

buffer *n* tampon *m*, mémoire *f* intermédiaire

◇ *buffer memory* mémoire tampon

bug *n* bogue *m*

bug-free *adj* (program) exempt d'erreurs *ou* de bogues

bug-ridden *adj* (program) bogué(e)

built-in *adj* (incorporated) incorporé(e)

built-to-order *adj* construit(e) sur mesure

bulk *n* (of information) volume *m*, masse *f*

bullet *n (symbol)* puce *f*

bulleted list *n* liste *f* à puces

bulletin board service *n* *Internet* serveur *m* télématique, *Can* babillard *m*

bundle 1 *n* plus *m* produit **2** *vt (software)* **it comes bundled with over £2000 worth of software** il est livré avec des logiciels pour une valeur de 2000 livres

burn *vt (CD-ROM)* graver

bus *n* bus *m*

◇ *bus board* carte *f* bus

◇ *bus controller* contrôleur *m* de bus

business *n*

◇ *business computing* informatique *f* de gestion

◇ *business graphics* graphiques *mpl* de gestion

◇ *business intelligence system* réactique *f*

busy *adj (telephone)* occupé(e); **the line or number is busy** la ligne est occupée; **I got the busy signal** ça sonnait occupé

button *n (on mouse)* bouton *m*; *(for menu selection)* case *f*

byte *n* **(eight-bit) byte** octet *m*

C++ *n (programming language)* C++ *m*

cable modem *n* modem-câble *m*

cabling *n* câbles *mpl*

cache 1 *n* **cache (memory)** antémémoire *f*, mémoire-cache *f*
2 *vt (data)* mettre en antémémoire *ou* en mémoire-cache

CAD *n (abbr* **computer-assisted design)** CAO *f*

CAD/CAM *n (abbr* **computer-assisted design/computer-assisted manufacture)** CFAO *f*

CAE *n (abbr* **computer-aided engineering)** ingénierie *f* assistée par ordinateur

CAL *n (abbr* **computer-aided learning)** EAO *m*

calculator *n* calculatrice *f*

call 1 *n* appel; **to take a call** prendre un appel; **to receive a call** recevoir un appel; **there was a call for you** il y a eu un appel pour vous; *Am* **to call collect** appeler en PCV, faire un appel en PCV
2 *vt* **to call sb** appeler qn

◊ *call connection* établissement *m* d'appel

◊ *call forwarding service* dispositif *m* de redirection d'appel

◊ *call waiting service* signal *m* d'appel

▶**call up** *vt sep* **(a)** *(on telephone)* téléphoner à, appeler **(b)** *(help screen, file)* rappeler

CAM *n (abbr* **computer-assisted manufacture)** FAO *f*

camera-ready copy *n DTP* copie *f* prête pour la reproduction

cancel 1 *vt* annuler; **cancel button** case *f* 'annuler'
2 *vi* s'annuler; **press 'esc' to cancel** appuyez sur 'Echap' pour annuler; **cancel entry** *(command)* annulation d'entrée

caps *npl (abbr* **capital letters)** majuscules *fpl*

◊ *caps lock* blocage *m* majuscule

◊ *caps lock key* touche *f* de verrouillage des majuscules

capture 1 *n (of data)* saisie *f*
2 *vt (data)* saisir

card *n* **(a)** *(with printed information)* carte *f* **(b)** *(circuit board)* carte *f*

◇ *card index* jeu *m* de fiches

◇ *card slot* emplacement *m* pour carte

caret *n* accent *m* circonflexe, symbole *m* '∧'

carpal tunnel syndrome *n* syndrome *m* du canal carpien

carriage return *n* retour *m* de chariot

carrier *n (for signal)* opérateur *m*

◇ *carrier (detect) signal* signal *m* de détection de por-teuse

cartridge *n (disk)* cartouche *f*; **ink/toner cartridge** cartouche d'encre /de toner

cascading menu *n* menu *m* en cascade

CASE *n (abbr* **computer-aided software engineering**) ingénie-rie *f* des systèmes assistée par ordinateur

case-insensitive *adj* qui ne distingue pas les majuscules des minuscules; **this URL is case-insensitive** le respect de majuscules et des minuscules n'est pas nécessaire pour cette URL

case-sensitive *adj* qui dis-tingue les majuscules des mi-nuscules; **this e-mail address is case-sensitive** il faut respecter les majuscules et les minus-cules dans cette adresse élec-tronique

CASM *n (abbr* **computer-aided sales and marketing**) vente *f* et marketing assistés par ordina-teur

cathode ray tube *n* tube *m* à rayons cathodiques, tube ca-thodique

◇ *cathode ray tube monitor* moniteur *m* à tube catho-dique

Cc *Internet (abbr* **carbon copy**) CC

CD-I, CDI *n (abbr* **compact disc interactive**) CD-I *m*

CD-R *n* **(a)** *(abbr* **compact disc recorder**) graveur *m* de disque compact **(b)** *(abbr* **compact disc recordable**) CD-R *m*

CD-ROM *n (abbr* **compact disc-read only memory**) CD-ROM *m*, JO cédérom *m*

◇ *CD-ROM burner* graveur *m* de CD-ROM

◇ *CD-ROM drive* lecteur *m* de CD-ROM, lecteur de disque optique

◇ *CD-ROM newspaper* journal *m* sur CD-ROM

◇ *CD-ROM reader* lecteur de CD-ROM

CD-RW *n (abbr* **compact disc rewritable**) CD *m* réinscriptible

cedilla *n* (symbole *m*) cédille *f*

cell *n (on spreadsheet)* cellule *f*

cellphone, cellular phone *n* téléphone *m* cellulaire

central processing unit *n* unité *f* centrale (de traite-ment), processeur *m* central

centre, *Am* **center** *vt (text)* centrer

CGA *n (abbr* **colour graphics adaptor**) CGA *m*

CGI *n* **(a)** *Internet (abbr* **common gateway interface**) CGI *f*, interface *f* commune de passerelle (**b**) (*abbr* **computer-generated images**) images *fpl* créées par ordinateur

channel *n* (*of communication, data flow, for IRC*) canal *m*

character *n* caractère *m*; **characters per inch** caractères par pouce; **characters per second** caractères par seconde

◇ *character code* code *m* de caractère

◇ *character generator* générateur *m* de caractères

◇ *character insert* insertion *f* de caractère

◇ *character recognition* reconnaissance *f* de caractères

◇ *character set* jeu *m* de caractères

◇ *character smoothing* lissage *m* de caractères

◇ *character space* espace *m*

◇ *character spacing* espacement *m* des caractères

chart *n* graphique *m*

chat *Internet* **1** *n* messagerie *f* de dialogue en direct, bavardage *m*, chat *m*
2 *vi* bavarder, chatter

◇ *chat room* site *m* de bavardage, salon *m*, *Can* bavardoir *m*

◇ *chat software* logiciel *m* de bavardage

check box *n* case *f* de pointage *ou* d'option

chip *n* puce *f*

chooser *n* sélecteur *m*

circuit *n* circuit *m*

◇ *circuit board* plaquette *f*,

carte *f* de circuits

circuitry *n* circuits *mpl*

circumflex accent *n* accent *m* circonflexe

clear *vt* **to clear the screen** vider l'écran

click 1 *n* clic *m*
2 *vt* cliquer
3 *vi* cliquer (**on** sur); **to click and drag** cliquer et glisser

clickable image *n Internet* image *f* cliquable

◇ *clickable image map* image *f* cliquable

client *n* (*part of network*) (ordinateur *m*) client *m*

client-server *adj*

◇ *client-server database* base *f* de données client-serveur

◇ *client-server model* modèle *m* client-serveur

clip art *n* clipart *m*

clipboard *n* (*for cut text*) presse-papiers *m*, bloc-notes *m*

clock *n* horloge *f*

◇ *clock speed* fréquence *f* d'horloge

◇ *clock speed doubler* doubleur *m* de fréquence (d'horloge)

clone *n* clone *m*

close box *n* case *f* de fermeture

closing tag *n* balise *f* de fin

cluster *n* cluster *m*, bloc *m*; (*of terminals*) grappe *f*

CMYK *DTP* (*abbr* **cyan, magenta, yellow, black**) CMJN

.co *Internet* = abréviation désignant les entreprises commerciales dans les adresses électroniques britanniques

co-ax(ial) cable *n* câble *m* coaxial

coated paper *n* papier *m* couché

COBOL *n* (*abbr* **Common Business-Oriented Language**) cobol *m*

code 1 *n* code *m*; *Tel* (**dialling**) **code** indicatif *f*
  2 *vt* coder

coded *adj* codé(e)

coding *n* (*providing codes*) codage *m*; (*system of codes*) codes *mpl*

◇ **coding error** erreur *f* de codage

cold *adj*

◇ **cold boot** démarrage *m* à froid

◇ **cold start** démarrage *m* à froid

collapse *vt* (*subdirectories*) réduire

collate *vt* (*documents, data*) rassembler

collect call *n* *Am Tel* communication *f* en PCV

colon *n* (*punctuation mark*) deux-points *m*

colour, *Am* **color** *n*

◇ **colour display** affichage *m* couleur

◇ **colour graphics** graphisme *m* en couleur

◇ **colour monitor** moniteur *m* couleur

◇ **colour printer** imprimante *f* couleur

◇ **colour printing** impression *f* couleur

◇ *DTP* **colour separation** séparation *f* des couleurs

column *n* (*in table, spreadsheet*) colonne *f*

◇ **column graph** histogramme *m*

.com *Internet* = abréviation désignant les entreprises commerciales dans les adresses électroniques

▸ **come out** *vi* (*exit*) sortir; **to come out of a document** sortir d'un document

comma *n* virgule *f*

command *n* commande *f*; (*from menu options*) article *m*

◇ **command code** code *m* de commande

◇ **command file** fichier *m* de commande

◇ **command key** touche *f* Commande

◇ **command language** langage *m* de commande

◇ **command line** ligne *f* de commande

◇ **command sequence** séquence *f* de commandes

common gateway interface *n* *Internet* interface *f* commune de passerelle

comms *n*

◇ **comms package** logiciel *m* de communication

◇ **comms port** port *m* de communication

communication *n*

◇ *communication network* réseau *m* de communication

◇ *communications software* logiciel *m* de communication

.comp *Internet* (*abbr* **computers**) *(in newsgroups)* = abréviation désignant les forums de discussion qui ont pour thème l'informatique

compact *vt (file)* comprimer

compacting *n (of file)* compression *f*

compatibility *n* compatibilité *f*

compatible *adj* compatible (**with** avec); **IBM-compatible** compatible IBM

◇ *compatible computer* ordinateur *m* compatible

compile *vt* compiler

compiler *n* compilateur *m*

compliant *adj* conforme (**with** à); **year 2000 compliant** conforme à l'an 2000

component *n* composant *m*

compose *vt (e-mail)* rédiger

compress *vt (file)* comprimer

compressed *adj (file)* comprimé

compression *n (of file)* compression *f*

computer *n* ordinateur *m*; **to put sth on computer** mettre qch sur ordinateur

◇ *computer analyst* analyste *mf*

◇ *computer animation* animation *f*

◇ *computer dating* = rencontres sélectionnées par

ordinateur

◇ *computer department* service *m* informatique

◇ *computer engineer* ingénieur-informaticien(enne) *m,f*

◇ *computer equipment* équipement *m* informatique

◇ *computer expert* informaticien(enne) *m,f*

◇ *computer game* jeu *m* informatique

◇ *Fam computer geek* allumé(e) *m,f* de l'informatique

◇ *computer graphics* graphiques *mpl*; *(technique)* infographie *f*

◇ *computer literacy* connaissances *fpl* informatiques

◇ *computer network* réseau *m* d'ordinateurs, réseau *m* informatique

◇ *computer operator* opérateur(trice) *m,f* de saisie

◇ *computer printout* sortie *f* papier

◇ *computer program* programme *m* informatique

◇ *computer programmer* programmeur(euse) *m,f*

◇ *computer programming* programmation *f*

◇ *computer science* informatique *f*

◇ *computer scientist* informaticien(enne) *m,f*

◇ *computer simulation* simulation *f* sur ordinateur

◇ *computer system* système *m* informatique

◇ *computer technician* technicien(enne) *m,f* en informatique

◇ *computer virus* virus *m* informatique

computer-aided,
computer-assisted *adj*
assisté(e) par ordinateur

◇ **computer-aided audit tech-**
niques techniques *fpl* d'audit
assistées par ordinateur

◇ **computer-aided design** conception *f* assistée par ordinateur

◇ **computer-aided engineer-**
ing ingénierie *f* assistée par
ordinateur

◇ **computer-aided learning**
enseignement *m* assisté par
ordinateur

◇ **computer-aided manufac-**
turing fabrication *f* assistée
par ordinateur

◇ **computer-aided presenta-**
tion présentation *f* assistée
par ordinateur

◇ **computer-aided sales and**
marketing vente *f* et marketing assistés par ordinateur

◇ **computer-aided translation**
traduction *f* assistée par
ordinateur

computer-based training
n enseignement *m* assisté par
ordinateur

computer-generated *adj*
généré(e) par ordinateur

computer-integrated
manufacturing *n* fabrication *f* intégrée par ordinateur

computerization *n* (of
organization, records etc) informatisation *f*

computerize *vt* (organization, filing system etc) informatiser

computerized *adj* (system,

records, information) informa-
tisé(e)

computer-literate *adj* to be
computer-literate avoir des connaissances en informatique

computing *n* informatique *f*;
she works in computing elle
travaille dans l'informatique

◇ **computing centre** centre *m*
de calcul

concatenated *adj* concaténé

concatenation *n* enchaînement *m*

conference call *n* téléconférence *f*

config.sys *n* fichier *m* con-
fig.sys

configurable *adj* configurable

configuration *n* configuration *f*, paramétrage *m*

configure *vt* configurer, paramétrer

connect 1 *n* connexion *f*
2 *vt* (component, cable) connecter (**to** à)
3 *vi* (**a**) (of component, cable) se
raccorder (**to** à) (**b**) (to Internet) se connecter (**to** à)

◇ **connect time** durée *f* (d'établissement) de la connexion

connection *n* (**a**) (of two
components) connexion *f*,
liaison *f*
(**b**) Tel communication *f*; **we**
had a very bad connection la
communication était très
mauvaise
(**c**) (to Internet) connexion *f*;
to establish a connection se

connecter; **to have a fast/slow connection** disposer d'une connexion rapide/lente

◇ *connection kit* kit *m* d'accès ou de connexion

connectivity *n* connectivité *f*

connector *n* connecteur *m*

console *n* pupitre *m* de commande

consumables *npl* consommables *mpl*

content provider *n* Internet fournisseur *m* de contenu

context-sensitive help *n* aide *f* contextuelle

continuous *adj*

◇ *continuous mode* mode *m* continu

◇ *continuous paper or stationery* papier *m* (en) continu

control *n* (key) touche *f* contrôle

◇ *control key* touche *f* contrôle

◇ *control character* caractère *m* de contrôle

◇ *control panel* panneau *m* de configuration

controller *n* contrôleur *m*

conventional memory *n* mémoire *f* conventionnelle

conversational *adj* (mode) dialogue

conversion *n* conversion *f*

◇ *conversion program* programme *m* de conversion

◇ *conversion software* logiciel *m* de conversion

convert *vt* (file, document) convertir (**to/into** en)

cookie *n* Internet cookie *m*,

cafteur *m*, Can témoin *m*

◇ *cookie file* fichier *m* de cookies ou Can témoins

co-processor *n* coprocesseur *m*

copy *n* (of document, letter) copie *f*; **to make a copy of sth** faire une copie de qch

2 *vt* (**a**) (document, letter) copier; (photocopy) photocopier

(**b**) (computer file, text) copier; **to copy sth to disk** copier qch sur disquette; **to copy and paste sth** faire un copier-coller sur qch

3 *vi* **to copy and paste** faire un copier-coller

◇ *copy and paste* copier-coller *m*

◇ *copy block* copie *f* de bloc

◇ *copy disk* disquette *f* de copie

◇ *copy protection* protection *f* contre la copie

copy-protect *vt* protéger contre la copie

copy-protected *adj* protégé(e) contre la copie

cordless *adj* sans fil

◇ *cordless mouse* souris *f* sans fil

◇ *cordless telephone* téléphone *m* sans fil

corrupt **1** *adj* (disk, file) altéré(e)

2 *vt* (disk, file) altérer

corruption *n* (of disk, file) altération *f*

counter *n* (on web page) compteur *m*

courseware *n* didacticiel *m*

cover page, cover sheet n *(of fax)* page f de garde

cpi *(abbr* **characters per inch)** cpp

cps *(abbr* **characters per second)** cps

CPU n *(abbr* **central processing unit)** unité f centrale

crack 1 n *(program)* = programme permettant de forcer un système informatique
2 vt craquer, déplomber

cracker n pirate m informatique

crash 1 n *(of computer)* panne f
2 vi *(of computer network, system)* sauter; *(of computer)* tomber en panne

crawler n Internet araignée f

CRC n DTP *(abbr* **camera-ready copy)** copie f prête pour la reproduction

crop vt DTP *(graphic)* rogner
◇ **crop mark** trait m de coupe

cross-platform adj multiplateforme

cross-post vt Internet faire un envoi multiple de

crossposting n Internet envoi m multiple

cross-reference n renvoi m

cross-refer n renvoyer

crunch vt *(numbers, data)* traiter à grande vitesse

CRT n *(abbr* **cathode ray tube)** tube m à rayons cathodiques, tube cathodique

cryptographic key n Internet clé f de chiffrement

curly quotes n guillemets mpl anglais

cursor n curseur m; **move the cursor to the right/left** déplacez le curseur vers la droite/gauche; **the word where the cursor is** le mot pointé
◇ **cursor blink rate** vitesse f de clignotement du curseur
◇ **cursor control** contrôle m du curseur
◇ **cursor key** touche f de curseur
◇ **cursor movement** déplacement m du curseur
◇ **cursor position** position f du curseur

CU-See Me n Internet logiciel m de vidéoconférence CU-See Me

customizable adj *(menu, program)* qui peut être personnalisé(e)

customize vt *(menu, program)* personnaliser

cut 1 vt couper; **to cut and paste sth** faire un couper-coller sur qch; **cut sheet feed** alimentation f feuille à feuille; **cut sheet feeder** dispositif m d'alimentation feuille à feuille
2 vi **to cut and paste** faire un couper-coller

cyber n cyber m

cyberbanking n transactions fpl bancaires en ligne

cybercafe n cybercafé m

cybercrime n cybercrime m

cyberculture *n* cyberculture *f*

cybernaut *n* cybernaute *m*

cybernetic *adj* cybernétique

cybernetics *n* cybernétique *f*

cyberpunk *n* cyberpunk *mf*

cybersex *n* cybersexe *m*

cyberspace *n* cyberespace *m*; **in cyberspace** dans le cyberespace

cycle *n* cycle *m*

daisy-chain *vt* connecter en boucle

daisy-chaining *n* connexion *f* en boucle

daisy-wheel printer *n* imprimante *f* à marguerite

dash *n* *(symbol)* tiret *m*; *DTP* **em-dash** tiret cadratin; *DTP* **en-dash** tiret demi-cadratin

DAT *n* *(abbr* **digital audio tape)** DAT *m*, bande *f* audionumérique

◇ **DAT cartridge** cartouche *f* DAT

◇ **DAT drive** lecteur *m* DAT, lecteur de bande audionumérique

data *n* données *fpl*; **an item of data** une information; **to collect data on sb/sth** recueillir des informations sur qn/qch

◇ **data acquisition** collecte *f* ou saisie *f* de données

◇ **data analysis** analyse *f* de données

◇ **data bank** banque *f* de données

◇ **data bus** bus *m* de données

◇ **data capture** saisie *f* de données

◇ **data carrier** support *m* de données

◇ **data collection** recueil *m* ou collecte de données

◇ **data communications** communication *f* ou transmission *f* de données, télématique *f*

◇ **data compression** compression *f* de données

◇ **data encryption** cryptage *m* ou codage *m* de données

◇ **data entry** entrée *f* de données

◇ **data exchange** échange *m* de données

◇ **data link** voie *f* de transmission de données

◇ **data loss** perte *f* de données

◇ **data management** gestion *f* de données

◇ **data path** chemin *m* d'accès aux données

◇ **data privacy** confidentialité *f* des données ou de l'information

◇ **data processing** informatique *f*, traitement *m* de l'information ou des données

◇ **data processor** machine *f* de traitement de l'information, processeur *m* de données

◇ **data protection** protection *f* de l'information

◇ **data recovery** récupération *f* de données

◇ *data security* sécurité *f* des données

◇ *data set* ensemble *m* de données

◇ *data storage* stockage *m* de données

◇ *data stream* flot *m* de données

◇ *data transfer* transfert *m* ou transmission *f* de données

database *n* base *f* de données; **to enter sth into a database** mettre qch dans une base de données

◇ *database integration* intégration *f* de bases de données

◇ *database management* gestion *f* de bases de données

◇ *database management system* système *m* de gestion de bases de données

datacomms *n* communication *f* ou transmission *f* de données, télématique *f*

◇ *datacomms software* logiciel *m* de communication

dbase *n* (*abbr* **database**) BD *f*

DBMS *n* (*abbr* **database management system**) SGBD *m*

DD *n* (*abbr* **double density**) double densité *f*

DDE *n* (*abbr* **dynamic data exchange**) DDE *m*

debug *vt* (*program*) déboguer

debugger *n* (*program*) débogueur *m*

debugging *n* (*of program*) débogage *m*

decode *vt* décoder; **the file is automatically decoded when it is received** le fichier est décodé automatiquement à la réception

decoder *n* décodeur *m*

decoding *n* décodage *m*

decompress *vt* (*file*) décompresser

decrypt *vt* déchiffrer

decryption *n* déchiffrement *m*

dedicated *adj* (*terminal*) spécialisé(e), dédié(e)

◇ *dedicated line* ligne *f* spécialisée

◇ *dedicated word processor* machine *f* servant uniquement au traitement de texte

default 1 *n* défaut *m*; **by default** par défaut
2 *vi* **to default to sth** sélectionner qch par défaut

◇ *default drive* lecteur *m* par défaut

◇ *default font* police *f* par défaut

◇ *default setting* configuration *f* par défaut

◇ *default value* valeur *f* par défaut

define *vt* (*value*) déclarer

defragment *vt* défragmenter

defragmentation *n* défragmentation *f*

deinstall *vt* désinstaller

deinstallation *n* désinstallation *f*

deinstaller *n* désinstallateur *m*

del key *n* touche *f* d'effacement

The Windows desktop
Le bureau Windows

See also «Le bureau Mac» on the French-English side

Voir aussi «Le bureau Mac» dans la partie français-anglais

applications
applications

Start button
bouton Démarrer

Quick launch bar
Barre de lancement rapide

Recycle bin
Corbeille

drives
unités

window
fenêtre

menu bar
barre de menu

close box
case de fermeture

MS Office bar
barre du MS Office

desktop
bureau

folders
dossiers

Taskbar
Barre des tâches

All Users

Select an icon to view its description.

Address C:\WINDOWS\All Users

File Edit View Go Favorites Help

Back   Up   Cut   Copy   Paste   Undo

Desktop   Start Menu

2 object(s)   My Computer

Programs   10:25

Microsoft Outlook   Control Panel   Recycle Bin

MS-DOS   Internet Explorer   Workstation

Network   Windows_95 (C:)   Windows Explorer

New Folder   CD-ROM Disc (D:)   3½ Floppy (A:)

Start   Eudora Light - [In]   MS-DOS Prompt   All Users

delete 1 *vt* effacer, supprimer 2 *vi* effacer

◇ *delete (key)* touche *f* d'effacement

deletion *n* effacement *m*

delimit *vt (field)* délimiter

delimiter *n (of field)* délimiteur *m*

demo *n (abbr* demonstration) démonstration *f*; **we have received a demo of the new software** nous avons reçu une version de démonstration du nouveau logiciel

◇ *demo disk* disquette *f* de démonstration *ou* d'évaluation

◇ *demo version* version *f* de démonstration *ou* d'évaluation

demodulator *n* démodulateur *m*

descending *adj*

◇ *descending order* ordre *m* décroissant

◇ *descending sort* tri *m* en ordre décroissant

descriptor *n* descripteur *m*

deselect *vt* désactiver

desk accessory *n* accessoire *m* de bureau

desktop *n (screen area)* bureau *m*; **you will find the icon on your desktop** l'icône se trouve sur le bureau

◇ *desktop calculator* calculatrice *f* de bureau

◇ *desktop computer or PC* ordinateur *m* de bureau *ou* de table

◇ *desktop publishing* publication *f* assistée par ordinateur, microédition *f*

◇ *desktop publishing operator* opérateur(trice) *m,f* de publication assistée par ordinateur

◇ *desktop publishing package* logiciel *m* de mise en page

destination *n* destination *f*

◇ *destination disk (hard disk)* disque *m*; *(floppy disk)* disquette *f* de destination

◇ *destination drive* lecteur *m* de destination

device *n (peripheral)* unité *f* périphérique, périphérique *m*

◇ *device driver* pilote *m* de périphérique

diagnostic *adj*

◇ *diagnostic disk* disquette *f* de diagnostic

◇ *diagnostic program* programme *m* de diagnostic

dialogue, *Am* **dialog** *n* dialogue *m*

◇ *dialogue box* boîte *f* de dialogue

◇ *dialogue mode* mode *m* dialogue

dial *vt (telephone number)* composer; **to dial a number** composer *or* faire un numéro; **the number you have dialled has not been recognized** il n'y a pas d'abonné au numéro que vous avez demandé

◇ *Am* **dial code** indicatif *m* (téléphonique)

◇ *Br* **dialling** or *Am* **dial tone** tonalité *f* d'appel

dialling code *n Tel* indicatif *m* (téléphonique)

dial-up *n Internet*

◇ *dial-up access* accès *m* commuté

◇ *dial-up account* compte *m* d'accès par ligne commutée

Dictaphone *n* Dictaphone *m*, appareil *m* à dicter

digest *n Internet (of newsgroup, mailing list)* synthèse *f*

digicash *n* monnaie *f* électronique

digit *n* chiffre *m*

digital *adj* numérique

◇ *digital analog(ue) converter* convertisseur *m* analogique numérique

◇ *digital audio tape* cassette *f* numérique

◇ *digital camera* appareil photo *m* numérique

◇ *digital display* affichage *m* numérique

◇ *digital readout* affichage digital

◇ *digital signal* signal *m* numérique

◇ *digital signature* signature *f* numérique

◇ *digital video* vidéo *f* numérique

◇ *digital versatile disk* disque *m* vidéo numérique

◇ *digital video camera* caméra *f* vidéo numérique

digitally *adv* numériquement

digitize *vt (data)* convertir en numérique, numériser

digitizer *n* numériseur *m*

dingbat *n* symbole *m* Dingbat

DIP switch *n* interrupteur *m* DIP

dir *n (abbr* **directory***)* répertoire *m*

direct line *n Tel* ligne *f* directe

directory *n* (a) *(of files)* répertoire *m* (b) *(of telephone numbers)* annuaire *m*

◇ *directory structure* structure *f* arborescente, arborescence, structure du répertoire

◇ *Br directory enquiries* renseignements *mpl*

disable *vt (option)* désactiver

disabled *adj (option)* désactivéc(e)

disconnect *vt (machine)* débrayer, désembrayer

discussion *n Internet*

◇ *discussion group* forum *m* de discussion

◇ *discussion list* liste *f* de diffusion

disk *n* disque *m*; *(floppy)* disquette *f*; **to get sth on disk** enregistrer qch sur disque/disquette

◇ *disk access time* temps *m* d'accès disque

◇ *disk box* boîte *f* à disquettes

◇ *disk capacity* capacité *f* de disque/disquette

◇ *disk controller* contrôleur *m* de disque

◇ *disk controller card* carte *f* contrôleur de disque

◇ *disk drive* unité *f* ou lecteur *m* de disque/disquette

◇ *disk file* fichier *m* disque

◇ *disk fragmentation* fragmentation *f* de disque

◇ *disk mailer* pochette *f* d'expédition de disquette

⋄ *disk memory* mémoire *f* à disque

⋄ *disk operating system* système *m* d'exploitation de disques

⋄ *disk space* espace *m* disque

diskette *n* disquette *f*; **on diskette** sur disquette

⋄ *diskette box* boîte *f* à disquettes

display 1 *n (screen)* écran *m*; *(screen, display unit)* afficheur *m*; *(text appearing)* affichage *m* 2 *vt* afficher, visualiser

⋄ *display area* surface *f* ou zone *f* d'affichage

⋄ *display card* carte *f* d'affichage

⋄ *display unit* unité *f* de visualisation

distribution list *n Internet* liste *f* de diffusion *ou* distribution

DNS *n Internet (abbr* **Domain Name System)** système *m* de nom de domaine, DNS

docking station *n (for notebook)* station *f* d'accueil

document *n* document *m*

⋄ *document file* fichier *m* document

⋄ *document reader* lecteur *m* de documents

documentation *n* documentation *f*

dollar sign *n* symbole *m* du dollar

domain *n Internet* domaine *m*

⋄ *domain name* nom *m* de domaine

⋄ *Domain Name System* système *m* de nom de domaine

dongle *n* fiche *f* gigogne, clé *f* gigogne

DOS *n (abbr* **disk operating system)** DOS *m*

⋄ *DOS command* commande *f* du DOS

⋄ *DOS prompt* indicatif *m* (du) DOS, invite *f* du DOS

dot *n* point *m*

dot-matrix printer *n* imprimante *f* matricielle

dotted quad *n Internet* adresse *f* IP

double-click 1 *n* double-clic *m* 2 *vt* cliquer deux fois sur, double-cliquer 3 *vi* cliquer deux fois, faire un double-clic (**on** sur)

double-density disk *n* disquette *f* (à) double densité

double-speed CD-ROM *n* lecteur *m* de CD-ROM *ou* JO cédérom double vitesse

down *adj (not working)* **to be down** *(of computer)* être planté; **the network is down/has gone down** le réseau est planté/a planté; **the lines are down** les lignes sont en dérangement

⋄ *down arrow* flèche *f* vers le bas

⋄ *down arrow key* touche *f* de déplacement vers le bas

download 1 *n* téléchargement *m* 2 *vt* télécharger 3 *vi* effectuer un téléchargement; **graphic files take a long**

time to download le télé-
chargement de fichiers graphiques est très lent

downloadable *adj* téléchargeable

◇ *downloadable font* police *f*
téléchargeable

downtime *n (of machine)*
période *f* de non-productivité

downward-compatible
adj compatible vers le bas

DP *n (abbr* **data processing)**
traitement *m* des données,
informatique *f*

dpi *(abbr* **dots per inch)** dpi, ppp

draft *n*

◇ *draft mode* mode *m* rapide *ou*
brouillon, mode d'impression
rapide, mode liste rapide

◇ *draft printout* brouillon *m*

◇ *draft quality (of printout)*
qualité *f* brouillon *ou* listing,
qualité liste rapide

◇ *draft quality printing* impression *f* en qualité brouillon

◇ *draft version* version *f* brouillon

drag 1 *vt (icon)* faire glisser
2 *vi* **to drag and drop** faire un
glisser-lâcher

drag-and-drop *n* glisser-
lâcher *m*

DRAM *n (abbr* **dynamic random
access memory)** DRAM *f*

draw program *n* logiciel *m* de
dessin

drive *n (for disk)* lecteur *m*,
unité *f*; **drive a:/b:** unité de
disque a:/b:

driver *n (software)* programme
m de gestion, pilote *m*, gestionnaire *m* (de périphérique)

drop *vt (icon)* lâcher

drop cap *n DTP* lettrine *f*

drop-down menu *n* menu
m déroulant

drum scanner *n DTP* scanner *m ou* scanneur *m* à tambour

DTP *n (abbr* **desktop publishing)**
PAO *f*

◇ *DTP operator* opérateur
(trice) *m,f* de PAO

◇ *DTP software* logiciel *m* de
PAO

dump 1 *n* cliché *m* mémoire;
(memory) dump vidage *m* (de)
mémoire; **(screen) dump** capture *f* d'écran
2 *vt (memory)* vider

DVD *n (abbr* **Digital Video Disk,
Digital Versatile Disk)** DVD *m*,
disque *m* vidéo numérique

dynamic *adj* dynamique

◇ *dynamic data exchange*
échange *m* dynamique de
données

◇ *dynamic HTML* HTML *m*
dynamique

◇ *dynamic RAM* mémoire *f*
RAM dynamique

e-business *n* commerce *m* électronique

e-cash *n* argent *m* électronique, argent virtuel, e-cash *m*

e-commerce *n* commerce *m* électronique

◊ *e-commerce site* site *m* marchand

edit 1 *n (menu heading)* Édition *f*
2 *vt (text)* modifier, éditer

◊ *edit keys* touches *fpl* de modification

◊ *edit mode* mode *m* Édition

editing *n* édition *f*

editor *n (software)* éditeur *m* (de texte)

.edu *Internet* = abréviation désignant les universités et les sites éducatifs dans les adresses électroniques

efficiency *n (of machine)* rendement *m*

efficient *adj (machine)* à haut rendement

EFT *n (abbr* **electronic funds transfer)** transfert *m* de fonds électronique

EFTPOS *n (abbr* **electronic funds transfer at point of sale)** transfert *m* de fonds électronique sur point de vente

EGA *n (abbr* **enhanced graphics adaptor)** EGA *m*

electronic 1 *adj* électronique
2 *nm* **electronics** électronique *f*

◊ *electronic banking* transactions *fpl* bancaires électroniques, bancatique *f*

◊ *electronic cash* argent *m* ou monnaie *f* électronique

◊ *electronic catalogue* catalogue *m* en ligne

◊ *electronic commerce* commerce *m* électronique

◊ *electronic computer* calculateur *m* électronique

◊ *electronic data interchange* échange *m* de données informatisé

◊ *electronic data processing* traitement *m* électronique de l'information

◊ *electronic funds transfer* transfert *m* de fonds électronique

◊ *electronic funds transfer at point of sale* transfert *m* de fonds électronique au point de vente

◊ *electronic journal* journal *m* en ligne

◊ *electronic mail* courrier *m* électronique

The Journey of an E-mail

1 Your computer
Your journey through the Internet begins in your computer. An **e-mail client** is used to write and send e-mail messages. The completed message travels between your computer and your **Internet Service Provider's** server via a telephone line through a **modem** or an **ISDN** connection.

2 Your Internet Service Provider (ISP)
Your ISP acts as an intermediary between you and the Internet. When a message arrives at your ISP, a **router** redirects it to one of the Internet **backbones** - the real information highway.

3 On the Internet
Data travels on the Net from router to router. Each time your message arrives at a router, it will be redirected to another router, getting closer each time to its destination. The longer the distance, the higher the number of routers through which your message may have to go.

4 The end of the trip
At the end of the process, your message arrives at your recipient's ISP router where it can be collected. Depending on the traffic conditions on the Net, and the distance travelled, the whole trip can take anything from a few seconds to several hours.

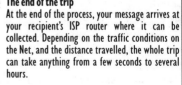

◇ *electronic mailbox* boîte *f* à ou aux lettres électronique

◇ *electronic mall* galeries *fpl* électroniques

◇ *electronic money* argent *m* électronique, argent virtuel

◇ *electronic office* bureau *m* informatisé

◇ *electronic point of sale* point *m* de vente électronique

◇ *electronic publishing* édition *f* électronique, ⟦JO⟧ éditique *f*

◇ *electronic shopping* téléachat *m*, achats *mpl* en ligne

e-mail 1 *n* courrier *m* électronique, ⟦JO⟧ mél *m*, *Can* courriel *m*; **to contact sb by e-mail** contacter qn par courrier électronique; **to send sth by e-mail** envoyer qch par courrier électronique

2 *vt (person)* envoyer un courrier électronique à; *(document)* envoyer par courrier électronique; **e-mail us at...** envoyez-nous vos messages à l'adresse suivante...

◇ *e-mail account* compte *m* de courrier électronique

◇ *e-mail address* adresse *f* électronique

◇ *e-mail client* client *m* de messagerie électronique

◇ *e-mail program* programme *m* de courrier électronique

◇ *e-mail software* logiciel *m* de courrier électronique

e-money *n* argent *m* électronique, argent virtuel

emoticon *n Internet* émoticon *m*, *Can* binette *f*

empty *vt (wastebasket, recycle bin)* vider

emulate *vt* simuler, émuler

emulation *n* émulation *f*

enable *vt (option)* activer

enabled *adj (option)* activé(e)

encode *vt* encoder

encoder *n* encodeur *m*

encoding *n* codage *m*, encodage *m*

encrypt *vt* crypter, chiffrer

encryption *n* chiffrement *m*

◇ *Internet* **encryption key** clé *f* de chiffrement

end *n*

◇ *end key* touche *f* fin

◇ *end user* utilisateur,-trice *m,f* final

endnote *n* note *f* de fin de document, NfD *f*

engaged *adj Br (telephone)* occupé(e); **the line** or **number is engaged** la ligne est occupée; **I got the engaged tone** or **signal** ça sonnait occupé

enhance *vt (image, quality)* améliorer

enhanced *adj (image, quality)* amélioré(e)

◇ *enhanced keyboard* clavier *m* étendu

enhancement *n (of image, quality)* amélioration *f*

enter 1 *n (key)* touche *f* (d')entrée

2 *vt (data)* entrer, introduire

◇ *enter key* touche (d')entrée

entry *n* (**a**) *(of data)* entrée *f* (**b**) **an entry level computer** un ordinateur d'entrée de gamme

environment n environnement m

EPS n (abbr encapsulated Post-Script) EPS

equal sign, equals sign n signe m égal

erasable adj effaçable

erase vt effacer

ergonomic adj ergonomique

ergonomics n ergonomie f

error message n message m d'erreur

esc key n touche f d'échappement, touche f Échap

escape 1 n (key) touche f d'échappement m
2 vi sortir
◇ **escape key** touche f d'échappement, touche f Échap

Ethernet ® n Ethernet ® m

exclamation mark, Am **exclamation point** n point m d'exclamation

ex-directory adj Br (telephone number) sur la liste rouge

executable file n fichier m exécutable

execute vt (command, program) exécuter

execution n (of command, program) exécution f

exit 1 n sortie f
2 vt (program, session) sortir de
3 vi sortir

expand vt (memory) étendre

expandable adj (memory) extensible; **4MB expandable to 64MB** 4 Mo extensible à 64 Mo

expanded adj
◇ **expanded keyboard** clavier m étendu
◇ **expanded memory** mémoire f paginée

expansion n (of memory) extension f
◇ **expansion board** carte f d'extension
◇ **expansion card** carte f d'extension
◇ **expansion slot** emplacement m pour carte d'extension

expert system n système m expert

export vt (file) exporter (**to** vers)

extended adj
◇ **extended keyboard** clavier m étendu
◇ **extended memory** mémoire f étendue

extension n (a) (for telephone) poste m; **extension 35** poste 35 (b) (of file) extension f
◇ **extension number** numéro m de poste

external adj externe
◇ **external device** dispositif m externe, périphérique m
◇ **external drive** unité f (de disque) externe
◇ **external modem** modem m externe

extract vt (zipped file) décompresser

ezine n magazine m électronique

facing pages *n DTP* pages *fpl* en regard

FAQ *n Internet* (*abbr* **frequently asked questions**) FAQ

◊ **FAQ file** fichier *m* FAQ

fatal error *n* erreur *f* fatale

favorites *npl Internet* favoris *mpl*

fax 1 *n* (*machine*) fax *m*, télécopieur *m*; (*message*) fax, télécopie *f*; **to send sb a fax** envoyer un fax à qn

2 *vt* (*message, document*) faxer, envoyer par fax; (*person*) envoyer un fax à

◊ **fax card** carte *f* fax

◊ **fax modem** modem-fax *m*

◊ **fax number** numéro *m* de fax

feed *vt* (*paper*) faire avancer, alimenter; **to feed data into a computer** entrer des données dans un ordinateur

feeder *n* (*for printer, scanner, photocopier*) chargeur *m*

fibre optic, *Am* **fiber optic** *adj* (*cable*) fibre *m* optique

field *n* (*in database*) champ *m*

file *n* fichier *m*

◊ **file compression** compression *f* de fichiers

◊ **file conversion** conversion *f* de fichiers

◊ **file (name) extension** extension *f* du nom de fichier

◊ **file format** format *m* de fichier

◊ **file management** gestion *f ou* tenue *f* des fichiers

◊ **file management system** système *m* de gestion de fichiers

◊ **file manager** gestionnaire *m* des fichiers

◊ **file name** nom *m* de fichier

◊ **file protection** protection *f* de fichiers

◊ **file server** serveur *m* de fichiers

◊ **file sharing** partage *m* de fichiers

◊ **file structure** structure *f* de fichiers

◊ **file transfer** transfert *m* de fichiers

◊ *Internet* **file transfer protocol** protocole *m* de transfert de fichiers

◊ *Internet* **file viewer** visualiseur *m*

filter *n* filtre *m*

filtering software *n Internet* logiciel *m* de filtrage

find *vt* **to find and replace** trouver et remplacer

⋄ *find command* commande *f* de recherche

finger *n Internet* = utilitaire de l'Internet permettant d'obtenir des informations sur un utilisateur du réseau

firewall *n Internet* mur *m* coupe-feu, garde-barrière *f*

firmware *n* firmware *m*, JO microprogramme *m*

fixed disk *n* disque *m* fixe

flag *vt (highlight)* sélectionner

flame *Internet* **1** *n* message *m* injurieux
2 *vt* descendre en flammes
3 *vi* rédiger un message injurieux

⋄ *flame war* guerre *f* d'insultes

flamer *n Internet* auteur *m* d'un message injurieux

flaming *n Internet* envoi *m* de messages injurieux

flatbed scanner *n* scanner *m* *ou* scanneur *m* à plat

flat *adj*

⋄ *flat file* fichier *m* de données non structurées

⋄ *flat monitor* écran *m* plat

⋄ *flat panel display* moniteur *m* à écran plat

⋄ *flat screen* écran *m* plat

flat-rate *adj*

⋄ *flat-rate connection (to Internet)* connexion *f* à tarif forfaitaire

⋄ *flat-rate monthly charge (to ISP)* forfait *m* mensuel

floating *adj*

⋄ *floating point* virgule *f* flottante

⋄ *floating point processor* coprocesseur *m* arithmétique

⋄ *floating window* fenêtre *f* flottante

floppy *n* disquette *f*; **on floppy** sur disquette

⋄ *floppy disk* disquette *f*

⋄ *floppy (disk) drive* unité *f* de disquettes

flowchart *n* ordinogramme *m*

folder *n (directory)* répertoire *m*, dossier *m*

follow-up message *n Internet (in newsgroups)* suivi *m* d'article

font *n* police *f*, fonte *f*

footer *n DTP* bas *m* de page

footnote *n* note *f* de bas de page

foreground *n* premier plan *m*

form *n Internet* formulaire *m*

form feed *n* avancement *m* du papier

format **1** *n (of page)* format *m*
2 *vt (disk)* formater; *(page, text)* mettre en forme, formater

formatting *n (of disk)* formatage *m*; *(of page, text)* mise *f* en forme, formatage

FORTRAN *n* FORTRAN *m*

forum *n Internet* forum *m* (de discussion)

forward **1** *vt (e-mail message)* faire suivre
2 *adj*

⋄ *forward search* recherche *f* avant

⋄ *forward slash* barre *f* oblique

four-colour *n DTP*

◇ *four-colour process* quadrichromie *f*

◇ *four-colour separation* séparation *f* quadrichromique

FPU *n* (*abbr* **floating-point unit**)
FPU *f*, coprocesseur *m* arithmétique

FQDN *n Internet* (*abbr* **Fully
Qualified Domain Name**) nom
m de domaine complet

fragmentation *n (of hard
disk)* fragmentation *f*

frame *n Internet (of web page)*
cadre *m*

franking machine *n* machine *f* à affranchir les lettres

freebie *n* produit *m* gratuit

Freefone® *n Br Tel* appel *m*
gratuit, ≃ numéro *m* vert; **call
Freefone 400** ≃ appelez le
numéro vert 400

freenet *n Internet* libertel *m*

freeware *n* logiciel *m* (du
domaine) public, gratuiciel *m*

freeze *vi (of screen, computer)*
être bloqué(e)

friction feed *n* avancement
m par friction

front-end *n* interface *f*

◇ *front-end computer* ordinateur *m* frontal

frozen *adj (screen)* bloqué(e)

FTP *Internet* **1** *n* (*abbr* **File
Transfer Protocol**) protocole *m*
de transfert de fichiers
2 *vt* télécharger par FTP

◇ *FTP server* serveur *m* FTP

◇ *FTP site* site *m* FTP

full *adj*

◇ *Tel full duplex* bidirectionnel
simultané, full duplex

◇ *full Internet access* accès *m*
à tout l'Internet

◇ *full page display* écran *m*
pleine page

◇ *full stop* point *m* final

function key *n* touche *f* de
fonction

gateway *n Internet* passerelle *f* (de connexion)

GB *n* (*abbr* **gigabyte**) Go *m*

geek *n Fam* allumé(e) *m,f*

generate *vt* créer, générer

GIF *n* (*abbr* **Graphics Interchange Format**) GIF *m*

gigabyte *n* gigaoctet *m*

glare *n*
◇ **glare filter** filtre *m* anti-reflet
◇ **glare screen** écran *m* anti-reflet

global search *n* recherche *f* globale

▸ **go down** *vi* (*of computer network*) planter

▸ **go into** *vt insep* (*file, program*) aller dans; **to go into a file** aller dans un fichier

gopher *n Internet* (serveur *m*) gopher *m*

.gov = abréviation désignant les sites gouvernementaux dans les adresses électroniques

grammar checker *n* correcteur *m* grammatical

graphical user interface *n* interface *f* utilisateur graphique

graphic interface *n* interface *f* graphique

graphics *npl* (*images*) graphismes *mpl*, graphiques *mpl*
◇ **graphics accelerator** accélérateur *m* graphique
◇ **graphics accelerator card** carte *f* accélérateur graphique
◇ **graphics card** carte *f* graphique
◇ **graphics display** affichage *m* graphique
◇ **graphics mode** mode *m* graphique
◇ **graphics package** grapheur *m*
◇ **graphics software** logiciel *m* graphique
◇ **graphics spreadsheet** tableur *m* de graphiques
◇ **graphics tablet** tablette *f* graphique

grave accent *n* accent *m* grave

Greek text *n DTP* texte *m* simulé

grey, *Am* **gray** *n* **shades of grey** niveaux *mpl* de gris

greyscale *Am* **grayscale** *n* niveau *m* de gris
◇ **greyscale monitor** moniteur *m* de niveau de gris

grid *n* grille *f*

gridline *n* quadrillage *m*

group dialling *n* numérotation *f* groupée

guarantee **1** *n (document, promise)* garantie *f*; **this computer has a five-year guarantee** cet ordinateur est garanti cinq ans; **under guarantee** sous garantie; **extended guarantee** extension *f* de la garantie; **on-site guarantee** garantie sur site; **return-to-base guarantee** garantie retour atelier

2 *vt (product, appliance)* garantir; **this computer is guaranteed for five years** cet ordinateur est garanti cinq ans

◇ *guarantee certificate* certificat *m* de garantie

guest *n* invité(e) *m,f*

guestbook *n (of web page)* livre *m* d'or

GUI *n (abbr* **graphical user interface***)* interface *f* utilisateur graphique

hack *vi* to hack into sth *(system, file)* s'introduire en fraude dans qch

hacker *n* (**a**) *(illegal user)* pirate *m* informatique (**b**) *(expert user)* bidouilleur(euse) *m,f*

half-tone *n* DTP demi-teinte *f*

hand-held *adj*
◇ *hand-held computer* ordinateur *m* de poche
◇ *hand-held scanner* scanner *m ou* scanneur *m* à main

handle *n* DTP poignée *f*

handshake *n* dialogue *m* d'établissement de liaison

hanging *adj*
◇ DTP *hanging indent* présentation *f* en sommaire
◇ DTP *hanging paragraph* paragraphe *m* en sommaire
▸ **hang up** *vi (on telephone)* raccrocher

hard *adj*
◇ *hard copy* copie *f* sur papier, sortie *f* papier
◇ *hard disk* disque *m* dur
◇ *hard drive* unité *f* de disque dur
◇ DTP *hard hyphen* césure *f* imposée, trait *m* d'union imposé

◇ *hard return* saut *m* de ligne manuel
◇ *hard space* espace *m* insécable

hardware *n* matériel *m*, hardware *m*
◇ *hardware problem* problème *m* de matériel

hash *n* symbole *m* '#', dièse *f*

HD (**a**) *(abbr hard disk)* DD (**b**) *(abbr high density)* HD

header *n* en-tête *m*

heading *n* titre *m*

help *n*
◇ *help button* case *f* d'aide
◇ *help desk (for computing queries)* service *m* d'assistance
◇ *help key* touche *f* d'aide
◇ *help line* service *m* d'assistance téléphonique
◇ *help menu* menu *m* d'aide
◇ *help screen* écran *m* d'aide

helper application *n* = utilitaire d'un logiciel de navigation capable de reconnaître et de gérer les différents formats de fichiers

Hex *adj (abbr hexadecimal)* hexadécimal(e)

hexadecimal *adj* hexadécimal(e)

hidden file n fichier m caché

hide vt (files, records) cacher

hierarchical adj hiérarchique

◇ *hierarchical file system* système m de fichiers hiérarchique

◇ *hierarchical menu* menu m hiérarchique

high-density adj (disk, graphics, printing) haute densité

high-end adj haut de gamme

highlight vt (text) sélectionner

high memory n mémoire f haute

hi-res adj Fam (abbr **high-resolution**) (à) haute résolution

high-resolution adj (à) haute résolution

high-speed adj à gran vitesse

history list n Internet historique m

hit 1 n Internet (visit to web site) hit m, accès m; (in search) occurrence f; **this web site counted 20,000 hits last week** ce site Web a été consulté 20 000 fois la semaine dernière 2 vt (key) appuyer sur

hold 1 n **to put sb on hold** (on telephone) mettre qn en attente; **to be on hold** être en attente

2 vt (a) (store) stocker; **how much data will this disk hold?** quelle quantité de données cette disquette peut-elle stocker?; **the commands are held in the memory** les instructions sont gardées en mémoire

(b) (on telephone) **hold the line please** ne quittez pas, s'il vous plaît; **hold all my calls** ne me passez aucun appel

3 vi (on telephone) attendre; **the line's** Br **engaged** or Am **busy, will you hold?** la ligne est occupée, voulez-vous patienter?

▸ **hold down** vt sep (key, mouse button) maintenir enfoncé(e)

home n (beginning of document) début m

◇ *home banking* banque f à domicile

◇ *home computer* ordinateur m familial

◇ *home key* touche f début

◇ Internet *home page* (initial page) page f d'accueil; (start page in browser) page f d'accueil; (personal page) page f personnelle

◇ *home shopping* téléachat m

horizontal orientation n (format m) paysage m

host 1 n host (computer) ordinateur-serveur m

2 vt Internet (web site) héberger

hosting n Internet (of web site) hébergement m

hot adj

◇ *hot key* touche f personnalisée

◇ Tel *hot line* numéro m d'urgence

◇ *hot line support* assistance f technique téléphonique, hot-line f

◇ *hot swap* (of devices) remplacement *m* à chaud

hotlist *n Internet* liste *f* de signets

HTML *n Internet* (*abbr* **Hyper Text Markup Language**) HTML

◇ *HTML editor* éditeur *m* HTML

HTTP *n Internet* (*abbr* **HyperText Transfer Protocol**) protocole *m* HTTP

◇ *HTTP server* serveur *m* Web

hub *n* hub *m*, concentrateur *m*

hybrid *adj (CD-ROM)* hybride

hyperlink *n Internet* hyperlien *m*

hypermedia *n* hypermédia *m*

hypertext *n* hypertexte *m*

◇ *hypertext link* lien *m* hypertexte

hyphen *n* trait *m* d'union

hyphenation *n* césure *f*

IAP *n Internet (abbr* **Internet Access Provider)** fournisseur *m* d'accès à l'Internet

IBM-compatible *adj* compatible IBM

icon *n* icône *f*
◊ *icon bar* barre *f* d'icônes
◊ *icon editor* éditeur *m* d'icônes

ID *n (abbr* **identification)** numéro *m* d'identification

IDE *n (abbr* **integrated drive electronics)** IDE

identifier *n* identificateur *m*

idle *adj (machine)* arrêté(e)

illegal *adj (character, file name, instruction)* non autorisé(e)

illustration *n* illustration *f*
◊ *illustration software* logiciel *m* graphique

image *n* image *f*
◊ *image bank* banque *f* d'images
◊ *image format* format *m* graphique
◊ *image processing* traitement *m* d'images

imagesetter *n DTP* photocomposeuse *f*

impact printer *n* imprimante *f* à impact

import *vt* importer (**from** depuis)

in box *n (for e-mail)* boîte *f* de réception, corbeille *f* d'arrivée

incoming *adj (telephone call)* de l'extérieur; *(fax)* en entrée; *(e-mail)* à l'arrivée

incompatibility *n* incompatibilité *f* (**with** avec)

incompatible *adj* incompatible (**with** avec)

indent *vt* mettre en retrait

indentation *n* alinéa *m*

index 1 *n (in book, database)* index *m*
2 *vt (database)* indexer

infect *vt (file, disk)* infecter

infoaddict *n Fam Internet* accro *mf* de l'Internet

infobahn *n* autoroute *f* de l'information, *Can* inforoute *f*

infohighway *n* autoroute *f* de l'information, *Can* inforoute *f*

information *n* **(a)** *(data)* information *f* **(b)** *Am Tel* renseignements *mpl*
◊ *information highway* autoroute *f* de l'information, *Can* inforoute *f*

◇ *information retrieval* recherche *f* documentaire

◇ *information society* société *f* de l'information

◇ *information storage* mémorisation *f* des informations

◇ *information superhighway* autoroute *f* de l'information, *Can* inforoute *f*

◇ *information technology* technologie *f* de l'information

infrared *n* infrarouge *m*

◇ *infrared mouse* souris *f* infrarouge

initialization *n* (*of computer, modem, printer*) initialisation *f*

initialize *vt* (*computer, modem, printer*) initialiser

inkjet printer *n* imprimante *f* à jet d'encre

inline image *n Internet* image *f* intégrée

input 1 *n* (*action*) entrée *f*, introduction *f*; (*data*) données *fpl* (en entrée) 2 *vt* (*data*) entrer

◇ *input device* périphérique *m* d'entrée

input/output *n* entrée/sortie *f*

◇ *input/output device* périphérique *m* d'entrée/sortie

insert 1 *n* insertion *f* 2 *vt* insérer

◇ *insert key* touche *f* d'insertion

◇ *insert mode* mode *m* (d')insertion

insertion point *n* point *m* d'insertion

install, *Am* **instal** *vt* (*equip-

ment, software*) installer

installation disk *n* disquette *f* d'installation

installer *n* (*program*) programme *m* d'installation

instruction *n* instruction *f*; **instructions** (*in program*) instructions *fpl*

◇ *instruction manual* guide *m* de l'utilisateur

integrated *adj* (*fax, modem*) intégré(e)

◇ *integrated package* logiciel *m* ou progiciel *m* intégré

◇ *integrated services digital network* Réseau *m* Numérique à Intégration de Services

◇ *integrated software* logiciel *m* intégré

intelligent terminal *n* terminal *m* intelligent

interactive *adj* interactif(ive)

◇ *interactive CD* CD-I *m*, disque *m* compact interactif

interface *n* interface *f*

internal *adj* interne

◇ *internal drive* unité *f* (de disque) interne

◇ *internal modem* modem *m* interne

international *n*

◇ *international call* communication *f* internationale

◇ *international Br dialling* or *Am dial code* indicatif *m* du pays

Internet *n* Internet *m*; **to surf the Internet** naviguer sur l'Internet

◇ *Internet 2* Internet 2

The Internet

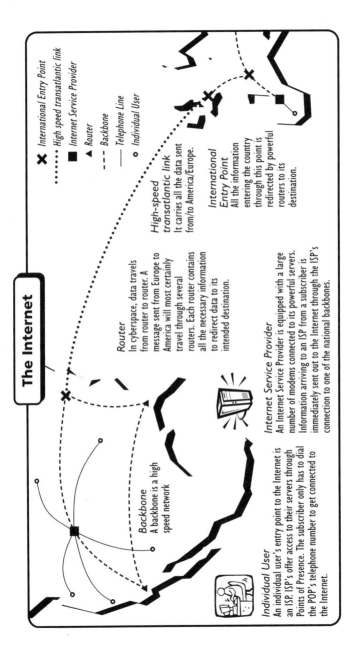

Legend:
- ✕ International Entry Point
- ••••••• High speed transatlantic link
- ■ Internet Service Provider
- ▲ Router
- --- Backbone
- — Telephone Line
- ○ Individual User

Router
In cyberspace, data travels from router to router. A message sent from Europe to America will most certainly travel through several routers. Each router contains all the necessary information to redirect data to its intended destination.

High-speed transatlantic link
It carries all the data sent from/to America/Europe.

International Entry Point
All the information entering the country through this point is redirected by powerful routers to its destination.

Backbone
A backbone is a high speed network

Internet Service Provider
An Internet Service Provider is equipped with a large number of modems connected to its powerful servers. Information arriving to an ISP from a subscriber is immediately sent out to the Internet through the ISP's connection to one of the national backbones.

Individual User
An individual user's entry point to the Internet is an ISP. ISP's offer access to their servers through Points of Presence. The subscriber only has to dial the POP's telephone number to get connected to the Internet.

◇ *Internet access provider* fournisseur *m* d'accès à l'Internet

◇ *Internet account* compte *m* Internet

◇ *Internet address* adresse *f* Internet

◇ *Internet banking* opérations *fpl* bancaires par l'Internet

◇ *Internet café* cybercafé *m*

◇ *Internet connection* connexion *f* à l'Internet

◇ *Internet number* numéro *m* Internet

◇ *Internet phone* téléphone *m* Internet

◇ *Internet presence provider* = fournisseur d'accès à l'Internet proposant l'hébergement de sites Web

◇ *Internet protocol* protocole *m* Internet

◇ *Internet Relay Chat* service *m* de bavardage Internet, dialogue *m* en direct

◇ *Internet service provider* fournisseur *m* d'accès à l'Internet

◇ *Internet Society* = organisation non gouvernementale chargée de veiller à l'évolution de l'Internet

◇ *Internet surfer* internaute *mf*

◇ *Internet telephone* téléphone *m* Internet

◇ *Internet telephony* téléphonie *f* sur l'Internet

◇ *Internet user* internaute *mf*

interpolation *n* interpolation *f*

interpreter *n* (*software*) interpréteur *m*

Intranet *n* Intranet *m*

invalid *adj* (*file name*) invalide

inverted commas *n* guillemets *mpl*

I/O *n* (*abbr* **input/output**) E/S *f*

IP *n* (*abbr* **Internet Protocol**)

◇ *IP address* adresse *f* IP

◇ *IP number* numéro *m* IP

IRC *n* Internet (*abbr* **Internet Relay Chat**) IRC *m*, service *m* de bavardage Internet, dialogue *m* en direct

◇ *IRC channel* canal *m* IRC, canal *m* de dialogue en direct

ISDN 1 *n* (*abbr* **integrated services digital network**) RNIS *m*

2 *vt Fam* **to ISDN sth** envoyer qch par RNIS

◇ *ISDN card* carte *f* RNIS

◇ *ISDN line* ligne *f* RNIS

◇ *ISDN modem* modem *m* RNIS *ou* Numéris

ISOC *n* Internet (*abbr* **Internet Society**) = organisation non gouvernementale chargée de veiller à l'évolution de l'Internet

ISP *n* Internet (*abbr* **Internet Service Provider**) fournisseur *m* d'accès à l'Internet

IT *n* (*abbr* **information technology**) technologie *f* de l'information

italic 1 *n* italic(s) italique *m*; **in italics** en italique

2 *adj* italique; **italic(s) face** or **type** caractères *mpl* italiques

item *n* (*on menu*) élément *m*

Java *n Internet* Java *m*
◇ **Java script** (langage *m*) Javascript *m*

Jaz ® *n*
◇ **Jaz disk** cartouche *f* Jaz ®
◇ **Jaz drive** lecteur *m* Jaz ®

job *n (task)* tâche *f*

joining fee *n Internet* frais
mpl d'accès au service

joystick *n* manette *f* de jeu,
manche *m* à balai

JPEG *n* (*abbr of* **Joint Photo-
graphic Experts Group**) (format *m*) JPEG *m*

jump *vi* to jump from one web
page to another passer d'une
page Web à une autre

jumper *n (pin)* cavalier *m*

junk e-mail *n Internet* messages *mpl* publicitaires

justification *n (of text)*
justification *f*; **left/right justification** justification *f* à
gauche/à droite; **vertical justification** justification *f* verticale

justified *adj (text)* justifié(e);
left/right justified justifié à
gauche/droite; **vertically justified** justifié verticalement

justify *vt (text)* justifier

K *n* (*abbr* **kilobyte**) Ko *m*; **how many K are left?** combien de Ko reste-t-il?; **720K diskette** disquette *f* de 720 Ko

KB *n* (*abbr* **kilobyte**) Ko *m*

Kb *n* (*abbr* **kilobit**) Kbit

Kbps (*abbr* **kilobits per second**) Kbit/s

kern *n DTP* approche *f*

kerning *n DTP* crénage *m*

key 1 *n* (*of sort, identification*) indicatif *m*, critère *m*; (*button*) touche *f*
2 *vt* (*data, text*) taper, saisir
◇ **key combination** combinaison *f* de touches
▸ **key in, key up** *vt sep* (*data, text*) taper, saisir

keyboard 1 *n* (*of typewriter, computer*) clavier *m*
2 *vt* (*data, text*) taper, saisir
3 *vi* introduire des données par clavier
◇ **keyboard layout** disposition *f* de clavier
◇ **keyboard map** schéma *m* de clavier
◇ **keyboard shortcut** raccourci *m* clavier
◇ **keyboard skills** compétences *fpl* de claviste

keyboarder *n* claviste *mf*, opérateur(trice) *m,f* de saisie

keying *n* (*of data text*) frappe *f*, saisie *f*
◇ **keying error** faute *f* de frappe
◇ **keying speed** vitesse *f* de frappe

keypad *n* pavé *m*

keystroke *n* frappe *f* (de touche); **keystrokes per minute/hour** vitesse *f* de frappe à la minute/à l'heure

keyword *n* mot *m* clé

kilobit *n* kilobit *m*

kilobyte *n* kilo-octet *m*

kiosk *n* borne *f* interactive

kit *n* kit *m*

knowledge base *n* base *f* de connaissances

knowledge-based system *n* système *m* basé sur les connaissances

The French keyboard layout

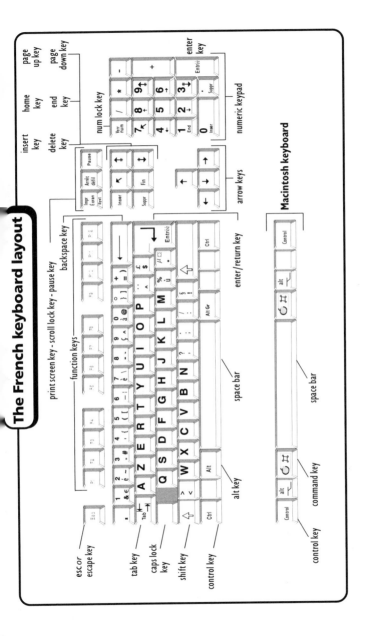

esc or escape key

tab key

caps lock key

shift key

control key

alt key

function keys

print screen key - scroll lock key - pause key

insert key

delete key

home key

end key

num lock key

page up key

page down key

enter key

backspace key

arrow keys

enter/return key

space bar

numeric keypad

Macintosh keyboard

space bar

control key

command key

LAN *n (abbr* **local area network**) réseau *m* local

landscape *n (paper format)* (format *m*) paysage *m* ; **to print sth in landscape** imprimer qch en paysage

◇ *landscape mode* mode *m* paysage

laptop *n* portable *m*

laser *n* laser *m*

◇ *laser disc* disque *m* laser

◇ *laser printer* imprimante *f* laser

launch *vt* lancer

layer *n* DTP couche *f*

LCD *n (abbr* **liquid crystal display**) affichage *m* à cristaux liquides, LCD *m*

◇ *LCD screen* écran *m* LCD

leading *n* DTP interlignage *m*

leased line *n* ligne *f* louée

LED *n (abbr* **light-emitting diode**) DEL *f*

left arrow *n* flèche *f* vers la gauche

◇ *left arrow key* touche *f* de déplacement vers la gauche

left-click 1 *vt* cliquer avec le bouton gauche de la souris sur

2 *vi* cliquer avec le bouton gauche de la souris (**on** sur)

legal *n (paper size)* = format de papier (8,5 x 14 pouces) employé surtout aux États-Unis

letter *n (paper size)* = format de papier (8,5 x 11 pouces) employé surtout aux États-Unis

◇ *letter quality* qualité *f* courrier

levels of grey *n* DTP échelle *f* des gris

library *n (of programs)* bibliothèque *f*

licence, *Am* **license** *n*

◇ *licence agreement* licence *f*

light pen *n* crayon *m* optique

line *n* **(a)** *(telephone connection)* ligne *f* ; **the line is** *Br* **engaged** *or Am* **busy** la ligne est occupée ; **there's someone on the line** il y a quelqu'un sur la ligne ; **hold the line please** ne quittez pas ; **the line's very bad** la communication est mauvaise ; **she's on the other line** elle est sur l'autre ligne **(b)** *(of text)* ligne *f*

◇ *line break* saut *m* de ligne

◇ *line end* fin *f* de ligne

◊ *line feed* changement *m* de ligne

◊ Tel *line noise* parasites *mpl*

◊ Tel *line rental* abonnement *m*

◊ *line spacing* interlignage *m*, espacement *m* de lignes

link 1 *n* (hyperlink) lien *m* (**to** avec)
2 *vt* lier, relier (**to** à)
3 *vi* **to link to** être relié à

liquid crystal display *n* affichage *m* à cristaux liquides

list *vt* lister

listing *n* listing *m*

◊ *listing paper* papier *m* continu, papier listing

live cam *n* Internet caméra *f* Internet

load 1 *vt* (disk, program) charger; **to load a program into the memory** charger un programme en mémoire
2 *vi* (of software, program) se charger

▸ **load up** *vt sep* (disk, program) charger

local *adj* local(e)

◊ *local area network* réseau *m* local;

◊ Tel *local call* communication *f* locale

◊ *local rate number* numéro *m* à tarification locale

localization *n* localisation *f*

localize *vt* localiser

location *n* Internet adresse *f* URL

lock *vt* (file, diskette) verrouiller

log file *n* fichier *m* compte-rendu

▸ **log in** *vi* (of user) entrer, ouvrir une session

▸ **log off 1** *vt sep* faire sortir
2 *vi* sortir

▸ **log on 1** *vt sep* faire entrer
2 *vi* (of user) entrer, ouvrir une session; (to remote system) entrer en communication; **to log onto a system** se connecter à un système

▸ **log out** *vi* (of user) sortir, se déconnecter

logical *adj* logique

logic circuit *n* circuit *m* logique

login name *n* nom *m* d'utilisateur, nom de login

long-distance 1 *adj* (telephone call) longue distance
2 *adv* **to telephone long-distance** faire un appel longue distance

look-up table *n* table *f* de recherche *ou* de référence

low-end *adj* bas de gamme

lower-case 1 *n* minuscule *f*, bas *m* de casse
2 *adj* minuscule, bas de casse

lurk *vi* Internet rôder

lurker *n* Internet rôdeur(euse) *m,f*, badaud(e) *m,f*

Mac *n* Mac *m*; **available for the Mac** disponible en version Mac
◇ *Mac disk* disquette *f* pour Mac
◇ *Mac OS* Mac-OS *m*
Mac-compatible *adj* compatible Mac

machine *n* *(computer)* machine *f*
◇ *machine code* code *m* machine
◇ *machine language* langage *m* machine
◇ *machine translation* traduction *f* assistée par ordinateur
machine-readable *adj* lisible par ordinateur

macro *n* macro *f*
◇ *macro language* macrolangage *m*
◇ *macro virus* virus *m* de macro
magnetic *adj*
◇ *magnetic card* carte *f* magnétique
◇ *magnetic card reader* lecteur *m* de cartes magnétiques
◇ *magnetic disk* disque *m* magnétique; *(floppy)* disquette *f* magnétique
◇ *magnetic strip* *(on card)* piste *f* magnétique

◇ *magnetic tape* bande *f* magnétique
magneto-optical *adj* magnéto-optique
magnify *vt* agrandir

mail *n* *(e-mail)* courrier *m* électronique, JO mél *m*, *Can* courriel *m*
◇ *mail address* adresse *f* électronique
◇ *mail bomb* = messages envoyés en masse pour bloquer une boîte aux lettres, *Can* bombard *m*
◇ *mail forwarding* réexpédition *f* du courrier électronique
◇ *mail gateway* passerelle *f* (de courrier électronique)
◇ *mail merge* publipostage *m*
◇ *mail path* chemin *m* du courrier électronique
◇ *mail reader* logiciel *m* de courrier électronique, client *m* de messagerie électronique
◇ *mail server* serveur *m* de courrier
mailbox *n* *(for e-mail)* boîte *f* à ou aux lettres
mailing *n* *(mailshot)* publipostage *m*, mailing *m*
◇ *Internet mailing list* liste *f* de diffusion

◇ *mailing shot* publipostage *m*, mailing *m*

mainframe *n*

◇ *mainframe (computer)* ordinateur *m* central

maintenance *n* maintenance *f*

management information system *n* système *m* intégré de gestion

manager *n* *(of disk)* gestionnaire *m*

master *adj*

◇ *master disk* disque *m* maître

◇ *master file* fichier *m* maître

maths co-processor *n* coprocesseur *m* mathématique

maximize *vt* *(window)* agrandir

MB *n* *(abbr* **megabyte**) Mo

Mb *n* *(abbr* **megabit**) Mb

Mbps *(abbr* **megabits per second**) mbps

media *n* *(hardware)* support *m*

meg *n* *Fam* méga *m*

megabit *n* mégabit *m*

megabyte *n* méga-octet *m*; **20 megabyte memory** mémoire *f* de 20 méga-octets

megahertz *n* mégahertz *m*

memory *n* mémoire *f*

◇ *memory card* carte *f* mémoire

◇ *memory chip* puce *f* à mémoire

◇ *memory upgrade* ajout *m* de mémoire

menu *n* menu *m*

◇ *menu bar* barre *f* de menu

◇ *menu item* élément *m* de menu

menu-driven *adj* commandé(e) par menu

merge *vt* *(files)* fusionner

message *n* *(e-mail)* message *m*

◇ *message body* corps *m* du message

◇ *message box* boîte *f* de dialogue

◇ *message handling* messagerie *f* (électronique)

◇ *message header* en-tête *m* de message

MHz *(abbr* **megahertz**) MHz

micro *n* *(microcomputer)* micro *m*

microchip *n* microprocesseur *m*

microcomputer *n* micro-ordinateur *m*

microprocessor *n* microprocesseur *m*

MIDI *(abbr* **musical instrument digital interface**) MIDI

millennium bug *n* bogue *m* de l'an 2000

MIME *n* *Internet* *(abbr* **Multipurpose Internet Mail Extensions**) (protocole *m*) MIME

MiniDisc® *n* MiniDisc® *m*

minimize *vt* *(window)* réduire

mini tower *n* mini-tour *f*

minus sign *n* signe *m* moins

mips *n* *(abbr* **million instructions per second**) MIPS *m*

mirror site n Internet site m miroir

MIS n (abbr **management information system**) système m intégré de gestion

MMX n (abbr **multimedia extensions**) MMX m

mobile phone n téléphone m mobile

mode n mode m

modem 1 n modem m; **to send sth to sb by modem** envoyer qch à qn par modem
2 vt **to modem sth to sb** envoyer qch à qn par modem
◇ **modem card** carte f modem

moderated list n Internet liste f de diffusion modérée, liste de diffusion gérée par un modérateur

moderator n Internet modérateur m

modifier key n touche f de modification

monitor n (screen) moniteur m

monospaced adj DTP non proportionnel(elle)

morph vt (image) transformer par morphing

motherboard n carte f mère

mouse n souris f
◇ **mouse button** bouton m de souris
◇ **mouse driver** programme m de commande de la souris
◇ **mouse mat** tapis m de souris
◇ **mouse pad** tapis m de souris

MP3 n (abbr **MPEG1 Audio Layer 3**) format m MP3

MPEG n (abbr **Moving Pictures Expert Group**) (format m) MPEG

MS-DOS n (abbr **Microsoft Disk Operating System**) MS-DOS m

MUD n Internet (abbr **multi-user dungeon**) environnement m MUD

multi-access adj à accès multiple

multicast n Internet multi-diffusion f

multifunctional key n touche f multifonction

multimedia 1 n multimédia m
2 adj multimédia
◇ **multimedia computer** ordinateur m multimédia

multiple mailboxes npl = possibilité d'avoir plusieurs boîtes aux lettres auprès d'un fournisseur d'accès à l'Internet

multiprocessor n multiprocesseur m

multi-station adj multipostes

multitasking 1 n multitâche m
2 adj multitâche

multithreading 1 n multithread m, multitraitement m
2 adj multithread, multitraitement

multi-user adj pour utilisateurs multiples
◇ **multi-user software** logiciel m multi-utilisateur
◇ **multi-user system** système m multi-utilisateur

The multimedia computer

CPU

CD-ROM drive

bay

disk drive

monitor

speaker

keyboard

mouse

graphics tablet

microphone

digital camera

joystick

scanner

fax modem

inkjet printer

navigate *Internet* **1** *vt* naviguer sur; **to navigate the Net** naviguer sur l'Internet **2** *vi (around web site)* naviguer

navigation *n Internet (around web site)* navigation *f*

◇ *navigation bar* barre *f* de navigation

◇ *navigation button* bouton *m* de navigation

Net *n Fam* **the Net** le Net

.net *Internet* = abréviation désignant les organismes officiels de l'Internet dans les adresses électroniques

nethead *n Fam Internet* accro *mf* de l'Internet

netiquette *n Internet* netiquette *f*

netizen *n Internet* internaute *mf*

netspeak *n Internet* langage *m* du Net, cyberjargon *m*

network **1** *n* réseau *m* **2** *vt* mettre en réseau

◇ *network administrator* administrateur *m* de réseau

◇ *network card* carte *f* réseau

◇ *Network Computer* ordinateur *m* de réseau

◇ *network driver* gestionnaire *m* de réseau

◇ *network manager* gestionnaire *m* de réseau

◇ *network server* serveur *m* de réseau

◇ *network software* logiciel *m* de réseau

◇ *network traffic* trafic *m* de réseau

networked systems *npl* systèmes *mpl* en réseau

networking *n (of computer system)* mise *f* en réseau; **to have networking capabilities** *(of terminal)* offrir la possibilité d'intégration à un réseau

neural network *n* réseau *m* neuronal

newbie *n Fam Internet* internaute *mf* novice, cybernovice *mf*

news *n Internet* nouvelles *fpl*

◇ *news article* article *m* Usenet

◇ *news reader* logiciel *m* de lecture de nouvelles

◇ *news server* serveur *m* de nouvelles

newsgroup *n Internet* forum *m* (de discussion), newsgroup *m*

nickname *n* surnom *m*

Network topologies

Centralized

A central computer controls access to the network

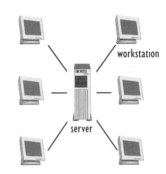

Star network
Its physical layout resembles a star. At its centre is a central network processor.

workstation

server

Decentralized

Each workstation can access the network independently and establish its own connections with other workstations

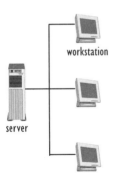

workstation

server

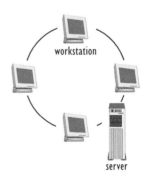

workstation

server

Bus network
A single connecting line, the bus, is shared by a number of nodes, including workstations and shared printers.

Ring network
A number of nodes are arranged around a closed loop cable.

node *n* nœud *m*

noise *n* bruit *m*

notebook (computer) *n* ordinateur *m* portable

notepad *n* ardoise *f* électronique

number *n* *(digit)* numéro *m*

◇ *number crunching* calculs *mpl* (rapides)

◇ *number key* touche *f* numérique

◇ *numbers lock* verrouillage *m* du pavé numérique

◇ *numbers lock key* touche *f* de verrouillage du pavé numérique

numeric **1** *n* numerics chiffres *mpl* *ou* caractères *mpl* numériques

2 *adj* numérique

◇ *numeric field* champ *m* numérique

◇ *numeric keypad* pavé *m* numérique

numerical keypad pavé *m* numérique

num lock *n* (*abbr* numbers lock) verr num; **the num lock is on** le pavé numérique est verrouillé

◇ *num lock key* touche *f* de verrouillage du pavé numérique

object *n (in document)* objet *m*

object-orientated *adj* orienté(e) objet

oblique *n* barre *f* oblique

OCR *n* (**a**) *(abbr* **optical character reader**) lecteur *m* (à reconnaissance) optique de caractères (**b**) *(abbr* **optical character recognition**) OCR *f*

◊ **OCR software** logiciel *m* d'OCR

office *n*

◊ **office automation** bureautique *f*

◊ **office IT** bureautique *m*

off-hook, offhook *adj* **off-hook signal** signal *m* de réponse *ou* de décrochage

off-line, offline **1** *adj* non connecté(e); *(processing)* en différé; *(printer)* déconnecté(e); **to be off-line** ne pas être connecté; **to go off-line** se déconnecter

2 *adv* hors ligne, hors connexion; **to work off-line** travailler sans se connecter à l'Internet

◊ **off-line mode** mode *m* autonome

◊ **off-line reader** lecteur *m* non connecté

one-step *adj* **one-step set-up/web access** installation *f* facile/accès *m* facile au Web

on-hook, onhook *adj* **on-hook signal** signal *m* de fin de communication *ou* de raccrochage

on-line, online **1** *adj* en ligne; **to be on-line** *(of person)* être connecté(e); **the disk contains all you need to get on-line** cette disquette contient tout ce qu'il vous faut pour vous connecter; **to go on-line** *(for the first time)* se raccorder à l'Internet; **to put the printer on-line** connecter l'imprimante

2 *adv* en ligne; **to buy/order on-line** acheter/commander qch en ligne; **to shop on-line** faire un achat en ligne; **to work on-line** travailler en étant connecté à l'Internet

◊ **on-line banking** transactions *fpl* bancaires en ligne

◊ **on-line help** aide *f* en ligne

◊ **on-line mode** mode *m* connecté

◊ **on-line registration** inscription *f* en ligne

◊ **on-line service** service *m* en ligne

◇ **on-line time** durée *f* de connexion

on-screen 1 *adj* à l'écran **2** *adv* sur (l')écran; **to work on-screen** travailler sur écran

◇ **on-screen help** aide *f* en ligne

on-site *adj* sur place

◇ **on-site guarantee** garantie *f* sur site

◇ **on-site service** maintenance *f* sur site

open line *n Tel* ligne *f* ouverte

opening tag *n* balise *f* de début

operating system *n* système *m* d'exploitation

operation *n* opération *f*

operator *n Tel (person)* opérateur(trice) *m,f*; **(switchboard) operator** standardiste *mf*

optical *adj* optique

◇ **optical character reader** lecteur *m* optique de caractères

◇ **optical character recognition** reconnaissance *f* optique des caractères

◇ **optical disk** disque *m* optique

◇ **optical drive** lecteur *m* optique

◇ **optical fibre** fibre *f* optique

◇ **optical mouse** souris *f* optique

◇ **optical scanner** scanner *m ou* scanneur *m* optique

optimizer *n* optimiseur *m*

option *n* option *f*

◇ **option box** case *f* d'option

◇ **option button** case *f* d'option

◇ **option key** touche *f* Option

.org *Internet* = abréviation désignant les organisations à but non lucratif dans les adresses électroniques

organizer *n (software)* organiseur *m*

orphan *n DTP* (ligne *f*) orpheline *f*

OS *n* (*abbr* **operating system**) système *m* d'exploitation

out box *n (for e-mail)* corbeille *f* de départ

outgoing *adj (telephone call)* sortant(e); *(e-mail)* à expédier, au départ

output 1 *n (of data, information)* sortie *f* **2** *vt (data, information)* sortir (**to** sur)

◇ **output device** périphérique *m* de sortie

outside line *n Tel* ligne *f* extérieure

overflow *n (of data)* dépassement *m* de capacité

overwrite *vt (file)* écraser

◇ **overwrite mode** mode *m* de superposition

package *n (software)* logiciel *m*

packet *n (of data)* paquet *m*

◇ *Internet* **packet switching** commutation *f* de paquets

page *n (of document, computer file)* page *f*

◇ *page break* saut *m* de page

◇ *page design* mise *f* en page

◇ *page down* page suivante

◇ *page down key* touche *f* page suivante

◇ *page format* format *m* de page

◇ *page layout* mise *f* en page

◇ *page preview* aperçu *m* avant l'impression

◇ *page scanner* lecteur *m* de pages

◇ *page setup* format *m* de page

◇ *page up* page précédente

◇ *page up key* touche *f* page précédente

▸ **page down** *vi* feuilleter en avant

▸ **page up** *vi* feuilleter en arrière

paginate *vt* paginer

pagination *n* pagination *f*

paint program *n* logiciel *m* de dessin bitmap

palette *n* palette *f*

palmtop *n* ordinateur *m* de poche

paper *n* papier *m*

◇ *paper advance* (on printer) entraînement *m* du papier

◇ *paper feed* alimentation *f* papier

◇ *paper jam* bourrage *m* papier

◇ *paper tray* bac *m* à feuilles

paperless office *n* bureau *m* entièrement informatisé

paragraph *n* paragraphe *m*

◇ *paragraph break* fin *f* de paragraphe

◇ *paragraph format* format *m* de paragraphe

◇ *paragraph mark* marque *f* de paragraphe

parallel *adj* parallèle

◇ *parallel interface* interface *f* parallèle

◇ *parallel port* port *m* parallèle

parameter *n* paramètre *m*

parity *n* parité *f*

park *vt (hard disk)* effectuer le parcage de

partition 1 *n (of disk)* partition *f* **2** *vt (hard disk)* diviser en partitions

PASCAL n PASCAL m

password n mot m de passe

◇ *password protection* protection f par mot de passe

password-protected adj protégé(e) par mot de passe

paste vt (text) coller (**into/onto** dans)

patch n (correction) correction f

path n chemin m (d'accès)

pathname n chemin m d'accès

pause n pause f

◇ *pause key* touche f Pause

PC n (abbr **personal computer**) PC m; **available for the PC** disponible en version PC

◇ *PC disk* disquette f pour PC

PC-compatible adj compatible PC

PCI n (abbr **peripheral component interface**) PCI m

PCMCIA n (abbr **PC memory card international association**) PCMCIA

PDA n (abbr **personal digital assistant**) agenda m électronique de poche, assistant m numérique de poche

PDF n (abbr **portable document format**) (format m) PDF m

period n Am (punctuation) point m

perforated paper n papier m à bandes perforées

peripheral 1 n périphérique m 2 adj périphérique

◇ *peripheral device, peripheral unit* unité f périphérique

Perl n (abbr **practical extraction and report language**) language m Perl

personal adj

◇ *personal computer* ordinateur m individuel

◇ *personal computing* informatique f individuelle

◇ *personal digital assistant* agenda m électronique de poche, assistant m numérique de poche

◇ Internet *personal home page* page f personnelle, page perso

◇ *personal organizer* (electronic) agenda m électronique

PGP n Internet (abbr **Pretty Good Privacy**) (logiciel m de chiffrement) PGP m

phonecard n carte f de téléphone

photo n

◇ *photo CD* CD-Photo m, Photo-CD m

◇ *photo editing* retouche f d'images

photocopier n photocopieuse f, photocopieur m

photocopy 1 n photocopie f 2 vt photocopier

photocopying machine n photocopieuse f, photocopieur m

phreaker n Fam pirate m du téléphone

pie chart n camembert m

pin n broche f

pipe 1 n (symbol) symbole m '|' 2 vt (commands) chaîner

pixel n pixel m

pixellated adj (image) bitmap, en mode point

platform n (hardware standard) plateforme f

plotter n (device) traceur m

plug n (electrical) prise f

plug-in n module m d'extension, Can plugiciel m

plug & play n plug and play m

plus sign n signe m plus

point n DTP point m
◇ **point size** corps m

pointer n pointeur m

point-to-point protocol n Internet protocole m point à point

POP n Internet (a) (abbr **post office protocol**) protocole m POP (b) (abbr **point of presence**) point m de présence, point m d'accès

pop-up menu n menu m local

port n (socket) port m

portable 1 n (computer) (ordinateur m) portable m
2 adj (computer) portable

portal n Internet portail m

portrait n (paper format) (format m) portrait m ; **to print sth in portrait** imprimer qch en portrait
◇ **portrait mode** mode m portrait

position vt (cursor, image) positionner

post vt Internet (to newsgroups) poster

postmaster n Internet (for e-mail) maître m de poste

post office protocol n Internet protocole m POP

PostScript ® n PostScript ® m
◇ **Postscript font** police f de caractères PostScript

pound sign n symbole m de la livre sterling

power n (electricity) courant m
◇ **power supply** transformateur m
◇ **power unit** dispositif m d'alimentation
◇ **power user** = personne qui sait utiliser au mieux les ressources de son ordinateur
▸ **power down** 1 vt sep éteindre
2 vi éteindre
▸ **power up** 1 vt sep allumer
2 vi allumer

power-down n mise f hors tension

power-on key n touche f d'alimentation

PPP n Internet (abbr **point-to-point protocol**) protocole m PPP, protocole m point à point

preformatted adj (disk) préformaté(e)

preinstall vt (software) préinstaller

preinstalled adj (software) préinstallé(e)

prepress n DTP prépresse m

preprogram vt préprogrammer

preprogrammed adj préprogrammé(e)

presentation graphics npl graphiques mpl de présentation

preview n prévisualisation f

print 1 vt imprimer
2 vi (of document) s'imprimer; (of printer) imprimer

◇ *print format* format m d'impression

◇ *print head* tête f d'impression

◇ *print job* fichier m à imprimer

◇ *print menu* menu m d'impression

◇ *print preview* aperçu m avant impression

◇ *print quality* qualité f d'impression

◇ *print queue* liste f de fichiers à imprimer

◇ *print screen* copie f d'écran

◇ *print screen key* touche f Impr écran

◇ *print speed* vitesse f d'impression

▶ **print out** vt sep imprimer

printer n imprimante f

◇ *printer cable* câble m d'imprimante

◇ *printer driver* programme m de commande d'impression

◇ *printer font* fonte f imprimante

◇ *printer paper* papier m d'impression

◇ *printer speed* vitesse f d'impression

printout n sortie f (sur) papier; (list, results of calculation) listing m

private line n Tel ligne f privée

privilege n (for access to network, database) droits mpl d'accès

proceed vi (in dialogue box) continuer

process 1 n procédé m, traitement m
2 vt (data) traiter

◇ DTP *process colours* impression f en quadrichromie

processing n (of data) traitement m

◇ *processing speed* vitesse f de traitement

◇ *processing time* temps m de traitement

processor n processeur m

◇ *processor speed* vitesse f du processeur

program 1 n programme m
2 vt programmer; **to program a computer to do sth** programmer un ordinateur pour qu'il fasse qch
3 vi programmer; **to program in assembly language** programmer en assembleur

◇ *program disk* disquette f programme

◇ *program language* langage m de programmation

◇ *program library* bibliothèque f de programmes

programmer n programmeur(euse) m,f

programming n programmation f

◇ *programming language* langage m de programmation

prompt n (on command line) invite f; (with wording) mes-

Types of printer

Dot-Matrix

- ▷ Uses an inked ribbon to make an impression on the paper
- ▷ able to print on multi-part forms and continuous paper
- ▷ low cost per printed page
- ▷ higher noise level
- ▷ lower print quality

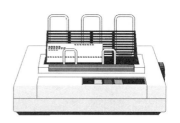

Inkjet

- ▷ Uses a fine jet of ink to form characters on the paper
- ▷ affordable colour printing
- ▷ high cost per printed page
- ▷ quiet printing

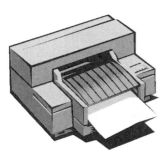

Laser

- ▷ Uses laser to print text on the paper
- ▷ low cost per printed page
- ▷ quiet printing
- ▷ fast
- ▷ colour laser printers are expensive

sage *m* d'invite *ou* d'attente;
return to the C:\ prompt
revenir au message d'attente
du DOS

protection *n* protection *f*

protocol *n* protocole *m*

provider *n* *Internet* fournisseur *m* d'accès à l'Internet

proxy *n* *Internet* mandataire *m*

◇ *proxy* *server* serveur *m*
proxy, serveur mandataire *ou*
de procuration

public domain *n* domaine *m*
public

◇ *public* *domain* *software*
logiciel *m* (du domaine)
public, *Can* publiciel *m*

publish *vt* *(web page)* publier

▸ **pull down** *vt sep* *(menu)*
dérouler

pull-down menu *n* menu *m*
déroulant

pulse *n* *Tel* impulsion *f*

push technology *n* *Internet*
technologie *f* du push de don-
nées

quality *n* qualité *f*

query 1 *n* interrogation *f*
2 *vt (database)* interroger
◇ *Am* **query mark** point *m*
d'interrogation

question mark *n* point *m*
d'interrogation

queue 1 *n* file *f* d'attente
2 *vt (print jobs)* mettre en file
d'attente

quick launch bar *n* barre *f* de
lancement rapide

quit 1 *vt (database, program)*
sortir de, quitter
2 *vi* sortir

quote *vt (in e-mail)* citer

quoting *n (in e-mail)* citation *f*

QWERTY keyboard *n* clavier
m QWERTY

radio button *n* bouton *m* radio, bouton *m* d'option

RAM *n* (*abbr* **random access memory**) mémoire *f* vive

random *adj*

◇ *random access* accès *m* aléatoire

◇ *random access memory* mémoire *f* vive

◇ *random error* erreur *f* aléatoire

raw *adj* (*data, statistics*) brut(e)

RDBMS *n* (*abbr* **relational database management system**) SGBDR *m*

read *vt* lire ; **this computer only reads double-density disks** cet ordinateur ne lit que les disquettes (à) double densité

▸ **read out** *vt sep* (*data*) sortir, extraire de la mémoire

readdress *vt* (*e-mail message*) faire suivre

read-me file *n* fichier *m* lisez-moi

read-only *adj* (à) lecture seule ; **that file is read-only** ce fichier est protégé en écriture ; **to make a file read-only** mettre un fichier en lecture seule

◇ *read-only memory* mémoire *f* morte

read-write head *n* tête *f* de lecture-écriture

Real Player *n* *Internet* lecteur *m* Real Media

real time *n* temps *m* réel

real-time *adj* en temps réel

reboot 1 *vt* réamorcer **2** *vi* se réamorcer

recipient *n* (*of e-mail message*) destinataire *mf*

reconfigure *vt* reconfigurer

record *n* (*in database*) article *m*, enregistrement *m*

recover *vt* (*file, data*) récupérer

recovery *n* (*of file, data*) récupération *f*

recycle bin *n* corbeille *f*

redial *Tel* **1** *n* **redial (feature)** rappel *m* du dernier numéro ; **the latest model has automatic redial** le dernier modèle est muni du système de rappel du dernier numéro
2 *vt* (*number*) refaire
3 *vi* refaire le numéro

redirect *vt* (*e-mail message*) faire suivre (**to** à)

redo vt rétablir, refaire

redraw vt actualiser, rafraîchir

reference vt référencer

refresh 1 n actualisation f, rafraîchissement m
2 vt (screen) actualiser, rafraîchir

◊ **refresh rate** taux m d'actualisation ou de rafraîchissement

register 1 n (of memory) registre m
2 vt (software) inscrire

registered user n utilisateur(trice) m,f disposant d'une licence

registration n
◊ **registration card** licence f
◊ **registration number** numéro m de licence

registry n (Windows file) registre m

reinitialize vt réinitialiser

reinsert vt (block) réinsérer

relational database n base f de données relationnelle

release n (of software) version f

reload vt recharger

remailer n Internet service m de courrier électronique anonyme

remote adj (user) à distance
◊ **remote access** accès m à distance
◊ **remote server** serveur m distant
◊ **remote terminal** terminal m distant

removable adj (disk) amovible, extractible

rename vt (file) changer le nom de, renommer

rendering n DTP rendu m

rental n (for telephone) abonnement m

repaginate vt repaginer

repeat-action key n touche f de répétition

repeat function n fonction f de répétition

repetitive strain injury n lésions fpl attribuables au travail répétitif

replace vt remplacer; **replace all** (command) tout remplacer

report n (of database) état m

reprogram vt reprogrammer

reprogrammable adj (key) reprogrammable

rerun vt (program) relancer

reset 1 n réinitialisation f
2 vt réinitialiser
◊ **reset button** bouton m de réinitialisation
◊ **reset switch** bouton m de réinitialisation

resize vt redimensionner

resolution n (of image) résolution f

restart 1 n (of system) redémarrage m; (of program) reprise f
2 vt (system) redémarrer; (program) reprendre
3 vi (of system) redémarrer; (of program) reprendre

restore 1 n restauration f
2 vt (file, text, data) restaurer

resume *vt* reprendre

retouch *vt (photograph)* retoucher

retrieval *n (of data, file)* recherche *f*; *(of lost data)* récupération *f*

retrieve *vt (data, file)* rechercher; *(lost data)* récupérer

retry *vi* réessayer

return *n (key)* touche *f* Retour
◇ *return address (of e-mail)* adresse *f* de l'expéditeur
◇ *return key* touche *f* Retour

reverse 1 *vt Br Tel* **to reverse the charges** appeler en PCV, faire un appel en PCV
2 *adj*
◇ *reverse mode* inversion *f* vidéo
◇ *reverse slash* barre *f* oblique inversée
◇ *reverse sort* tri *m* en ordre décroissant

reverse-charge call *n Br Tel* communication *f* en PCV

revert *vi (undo)* défaire; **to revert to the previous settings** rétablir les paramètres précédents

rewritable *adj (media)* réinscriptible

RGB *n (abbr* **red, green and blue)** RVB *m*

ribbon *n (under menu bar)* ruban *m*, barre *f* d'outils

right arrow *n* flèche *f* vers la droite
◇ *right arrow key* touche *f* de

déplacement vers la droite

right-click 1 *vt* cliquer avec le bouton droit de la souris sur
2 *vi* cliquer avec le bouton droit de la souris (**on** sur)

ring network *n* réseau *m* en anneau

RISC *n (abbr* **reduced instruction set chip** *or* **computer)** RISC

ROM *n (abbr* **read only memory)** mémoire *f* morte, (mémoire) ROM *f*

root directory *n* racine *f*, répertoire *m* principal

router *n Internet* routeur *m*

routine *n* sous-programme *m*

row *n (in spreadsheet)* ligne *f*

RSI *n (abbr* **repetitive strain injury)** lésions *fpl* attribuables au travail répétitif

ruler *n* (**a**) *(in word processor)* règle *f* (**b**) *DTP* règle *f*
◇ *ruler line* règle *f*

run 1 *vt (program)* exécuter, faire tourner; **this computer runs most software** on peut utiliser la plupart des logiciels sur cet ordinateur
2 *vi* **this software runs on DOS** ce logiciel tourne sous DOS; **do not interrupt the program while it is running** ne pas interrompre le programme en cours d'exécution; **running at...** cadencé à...

runtime (version) *n* version *f* exécutable

save 1 *vt (document)* sauvegarder, enregistrer; **to save sth to disk** sauvegarder qch sur disquette; **do you want to save changes?** voulez-vous enregistrer les modifications?; **save as...** enregistrer sous…

2 *vi* sauvegarder, enregistrer; **this file is taking a lot of time to save** ça prend beaucoup de temps pour sauvegarder ce fichier

scan 1 *n* lecture *f* au scanner *ou* scanneur

2 *vt* passer au scanner *ou* scanneur

▸**scan in** *vt sep (graphics)* insérer par scanner *ou* scanneur, capturer au scanner *ou* scanneur

scanner *n* scanner *m*, scanneur *m*

scheduler *n (package)* logiciel *m* de planification (de projets)

.sci *Internet (abbr* **science)** *(in newsgroups)* = abréviation désignant les forums de discussion scientifiques

scrapbook *n (on Macintosh)* album *m*

scratchpad *n Am* bloc-notes *m*

◇ *scratchpad memory* mémoire *f* bloc-notes

screen *n* écran *m*; **to work on screen** travailler sur écran; **to bring up the next screen** amener l'écran suivant

◇ *screen capture* capture *f* d'écran

◇ *screen display* affichage *m*

◇ *screen dump* capture *f* d'écran

◇ *screen refresh* actualisation *f* *ou* régénération *f* de l'écran

◇ *screen saver* économiseur *m* d'écran

◇ *screen shot* capture *f* d'écran

scroll 1 *n* défilement *m*
2 *vt* faire défiler
3 *vi* défiler

◇ *scroll bar* barre *f* de défilement

◇ *scroll box* ascenseur *m*

◇ *scroll button* bouton *m* de défilement

◇ *scroll lock key* touche *f* arrêt défil

▸**scroll down 1** *vt insep* **to scroll down a document** faire défiler un document vers le bas
2 *vi (of person)* faire défiler de haut en bas; *(of text)* défiler de haut en bas

▸ **scroll through** *vt insep* *(text)* parcourir

▸ **scroll up 1** *vt insep* **to scroll up a document** faire défiler un document vers le haut
2 *vi (of person)* faire défiler de bas en haut; *(of text)* défiler de bas en haut

SCSI *n (abbr* **small computer systems interface)** SCSI *f*
◇ **SCSI card** carte *f* SCSI

SDRAM *n (abbr* **synchronous dynamic random access memory)** SDRAM *f*

search 1 *n* recherche *f*; **to do a search** faire une recherche; **to do a search for sth** rechercher qch; **search and replace** recherche et remplacement *m*
2 *vt (file, directory)* rechercher dans; **to search and replace sth** rechercher et remplacer qch
3 *vi* faire une recherche
◇ *Internet* **search engine** moteur *m* de recherche

sector *n (of disk)* secteur *m*

secure *adj Internet*
◇ **secure electronic transaction** protocole *m* SET
◇ **secure HTTP** protocole *m* HTTP sécurisé
◇ **secure server** serveur *m* sécurisé
◇ **secure sockets layer** protocole *m* SSL

security *n* sécurité *f*
◇ *Internet* **security certificate** certificat *m* de sécurité
◇ **security level** niveau *m* de sécurité

seek time *n* temps *m* d'accès

select *vt* sélectionner; **select "enter"** tapez entrée; **to select an option** activer une option

selection *n* sélection *f*
◇ **selection box** rectangle *m* de sélection

self-extracting archive *n* archive *f* autodécompactable

self-test 1 *n* autotest *m*
2 *vi* s'autotester

semicolon *n* point-virgule *m*

separator *n* séparateur *m*

sequence *n* séquence *f*

sequential *adj* séquentiel(elle)
◇ **sequential access** accès *m* séquentiel
◇ **sequential processing** traitement *m* séquentiel

serial *adj*
◇ **serial cable** câble *m* série
◇ **serial interface** interface *f* série
◇ **serial port** port *m* série
◇ **serial printer** imprimante *f* série

server *n* serveur *m*
◇ **server administrator** administrateur *m* de serveur

service *n*
◇ **service bureau** société *f* de traitement à façon
◇ *Internet* **service provider** fournisseur *m* d'accès

session *n Internet* session *f*

SET® *n Internet (abbr* **secure electronic transaction)** SET *f*

set 1 *n (of characters, instructions)* jeu *m*, ensemble *m*
2 *vt (tabs, format)* poser

▸**set up** *vt sep (computer, system)* configurer

settings *n* paramètres *mpl*, réglages *mpl*

setup *n* configuration *f*

◇ *setup CD-ROM* CD-ROM *m* ou JO cédérom *m* d'installation

◇ *Internet setup charge* frais *mpl* d'inscription

◇ *Internet setup fee* frais *mpl* d'inscription

◇ *setup program* programme *m* d'installation

SGML *n* (*abbr* **Standard Generated Markup Language**) SGML *m*

shade *n* ombre *f*

◇ *shades of grey* niveaux *mpl* ou tons *mpl* de gris

shadow printing *n* impression *f* ombrée

shareware *n* shareware *m*, partagiciel *m*, logiciel *m* contributif

sheetfeed *n* avancement *m* du papier

sheet feeder *n* bac *m* d'alimentation papier

shift *n* touche *f* Majuscule; **an asterisk is shift 8** pour un astérisque, il faut taper simultanément la touche majuscule et la touche 8

◇ *shift key* touche *f* Majuscule

shopping basket, *Am* **shopping cart** *n Internet* caddie

shortcut *n* raccourci *m*

◇ *shortcut key* touche *f* de raccourci

show *vt (files, records)* afficher

▸**shut down** 1 *vt sep (computer)* éteindre
2 *vi (of system)* s'arrêter

shutdown *n* fermeture *f*, arrêt *m* de fin de session

signature *n (on e-mail)* signature *f*

SIMM *n* (*abbr* **single in-line memory module**) SIMM *m*

simulate *vt* simuler

simulation *n* simulation *f*

simulator *n* simulateur *m*

single user licence *n* licence *f* individuelle d'utilisation

singletasking 1 *n* monotâche *m*
2 *adj* monotâche

site *n Internet* site *m*

size 1 *n (of file)* taille *f*; *(of font)* corps *m*, taille *f*
2 *vt* dimensionner

◇ *size box* case *f* de dimensionnement

skip *vt (command)* sauter

slash *n* barre *f* oblique

sleep *vi* être en veille; **to put a notebook to sleep** mettre un portable en veille

◇ *sleep mode* veille *f*

slider *n* languette *f*

slide show *n* diaporama *m*, projection *f* de diapositives

SLIP *n* (*abbr* **serial line Internet protocol**) protocole *m* SLIP

slot *n* emplacement *m*

small caps *n* petites capitales *fpl*

smart *adj*

◇ *smart card* carte *f* à puce

◇ *smart quotes* = conversion automatique des guillemets saisis au clavier en guillemets typographiques

smiley *n Internet* souriant *m*, émoticon *m*, *Can* binette *f*

SMTP *n Internet* (*abbr* **Simple Mail Transfer Protocol**) protocole *m* SMTP

snail mail *n Fam* courrier *m* escargot, = courrier postal

.soc *Internet* (*abbr* **social**) (*in newsgroups*) = abréviation désignant les forums de discussion qui ont pour thème les faits de société

socket *n* (**a**) (*slot*) prise *f* (femelle) (**b**) *Internet* socket *f*, port *m*

soft *adj*

◇ *soft copy* visualisation *f* sur écran

◇ *soft hyphen* césure *f* automatique, tiret *m* conditionnel

◇ *soft return* saut *m* de ligne automatique

software *n* logiciel *m*, software *m*

◇ *software company* éditeur *m* de logiciels

◇ *software developer* développeur(euse) *m,f*

◇ *software error* erreur *f* de logiciel

◇ *software house* éditeur *m* de logiciel

◇ *software package* logiciel

◇ *software piracy* piratage *m* de logiciels

◇ *software problem* problème *m* de logiciel

sort 1 *n* (*arranging in list*) tri *m*; **the program will do an alphabetical sort** le programme exécutera un tri alphabétique

2 *vt* (*arrange in list*) trier; **to sort sth alphabetically** trier qch par ordre alphabétique; **to sort sth in ascending/descending order** trier qch par ordre croissant/décroissant

3 *vi* (*arrange in list*) trier; (*of file, data*) se trier

sound card *n* carte *f* son

source *n*

◇ *source disk* disque *m* source; (*floppy*) disquette *f* source

◇ *source document* document *m* de base, document source

◇ *source file* fichier *m* source

◇ *source text* texte *m* de départ

space *n* (*in text*) espace *m ou f*

◇ *space bar* barre *f* d'espacement

spacing *n* (*horizontal*) espacement *m*; (*vertical*) interligne *m ou f*

spam *Internet* 1 *n* messages *mpl* publicitaires

2 *vi* envoyer des messages publicitaires en masse

spammer *n Internet* = personne qui envoie des messages publicitaires en masse

spamming *n Internet* envoi *m* de messages publicitaires en masse

speaker *n* (*loudspeaker*) haut-parleur *m*

specs n spécifications *fpl*

specification n spécifications *fpl*

speech recognition n reconnaissance *f* de la parole

speed n vitesse *f*; **32 speed CD-ROM** lecteur *m* de CD-ROM 32 x

◇ Tel **speed dial** numérotation *f* abrégée

spellcheck n correction *f* orthographique ; **to do** or **run a spellcheck on a document** effectuer une correction orthographique sur un document

spellchecker n correcteur *m* orthographique ou d'orthographe

split vt *(file, image)* découper

◇ **split screen** écran *m* divisé, multi-écran *m*

spooler n *(for printing)* spouleur *m*, pilote *m* de mise en file d'attente

spot colour n DTP couleur *f* (du nuancier) Pantone

spreadsheet n *(document)* feuille *f* de calcul; *(software)* tableur *m*

SSL n Internet (abbr **secure sockets layer**) protocole *m* SSL

stand-alone n poste *m* autonome

◇ **stand-alone computer** ordinateur *m* autonome

standby mode n *(of printer, computer)* veille *f*

star n

◇ **star network** réseau *m* en étoile

◇ **star structure** structure *f* en étoile

start button n *(in Windows)* bouton *m* Démarrer

starter pack n Internet kit *m* de connexion

▸ **start up** 1 vt sep *(computer)* mettre en route
2 vi *(of computer)* se mettre en route

start-up n démarrage *m*

◇ **start-up disk** disquette *f* de démarrage

◇ **start-up screen** écran *m* d'accueil

status n

◇ **status bar** barre *f* d'état

◇ **status line** ligne *f* d'état

◇ **status report** état *m* du projet

storage n *(of data)* mémoire *f*

◇ **storage capacity** capacité *f* de stockage

◇ **storage device** dispositif *m* de stockage

◇ **storage medium** support *m* de stockage

store 1 n *(of data)* mémoire *f*
2 vt *(data)* stocker

string n *(of characters)* chaîne *f*

style n

◇ **style bar** barre *f* de style

◇ **style sheet** feuille *f* de style

subdirectory n sous-répertoire *m*

subject n *(of e-mail message)* objet *m*

submenu n sous-menu *m*

subroutine n sous-programme *m*

subscribe vi (to ISP) s'abonner

subscriber n (to ISP, telephone network) abonné(e) m,f

subscription n (to ISP) abonnement m

suite n (of software) suite f logicielle, ensemble m logiciel

supercomputer n super-ordinateur m

superhighway n autoroute f

support vt (file format, device, technology) permettre l'utilisation de, supporter; **this package is supported by all workstations** ce progiciel peut être utilisé sur tous les postes de travail; **56K supported** gère l'accès en 56 kbit/s

◊ *support line* assistance f technique téléphonique

surf vt **to surf the Net** naviguer sur l'Internet

surround sound n son m 3D

SVGA n (abbr **Super Video Graphics Array**) SVGA m

switch n (in DOS) clé f

switchboard n Tel standard m

◊ *switchboard operator* standardiste mf

symbol n symbole m

syntax n syntaxe f

◊ *syntax error* erreur f de syntaxe

SYSOP n (abbr **Systems Operator**) sysop m, opérateur m système

system n système m

◊ *systems analysis* analyse f des systèmes

◊ *systems analyst* analyste-programmeur(euse) m,f

◊ *system crash* panne f du système

◊ *system disk* disque f système

◊ *system error* erreur f système

◊ *system failure* panne f du système

◊ *system file* fichier m système

◊ *system folder* dossier m système

◊ *systems management* direction f systématisée

◊ *system software* logiciel m d'exploitation, logiciel système

tab 1 *n* tabulation *f*
2 *vt (text)* mettre en colonnes (avec des tabulations)
◊ *tab key* touche *f* de tabulation

tab-delimited *adj* délimité(e) par des tabulations

table *n (diagram)* tableau *m*

tabulate *vt* mettre en colonnes *(avec des tabulations)*

tabulator *n* tabulation *f*
◊ *tabulator key* touche *f* de tabulation

tag 1 *n (code)* balise *f*
2 *vt* baliser

tape *n* bande *f*
◊ *tape backup* sauvegarde *f* sur bande
◊ *tape backup system* système *m* de sauvegarde sur bande
◊ *tape backup unit* unité *f* de sauvegarde sur bande
◊ *tape unit* unité *f* de bande

target disk *n (hard)* disque *m* cible ; *(floppy)* disquette *f* cible

task *n* tâche *f*

taskbar *n* barre *f* des tâches

TCP/IP *n* *Internet* (*abbr* **transmission control protocol/Internet protocol**) TCP-IP

tear-off menu *n* menu *m* flottant

techie *n Fam* = terme péjoratif ou humoristique désignant les informaticiens

technical support *n* support *m* technique

teleconference *n* téléconférence *f*

teleconferencing *n* téléconférence *f*

telematics *n* télématique *f*

telephone 1 *n* téléphone *m*
2 *vt* téléphoner à; **to telephone New York** appeler New York
3 *vi* téléphoner
◊ *telephone banking* opérations *fpl* bancaires par téléphone
◊ *telephone bill* facture *f* de téléphone
◊ *telephone book* annuaire *m* (téléphonique)
◊ *telephone call* appel *m* téléphonique, coup *m* de téléphone
◊ *telephone directory* annuaire *m* (téléphonique)
◊ *telephone exchange* central *m* téléphonique
◊ *telephone line* ligne *f* téléphonique

◇ *telephone message* message *m* téléphonique

◇ *telephone number* numéro *m* de téléphone

◇ *telephone order* commande *f* téléphonique *ou* par téléphone

◇ *telephone subscriber* abonné(e) *m,f* du téléphone

teleprocessing *n* télégestion *f*

teletex *n* télétex *m*

Telnet *n Internet* Telnet *m*

template *n (for keyboard)* réglette *f*; *(for program)* modèle *m*; *DTP (for document)* gabarit *m*

temporary file *n* fichier *m* temporaire

terminal *n* (poste *m*) terminal *m*

◇ *terminal emulation* émulation *f* de terminal

◇ *terminal emulator* émulateur *m* de terminal

◇ *terminal server* serveur *m* de terminaux

terminator *n (of chain)* terminateur *m*

text *n* texte *m*

◇ *text block* bloc *m* de texte

◇ *text buffer* mémoire *f* tampon de texte

◇ *text editor* éditeur *m* de texte

◇ *text field* champ *m* de text

◇ *text file* fichier *m* texte

◇ *text layout* disposition *f* de texte

◇ *text mode* mode *m* texte

◇ *text processing* traitement *m* de texte

◇ *text processor* (unité *f* de) traitement de texte

◇ *text wrap* habillage *m* du texte

thermal *adj*

◇ *thermal paper* papier *m* thermique *ou* thermosensible

◇ *thermal printer* imprimante *f* thermique *ou* thermoélectrique

thread *n (in newsgroup)* fil *m* de discussion

three-button mouse *n* souris *f* à trois boutons

throughput *n* capacité *f* de traitement

thumbnail *n* vignette *f*

TIFF *n (abbr* **Tagged Image File Format)** format *m* TIFF

tile *vt (windows)* afficher en mosaïque

time sharing *n* partage *m* de temps

title bar *n* barre *f* de titre

toggle *vi* basculer; **to toggle between two applications** alterner entre deux applications

◇ *toggle key* touche *f* à bascule

◇ *toggle switch* commande *f* à bascule

token ring *n* anneau *m* à jeton

toll *n Am Tel* frais *mpl* d'interurbain

◇ *toll call* communication *f* interurbaine

toll-free *Am Tel* **1** *adj* **toll-free number** numéro *m* vert
2 *adv* **to call toll-free** appeler un numéro vert

tone *n Tel* tonalité *f*

toner *n* toner *m*

◦ **toner cartridge** cartouche *f* de toner

tool bar *n* barre *f* d'outils

toolbox *n* boîte *f* à outils

touch screen *n* écran *m* tactile

touch-sensitive *adj (screen)* tactile ; *(key, switch)* à effleurement

touch-tone telephone *n* téléphone *m* à touches

tower *n (CPU)* boîtier *m* vertical, tour *f*

◦ **tower system** système *m* à boîtier vertical *ou* à tour

track *n (of disk)* piste *f*

trackball *n* boule *f* de commande, trackball *m ou f*

trackpad *n* tablette *f* tactile

transfer **1** *n (of data)* transfert *m*
2 *vt* (**a**) *Tel (call)* transférer ; **I'm transferring you now** je vous mets en communication (**b**) *(data)* transférer

◦ *Br* **transfer charge call** communication *f* en PCV

◦ **transfer rate** taux *m* de transfert

◦ **transfer speed** vitesse *f* de transfert

translate *vt (software)* traduire

translator *n (software)* traducteur *m*

transmission *n (of data)* transmission *f*

trash *n Am* poubelle *f*

tree *n (of data)* arbre *m*

◦ **tree diagram** *or* **structure** arborescence *f*

troubleshooter *n* expert *m*

troubleshooting *n* dépannage *m*

trusted third party *n (for Internet transactions)* tierce partie *f* de confiance

TTP *n (abbr* **trusted third party***) (for Internet transactions)* TPC *f*

tutorial *n* didacticiel *m*

◦ **tutorial program** didacticiel

type **1** *n (text)* caractères *mpl*
2 *vt* taper (à la machine) ; **to type sth into a computer** saisir qch à l'ordinateur
3 *vi* taper (à la machine)

◦ **type size** corps *m* des caractères

typeface *n* police *f* (de caractères)

typesetter *n DTP* photocomposeuse *f*

unauthorized *adj* non autorisé(e)

◇ *unauthorized access* accès *m* non autorisé

undo *vt (command)* annuler, défaire; **undo changes** annuler les révisions; **undo last** annuler dernière opération

◇ *undo command* commande *f* d'annulation

unedited *adj (text)* non édité(e)

unformatted *adj (disk)* non formaté(e)

uninitialized *adj* non initialisé(e)

uninstall *vt* désinstaller, supprimer

Unix *n* UNIX *m*

Unix-based *adj* basé(e) sur UNIX

unlimited e-mail addresses *npl* nombre *m* d'adresses électroniques illimité

unlisted *adj Am (telephone number)* sur la liste rouge

unlock *vt (file, diskette)* déverrouiller

unreadable *adj (file, data)* illisible

unzip *vt (file)* dézipper, décompresser

up arrow *adj* flèche *f* vers le haut

◇ *up arrow key* touche *f* de déplacement vers le haut

update 1 *n (of software package)* mise *f* à jour, actualisation *f*
2 *vt* mettre à jour, actualiser

upgradability *n* possibilités *fpl* d'extension

upgradable *adj (hardware, system)* évolutif(ive); *(memory)* extensible

upgrade 1 *n (of hardware, system)* augmentation *f* de puissance; *(of software)* mise *f* à jour, actualisation *f*
2 *vt (hardware, system)* optimiser; *(software)* améliorer, perfectionner

◇ *upgrade kit* kit *m* d'évolution *ou* d'extension

upload 1 *n* téléchargement *m*
2 *vt* télécharger *(vers un gros ordinateur)*

upper-case 1 *n* majuscule *f*
2 *adj* majuscule

UPS *n (abbr* **uninterruptible power supply)** onduleur *m*

upward-compatible *adj* compatible vers le haut

URL *n Internet* (*abbr* **uniform resource locator**) (adresse *f*) URL *m*

USB *n* (*abbr* **universal serial bus**) norme *f* USB, port *m* série universel

Usenet *n Internet* Usenet *m*

user *n* (*of computer*) utilisateur(trice) *m,f*; (*of telephone*) abonné(e) *m,f*

◇ **user ID, user identification** identification *f* de l'utilisateur

◇ **user interface** interface *f* utilisateur

◇ **user language** langage *m* utilisateur

◇ **user manual** manuel *m* d'utilisation

◇ **user name** nom *m* de l'utilisateur

◇ **user network** réseau *m* d'utilisateurs

◇ **user software** logiciel *m* utilisateur

◇ **user support** assistance *f* à l'utilisateur

user-definable *adj* (*characters, keys*) définissable par l'utilisateur

user-friendliness *n* convivialité *f*

user-friendly *adj* convivial(e)

utility *n* (*program*) programme *m* utilitaire, utilitaire *m*

◇ **utility program** (logiciel *m*) utilitaire

variable *n* variable *f*

VDU *n* (*abbr* **visual display unit**) moniteur *m*

◊ **VDU operator** personne *f* travaillant sur écran

vector graphics *n DTP* image *f* vectorielle

vendor *n* fournisseur *m*

vertical justification *n* justification *f* verticale

VGA *n* (*abbr* **Video Graphics Array**) VGA *m*

video *n* vidéo *f*

◊ **video accelerator card** carte *f* vidéo accélératrice

◊ **video board** carte *f* vidéo

◊ **video card** carte *f* vidéo

videoconference *n* visio-conférence *f*, vidéoconférence *f*

view *vt* (*codes, document*) visualiser

viewable area *n* (*of monitor*) zone *f* d'affichage

viewer *n* (*program*) visualiseur *m*

virtual *adj* virtuel(elle)

◊ **virtual reality** réalité *f* virtuelle

◊ **virtual reality simulator** simulateur *m* de réalité virtuelle

virus *n* virus *m*; **to disable a virus** désactiver un virus

◊ **virus check** détection *f* de virus; **to run a virus check on a disk** faire tourner le programme détecteur de virus sur une disquette

◊ **virus detector** détecteur *m* de virus

◊ **virus program** programme *m* virus

virus-free *adj* dépourvu(e) de virus

visual display unit *n* écran *m* ou console *f* de visualisation

voice *n*

◊ **voice mail** messagerie *f* vocale

◊ **voice recognition software** logiciel *m* de reconnaissance vocale

◊ **voice synthesizer** synthétiseur *m* de paroles

voice-activated *adj* à commande vocale

volume *n* volume *m*

◊ **volume label** label *m* de volume

VRAM *n* (*abbr* **video random access memory**) VRAM *f*

VRML *n* (*abbr* **virtual reality modelling language**) VRML *m*

W3 *n* (*abbr* **World Wide Web**) W3 *m*, le Web *m*

wallpaper *n* (*for screen*) papier *m* peint

WAN *n* (*abbr* **wide area network**) réseau *m* longue distance

warm *adj*
◊ *warm boot* redémarrage *m* à chaud
◊ *warm start* redémarrage à chaud *m*

warranty *n* garantie *f*; **this computer has a five-year warranty** cet ordinateur est garanti cinq ans; **under warranty** sous garantie; **extended warranty** extension *f* de la garantie; **on-site warranty** garantie sur site; **return-to-base warranty** garantie retour atelier

◊ *warranty certificate* certificat *m* de garantie

wastebasket *n* poubelle *f*

watchdog program *n* programme *m* sentinelle

Web *n* **the Web** le Web, la Toile

---

faq

Web site ou **Website**, **web site** ou **website**? Telle est la question. Dans les expressions "the World Wide Web" et "le Web", le terme "Web" s'écrit toujours avec une majuscule; par contre la situation est beaucoup moins claire en ce qui concerne les noms composés où figure ce terme, et l'on trouvera en divers endroits un même terme écrit en deux mots distincts ou en un seul mot, avec un "w" majuscule ou minuscule. Nous avons choisi dans cet ouvrage d'utiliser le "w" minuscule et la présentation en deux mots distincts pour les noms composés tels que **"web site"**, mais il faut noter que la forme **"Web site"** se rencontre également et que l'on peut utiliser l'une ou l'autre sans crainte de se tromper.

◇ *web authoring* création *f* de pages Web

◇ *web authoring program* programme *m* de création de pages Web

◇ *web authoring tool* outil *m* de création de pages Web

◇ *web browser* navigateur *m*, logiciel *m* de navigation

◇ *web cam* caméra *f* Internet

◇ *web consultancy* société *f* conseil pour la création et l'administration de sites Web

◇ *web design agency* société *f* spécialisée dans la conception de sites Web

◇ *web designer* concepteur-(trice) *m,f* de sites Web

◇ *web hosting* hébergement *m* de sites Web

◇ *web master* Webmaster *m*, Webmestre *m*, responsable *mf* de site Web

◇ *web page* page *f* Web

◇ *web server* serveur *m* Web

◇ *web site* site *m* Web

◇ *web space* espace *m* Web

welcome message *n* message *m* d'accueil

wide area network *n* réseau *m* longue distance

widow *n* DTP (ligne *f*) veuve *f*

wildcard *n* joker *m*

◇ *wildcard character* caractère *m* joker

WIMP *n* (*abbr* **windows, icon, mouse, pointer**) interface *f* WIMP

window *n* (*on screen*) fenêtre *f*

wireless mouse *n* souris *f* sans fil

wizard *n* assistant *m*

Word *n* Word; **it's in Word** c'est un document Word; **a Word document/file** un document/fichier Word

word *n* mot *m*

◇ *word count* nombre *m* de mots; **to do a word count** compter les mots

◇ *word count facility* fonction *f* de comptage de mots

◇ *word processor* logiciel *m* de traitement de texte

word-process *vt* réaliser par traitement de text

word-processing *n* traitement *m* de texte

◇ *word-processing program* logiciel *m* de traitement de texte

wordwrap *n* passage *m* automatique à la ligne suivante

work area *n* zone *f* de travail

workstation *n* station *f* ou poste *m* de travail

World Wide Web *n* le World Wide Web

WORM (*abbr* **write once read many times**) WORM

WP *n* (**a**) (*abbr* **word processing**) traitement *m* de texte (**b**) (*abbr* **word processor**) machine *f* à traitement de texte

wrap *vi* (*of lines*) se boucler

wrist rest *n* repose-poignets *m*

write **1** *vt* (*CD-ROM*) graver, enregistrer; **to write sth to disk** écrire qch sur disque **2** *vi* écrire; **to write to sb** écrire à qn

◇ *write protection* protection *f* contre l'écriture *ou* en écriture

◇ *write speed* vitesse *f* d'écriture

write-protect *vt* protéger contre l'écriture *ou* en écriture

write-protected *adj* protégé(e) contre l'écriture *ou* en écriture

WWW *n* (*abbr* World Wide Web) WWW, W3

WYSIWYG *n* (*abbr* **what you see is what you get**) tel écran-tel écrit *m* , tel-tel *m*, Wysiwyg *m*

◇ *WYSIWYG display* affichage *m* tel écran-tel écrit *ou* tel-tel *ou* Wysiwyg

XML *n* (*abbr* **Extensible Markup Language**) XML *m*

Y2K compliant *adj* (*abbr* **year 2000 compliant**) conforme à l'an 2000

year 2000 compliant *adj* conforme à l'an 2000

Yellow Pages *npl* **the Yellow Pages** les pages jaunes

zap *vt* (*file*) écraser

Zip ® *n*
 ◇ *Zip disk* cartouche *f* Zip ®
 ◇ *Zip drive* lecteur *m* Zip ®

zip *vt* (*file*) zipper, compresser

zoom box *n* case *f* zoom

L'INTERNET ET LE MONDE DES AFFAIRES: MODE D'EMPLOI

Petit guide de l'Internet à l'usage de l'homme d'affaires utilisant l'anglais comme langue de travail
par Bob Norton et Cathy Smith
traduit de l'anglais par Rose Rociola

Bob Norton dirige le service de documentation de l'Institut de Management de Corby, en Angleterre. Cathy Smith est chef du service informatique du centre de documentation sur le management du même institut. Bob et Cathy sont responsables de l'élaboration et de la gestion du site Internet de l'Institut. Chacun est l'auteur de nombreux articles sur la gestion de l'information et ils ont signé ensemble l'ouvrage *Understanding Business on the Internet*.

Table des Matières

Qu'est-ce que l'Internet?

L'Internet, réseau mondial ouvert, est constitué d'une multitude de réseaux informatiques reliés entre eux par l'intermédiaire de lignes téléphoniques publiques et privées. Ces réseaux sont la propriété d'organismes divers, agences gouvernementales, universités, sociétés privées et organisations bénévoles, qui autorisent ainsi l'accès à leurs ordinateurs – appelés dans ce cas serveurs – et aux informations qu'ils contiennent.

Le courrier électronique, qui peut se substituer au courrier postal, au téléphone ou à la télécopie, est le service le plus utilisé de l'Internet. D'autres services, tels que les groupes de nouvelles ou forums et les groupes de discussion, donnent à des utilisateurs ayant un intérêt commun la possibilité de dialoguer dans le monde entier. Quant au World Wide Web, service le plus célèbre, il permet de consulter des pages d'informations pouvant contenir du texte, des graphiques, des images et du son. Ces pages, bien que situées sur différents serveurs, sont reliées entre elles.

L'Internet n'appartient à personne et n'est régi par aucun organisme. Cependant, un certain nombre d'organisations bénévoles, telles que l'ISOC (Internet Society) ou l'IETF (Internet Engineering Taskforce), veillent à son évolution.

Les origines du réseau des réseaux

Au début des années soixante, en pleine guerre froide, le gouvernement américain veut mettre au point un système de communication efficace dans l'éventualité d'une attaque nucléaire. En effet, pour l'armée du Pentagone, il est bien trop risqué de garder des informations stratégiques dans un seul site, en cas de destruction de ce site. C'est ainsi que la société Rand Corporation eut l'idée d'un réseau décentralisé qui continuerait de fonctionner même en cas de destruction partielle. Pour plus de sécurité, les informations ne circuleraient pas sur le réseau dans leur intégralité, mais seraient décomposées en paquets et reconstituées une fois arrivées à destination.

En 1969, le réseau ARPANET voit le jour. Quatre universités sont reliées au moyen de lignes et de modems à grande vitesse, permettant ainsi aux chercheurs du gouvernement et des universités de communiquer par courrier électronique. Suite au succès de ce moyen de communication rapide, d'autres centres de recherches ainsi que des sociétés, d'abord aux États-Unis puis dans le monde entier, se connectent. C'est la naissance de l'Internet.

Dans les années quatre-vingt, les grandes entreprises commencent à utiliser l'Internet pour communiquer. À partir de 1990, dans le monde entier, un grand nombre d'entreprises de toutes sortes ainsi que de plus en plus de particuliers viennent se connecter.

Selon des estimations récentes, il y aurait plus de 50 millions d'utilisateurs aux États-Unis et ce chiffre ne cesse de croître. En Europe, on estime que de 2 à 3 % des ménages ont accès à l'Internet. Avec un million d'utilisateurs, la France vient en troisième position, après l'Allemagne et le Royaume-Uni, qui compte à ce jour trois millions d'utilisateurs en constante augmentation. La France est suivie de près par les Pays-Bas, la Suède, l'Italie et l'Espagne. À la fin des années 90, on estime que les communications sur l'Internet, et notamment la quantité de courriers électroniques échangés, doublent tous les cent jours; quant au World Wide Web, il double de volume tous les six mois. Certains estiment qu'il y aura 250 millions d'utilisateurs d'ici à l'an 2000. Pour d'autres, à ce rythme là, tous les habitants de la planète seront connectés d'ici à 2003!

Quatre facteurs expliquent ce taux de croissance exceptionnel:

• le rapprochement des technologies de l'informatique et des télécom-munications;

• la baisse des prix des micro-ordinateurs et l'augmentation des ventes qui s'en est suivie;

• la médiatisation importante de l'Internet;

• l'amélioration de la convivialité de l'Internet, en particulier depuis l'apparition du World Wide Web en 1993-94.

Au départ, l'internaute type était un homme instruit de 35 ans, partisan de la liberté individuelle et de la liberté d'expression. À partir de 1995, parmi les utilisateurs types on trouve également le cadre d'entreprise, homme ou femme pouvant avoir la quarantaine et utilisant l'Internet pour communiquer à distance avec des clients et des fournisseurs ainsi que pour rechercher et envoyer des informations relatives à son travail.

Les enjeux de l'Internet

L'utilisation de l'Internet présente de nombreux avantages pour les entreprises: la possibilité de communiquer mieux et moins cher, de travailler efficacement à distance et, quelle que soit la taille de l'entreprise, de se faire connaître sur le marché international à moindre frais.

Cependant, au début des années quatre-vingt-dix, de nombreuses entreprises se sont laissé prendre par l'illusion d'un marché électronique facile où de nombreux clients les attendaient. Certains articles parus dans la presse ont contribué à répandre la peur que ceux qui ne se reliaient pas à l'Internet seraient vite dépassés et évincés de ce marché prometteur.

De nombreuses entreprises ont suivi le mouvement sans toutefois réaliser que cette nouvelle opportunité devait être planifiée, organisée et gérée, au même titre que tout projet professionnel. De nombreuses sociétés qui n'ont pas su adapter l'utilisation de l'Internet à leurs besoins réels se demandent maintenant comment y parvenir et combien de ressources y consacrer.

L'Internet peut-il vraiment être utile au monde des affaires et changer notre façon de travailler ou ne correspond-il qu'à une simple lubie? Force est de constater qu'il s'agit d'un phénomène durable. L'Internet est en pleine expansion et le grand public sait de mieux en mieux s'en servir.

- L'Internet n'est plus uniquement l'apanage de jeunes gens boutonneux toujours rivés à leur écran. La standardisation de l'équipement nécessaire, micro-ordinateur, modem et logiciel du fournisseur d'accès, a contribué à mettre le réseau à la portée du grand public.

- L'Internet représente une solution souvent plus économique que les méthodes classiques pour obtenir, envoyer, recevoir et stocker des informations. Nul ne peut aujourd'hui ignorer la société de l'information.

- De nombreuses entreprises, de la PME à la grosse multinationale, expérimentent sur l'Internet de nouvelles approches pour la gestion du personnel, la communication externe, la promotion de leurs produits ou services et les transactions commerciales. D'autres sociétés, ne voyant pas de rentabilité immédiate, se contentent d'une utilisation plus réduite. Les investissements des grandes banques viennent cependant renforcer la promesse d'un marché électronique. Des entreprises commencent à obtenir des résultats financiers. Selon des chiffres récents, aux États-Unis, les transactions commerciales sur l'Internet s'élèvent à trois milliards de dollars chaque année et ce chiffre ne cesse de croître.

• Même si tous ne l'utilisent pas, l'Internet a modifié nos comportements, dans notre vie professionnelle comme dans notre vie privée. L'Internet est aujourd'hui au cœur de nombreux débats:
  – l'impact de l'évolution technologique sur le monde des affaires, la société et l'État;
  – les nouvelles techniques de marketing et les relations avec la clientèle;
  – la question sociale des laissés-pour-compte du monde de l'information dans une société où l'information est devenue un bien commercial et le savoir un avantage concurrentiel;
  – les implications légales du transfert d'informations au-delà des frontières.

Le Parlement européen et le Sénat américain se penchent aujourd'hui sur les opportunités offertes par l'Internet ainsi que sur les problèmes que son utilisation soulève. Les gouvernements ne peuvent plus ignorer les enjeux stratégiques du réseau.

L'Internet évolue très rapidement, mais une utilisation optimale requiert du temps et des efforts. Il faut en effet envisager de nouvelles approches pour en tirer le meilleur parti. Bien que l'on ne puisse pas affirmer aujourd'hui que ceux qui attendent trop longtemps seront évincés, il est certain qu'ils devront fournir beaucoup d'efforts pour rester compétitifs. En effet, nombreux sont ceux qui voient en l'Internet, et dans les technologies qui en découlent, l'outil d'avenir incontournable de toute stratégie commerciale.

La gestion du réseau

Afin d'exploiter au mieux les possibilités qu'offre l'Internet, il est important de ne pas se laisser influencer par l'attrait de la technologie et de planifier avec soin son utilisation. Il est donc utile dans un premier temps de répondre à certaines questions essentielles:

Pourquoi voulons-nous utiliser l'Internet?

- Par peur d'être dépassé?

- Pour découvrir les opportunités offertes?

- Pour explorer les possibilités commerciales?

- Pour évaluer les avantages que l'entreprise peut en tirer?

Dans quel but voulons-nous utiliser l'Internet?

- Pour améliorer la communication externe de l'entreprise?

- Pour interroger des bases de données? Pour entrer en contact avec des experts? Pour obtenir des informations sur des sociétés et leurs produits?

- Pour tirer parti des possibilités de commercialisation? Pour prendre de l'avance sur la concurrence?

- Pour améliorer les relations avec la clientèle ou attirer de nouveaux clients?

Qui va utiliser l'Internet?

- Quelles sont les compétences requises?

- Est-il nécessaire de recruter du personnel expérimenté ou vaut-il mieux former le personnel interne?

- Est-il préférable de faire appel à un consultant extérieur ou de sous-traiter tout le projet à une société spécialisée?

- Qui doit avoir accès à l'Internet?

- Qui a le temps de s'occuper de l'Internet? Comment trouver le temps nécessaire?

Quel mode d'accès choisir?

- Vaut-il mieux opter pour une ligne spécialisée, une ligne RNIS ou un simple accès commuté?

- Comment choisir le service correspondant le mieux à nos besoins?

Communication

Le *courrier électronique* ["e-mail"] est le service le plus utilisé de l'Internet: des centaines de millions de messages sont échangés chaque jour. Le succès de ce service tient à sa facilité d'emploi, à son faible coût (tarif d'une communication locale) quelle que soit la destination, et à la possibilité de joindre des fichiers informatiques aux messages (graphiques, documents annexes ou même logiciels). Le décalage horaire ou la peur de déranger ne sont plus un problème car le destinataire n'a pas besoin d'être connecté au même moment pour recevoir son message. L'envoi d'un message à de multiples destinataires est une procédure simple et bon marché. Il est également possible d'échanger des informations avec des personnes que l'on ne connaît pas grâce aux groupes d'intérêt appelés *groupes de nouvelles* ou *forums* ["newsgroups"] et *groupes de discussion* ["discussion groups"].

> Une adresse électronique se présente généralement sous la forme suivante:
>   nom@domaine.pays
>   Par exemple, jdurand@club-internet.fr

Bien que le courrier électronique offre de nombreux avantages, il comporte également des risques qui ne doivent pas être ignorés:

1. Le courrier électronique n'est pas encore totalement sûr. N'importe quelle personne suffisamment déterminée peut intercepter votre courrier. Des enquêtes réalisées au hasard révèlent que jusqu'à un quart des paquets d'information dont sont composés les messages électroniques peuvent ne pas parvenir à leur destinataire, notamment durant les heures de pointe, lorsque les réseaux sont très embouteillés. Dans la plupart des cas cependant, les messages ne sont pas perdus, ils sont renvoyés

à l'expéditeur.

2. Le courrier électronique ne garantit pas une réponse immédiate. Certaines personnes lui préfèrent le téléphone pour les informations de nature urgente.

3. La convivialité du courrier électronique encourage une certaine familiarité, que l'on peut parfois regretter après-coup. Cette caractéristique a répandu le sentiment que les messages électroniques sont peu fiables, non durables, voire même inexacts, et ne valent donc pas la peine d'être cités. Il faut savoir pourtant que le courrier électronique est une forme de publication qui est donc soumise en tant que telle à la législation relative aux droits d'auteur et à la diffamation. Un message électronique doit par conséquent être considéré de la même façon que tout autre forme de communication écrite.

4. Les fichiers joints aux messages peuvent contenir des virus. Cependant, il est difficile de savoir si un fichier est infecté ou non tant que l'on ne l'a pas ouvert. Étant donné qu'un virus peut détruire toutes les informations contenues sur le disque dur de l'ordinateur, certaines organisations vérifient tous les fichiers joints avant de les ouvrir; d'autres vont même jusqu'à interdire la réception de fichiers.

Avant d'utiliser le courrier électronique au sein d'une organisation, il est important de tenir compte des points suivants:

1. Utilisation optimale – Il faut diminuer le risque d'utilisation inappropriée, de perte de temps et de surcharge d'information.

2. Priorité – Le courrier électronique doit-il être prioritaire par rapport aux autres moyens de communication? Si tel est le cas, quelle est la procédure à suivre?

3. Responsabilité par rapport au contenu – Cette question ne doit pas être négligée, étant donné la portée du courrier électronique qui permet d'atteindre le plus grand nombre à moindre frais.

Accès à l'information

Sur le *World Wide Web*, ou tout simplement le *Web*, on peut accéder, la plupart du temps gratuitement, à des informations sur une multitude de sujets et sous différentes formes. Ce service permet de consulter des *sites Web* ["web sites"] contenant des pages de texte, mais aussi des images et du son, à l'aide d'un logiciel spécifique appelé *navigateur* ["browser"]. Il est possible de naviguer d'une page à l'autre grâce à des liens appelés *liens hypertexte* ["hypertext-links"]. Chaque site Web a son adresse, connue sous le nom *d'adresse URL* ["Uniform Resource Locator, URL"], par exemple: http://www.renault.fr

- http://["HyperText Transfer Protocol"] signifie protocole de transfert des pages hypertextes;

- www.renault.fr indique le nom du serveur, celui de l'organisme ainsi que le code du pays, dans ce cas la France.

Figure 1: La page d'accueil du site institutionnel de Renault, en français et en anglais (www.renault.com)

Chaque site s'ouvre sur un menu principal ou *page d'accueil* ["home page"]. La plupart des adresses citées correspondent à la page d'accueil, mais il peut arriver que l'adresse renvoie à une section spécifique du site. On appelle *nom de domaine* ["domain name"] la partie de l'adresse comprenant le nom de l'organisation et le code du pays, par exemple *renault.fr*.

Il existe un très grand nombre de sites susceptibles d'intéresser une entreprise, il serait impossible de tous les recenser. Le site francophone *(e)-business: la lettre du commerce électronique* (http:\\www.ebusiness.org) représente un bon point de départ pour obtenir des informations sur le commerce électronique. Un lien hypertexte renvoie à une sélection de sites sur le commerce électronique. Il faut s'abonner pour avoir accès à tous les services, mais un espace grand public peut être consulté gratuitement.

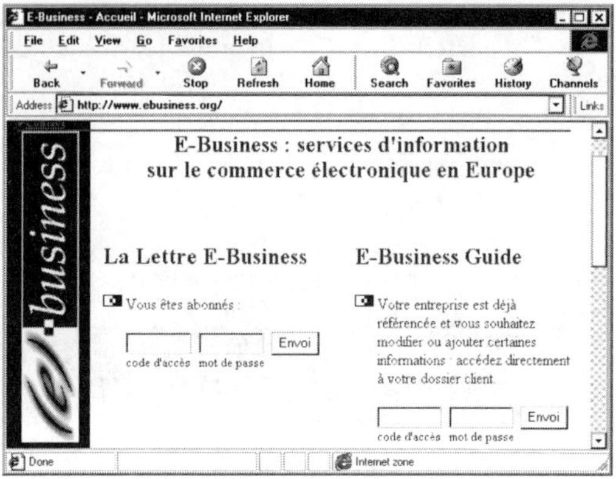

Figure 2: La page d'accueil de (e)-business

Le moyen le plus rapide d'accéder aux informations désirées est d'obtenir les adresses des sites dans la presse ou par le bouche à oreille. Les deux principaux navigateurs, Netscape Navigator et Internet Explorer de Microsoft, permettent de garder en mémoire les adresses des sites désirés, au moyen des options respectives Signets et Favoris. Si vous ne connaissez pas l'adresse du site recherché, vous pouvez utiliser l'un des nombreux outils de recherche proposés sur le Web. Il peut s'agir d'annuaires, où des mots-clés ont été sélectionnés et indexés, ou de moteurs de recherche ("search engines"), programmes explorant régulière-ment le Web à la recherche de nouvelles informations.

Il est important de garder à l'esprit qu'une recherche peut déboucher sur des centaines, voire parfois des milliers, de résultats différents, appelés *hits* ou *contacts de page* ["hits"]. En effet, le Web est si vaste que les outils de recherche ne réussissent pas toujours à faire le tri entre les informations pertinentes et celles qui ne le sont pas. Bien que la plupart des outils de recherche classent les informations par catégories (affaires, sports, art, actualité, loisirs, etc.), mieux vaut être le plus précis possible lors d'une recherche.

Les adresses suivantes renvoient à des outils de recherche sur le Web:
   Yahoo – (http://www.yahoo.fr) ou (http://www.yahoo.co.uk)
   Excite – (http://www.excite.fr) ou (http://www.excite.co.uk)

Altavista – (http://www.altavista.com)
AltaVista propose également un outil pour la traduction de
documents en français et en anglais ainsi que dans de
nombreuses autres langues.
Ecila – (http://ecila.ceic.com)
Eureka – (http://www.eureka-fr.com)
Lokace – (http://lokace.iplus.fr)
Francite – (http://francite.com)

Figure 3: La version française de Yahoo avec les principaux domaines de
recherche de l'information

Marketing

Le Web n'est pas qu'une gigantesque source d'informations. C'est
également un endroit où particuliers et sociétés peuvent faire
connaître et vendre leurs produits ou leurs services. Très vite, des
fleurs, des livres et des logiciels ont été commercialisés avec
succès. Le Web est un monde égalitaire où les PME côtoient les
plus grandes sociétés. Certains sites sont très professionnels,
d'autres ont une apparence beaucoup plus artisanale, mais tous
en sont encore au stade expérimental.

Le Web est un marché interactif où le client potentiel choisit le
lieu, le moment et la durée de sa visite. Ce marché, ouvert 24
heures sur 24 et sept jours sur sept, peut recevoir aussi bien la
visite de votre voisin que d'une personne se trouvant à l'autre
bout du monde.

Il est possible de commercialiser ses produits sur le Web en plaçant des annonces publicitaires dans d'autres sites Web. Il existe différents types d'annonces:

- *Bandeaux publicitaires*: ces encadrés graphiques ressemblent à des panneaux d'affichage. Ils sont de plus en plus souvent animés et interactifs.

- *Boutons*: semblables aux bandeaux, les boutons affichent en général le nom d'une société, d'une marque ou même d'un secteur d'activité. Il suffit de cliquer sur le bouton pour atteindre le site Web correspondant.

- *Mots-clés*: les annonceurs ont même la possibilité d'acheter des mots. Par exemple, si Moet-Chandon achetait le mot «champagne», à chaque fois que quelqu'un recherche ce mot, le nom Moet-Chandon s'afficherait à l'écran.

La première étape pour se faire connaître consiste à créer un site Web. Le succès d'un site dépend de sa présentation, de l'utilité de son contenu et de la fréquence des mises à jour. L'interactivité du Web permet à une entreprise de découvrir les préférences de ses clients et de développer ses relations commerciales. Pour plus de détails sur la création d'un site Web, reportez-vous au chapitre suivant.

Figure 4: ces "boutons" publicitaires sont situés au bas de la page d'accueil d'Ecila. Les sociétés en question ont acheté cet espace de façon à fournir un lien direct avec leur propre site Web. Reportez-vous à la Figure 3 pour un exemple de bandeau publicitaire pour Sicav.

Accès à l'Internet

Il existe deux façons principales de se connecter à l'Internet: par accès commuté ou par une ligne spécialisée.

Accès commuté

Pour l'accès commuté, c'est-à-dire ponctuel, il suffit d'avoir un modem relié à l'ordinateur, une ligne téléphonique et un abonnement auprès d'un fournisseur d'accès ["Internet Service Provider"]. Ce type d'accès ne requiert pas d'investissement majeur, il convient donc essentiellement aux particuliers et aux sociétés qui n'utilisent pas l'Internet de manière intensive. Son principal inconvénient est qu'il peut être lent, notamment aux heures de pointe lorsque des millions d'utilisateurs se connectent dans le monde entier.

De nombreuses sociétés choisissent d'installer une ligne de type RNIS (Réseau Numérique à Intégration de Service) afin d'obtenir un accès rapide et de qualité supérieure aux lignes téléphoniques. Une ligne RNIS, bien que coûteuse, est tout de même moins chère qu'une ligne spécialisée (voir ci-dessous) et les prix commencent à baisser.

L'efficacité d'une connexion à l'Internet dépend de toute la chaîne qui relie les deux ordinateurs: la puissance des ordinateurs, la rapidité du modem, la capacité des lignes téléphoniques ainsi que la rapidité de la connexion entre le fournisseur d'accès et l'Internet.

Ligne spécialisée

Cet accès se fait au moyen d'un câble fournissant une connexion permanente et rapide à l'Internet. La connexion peut se faire directement à un réseau de l'Internet ou passer par un fournisseur d'accès. L'installation d'une ligne spécialisée est beaucoup plus coûteuse que l'accès commuté et convient par conséquent aux sociétés qui utilisent l'Internet de manière intensive.

3: LA CREATION D'UN SITE WEB

1. Définition des objectifs

Pourquoi voulez-vous créer votre propre site ?

- Pour élargir votre clientèle ?
- Pour vous faire connaître ?
- Pour proposer un service ?
- À titre expérimental ?

Demandez-vous également quels sont les avantages que vous aimeriez tirer de votre site Web tout en tenant compte des ressources financières, techniques et humaines que vous voulez y investir. Définissez les critères qui vous permettront d'évaluer le succès du site. Prévoyez d'analyser les données de fréquentation du site et de consultation des pages.

2. Choix de l'emplacement du site

Une des méthodes les plus utilisées consiste à louer de l'espace auprès d'un fournisseur d'accès à l'Internet. La plupart des fournisseurs d'accès offrent gratuitement à leurs abonnés un espace pour créer quelques pages sur le Web. Cette option, peu coûteuse, permet de faire des essais sans prendre trop de risques. Une fois que vous avez choisi votre fournisseur d'accès, pensez à vous renseigner sur les possibilités d'évolution de votre site, sur les rapports détaillant la consultation du site et sur les transactions commerciales. Une autre possibilité consiste à faire appel à une société spécialisée pour la conception et l'hébergement de votre site, moyennant une redevance.

Beaucoup de grandes entreprises ont leur propre serveur Web. Cette solution cependant requiert des compétences techniques très poussées et un investissement considérable tant au niveau du matériel que des logiciels.

3. Recours à un prestataire ou réalisation en interne?

Le recours à un prestataire doit aboutir à la création d'un site professionnel. Renseignez-vous sur les projets déjà réalisés par la société et sur leur succès. Il vous faudra décider si vous voulez assurer la maintenance et la mise à jour du site ou si vous préférez sous-traiter cet aspect également. Le recours à une société spécialisée n'est pas forcément une solution bon marché car il faut tenir compte des efforts et du temps passés à décrire votre activité au prestataire.

La conception en interne peut également être coûteuse, que vous fassiez appel à des spécialistes ou que vous preniez le temps de créer vous-même le site. Si vous mettez en place un site important en interne, il peut être nécessaire de faire appel à un responsable de site Web ou *webmestre* ("web master") expérimenté. Le webmestre se charge de la conception, de l'évolution et de la maintenance d'un site, aussi bien au niveau du contenu que pour les aspects techniques. Cela nécessite un éventail de compétences rare: maîtrise des aspects techniques et graphiques, connaissance des systèmes d'information et qualités relationnelles.

4. Enregistrement du nom de domaine

Le nom de domaine doit permettre de vous identifier rapidement. Choisissez un nom en rapport avec votre activité ou votre raison sociale. Le nom choisi doit être enregistré avant de pouvoir être utilisé, cela permet de vérifier qu'il n'est pas déjà pris. Le fournisseur d'accès peut généralement se charger de l'enregistrement du nom de domaine pour une somme minime. Les noms sont enregistrés auprès des organisations suivantes:

- En France: AFNIC – Association Française pour le Nommage Internet en Coopération (http://www.nic.fr)

- Au Royaume-Uni: Nominet (http://www.nic.uk).

- Aux États-Unis: Internic (http://www.internic.net).

5. Présentation du site

Lors de la création du site, il est nécessaire de prendre en considération les deux aspects suivants:

- Conception – comment comptez-vous projeter l'image voulue?

- Navigation à l'intérieur du site – combien de fois faut-il cliquer sur la souris avant d'arriver à une information pertinente?

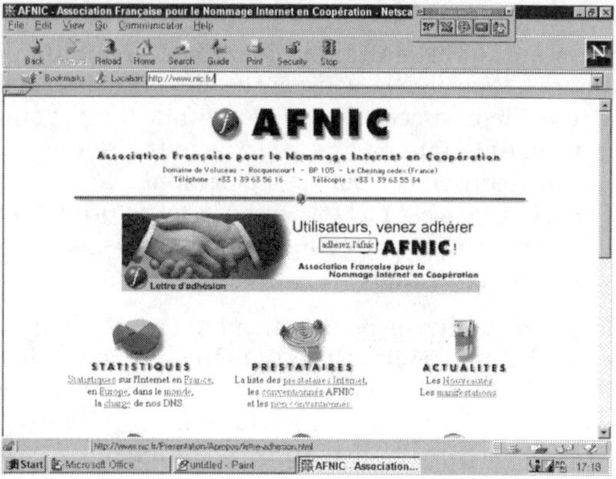

Figure 5: La page d'accueil de l'AFNIC

Il peut être utile d'observer les sites Web de différentes organisations et de noter ce qui vous plaît ou non. Consultez également des utilisateurs potentiels, leur avis peut être précieux pour rendre la présentation du site plus pratique.

Figure 6: La page d'accueil de la "Confederation of British Industry"

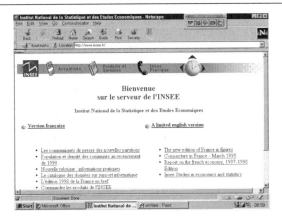

Figure 7: La page d'accueil de l'INSEE

6. Contenu du site

Les suggestions suivantes peuvent aider à rendre votre site plus intéressant et convivial:

- Affichez les réponses aux questions qui reviennent le plus fréquemment.

- Affichez des informations supplémentaires pertinentes.

- Assurez la maintenance et la mise à jour constante du site.

Une utilisation modérée de la couleur et de graphiques peut mettre en valeur votre site. N'en abusez pas cependant car cela pourrait ralentir les temps de consultation. Certains sites Web proposent en option une version texte seulement, d'autres un affichage dans d'autres langues pour toucher une clientèle internationale. Si vous souhaitez intégrer des séquences vidéo et du son, n'oubliez pas que tous les utilisateurs n'y ont pas accès.

Bien que le coût de l'espace disque soit dérisoire, il ne faut pas oublier que la surcharge d'information sur le Web est devenue un problème. Mettez-vous à la place de l'utilisateur afin de créer une présentation qui facilite la lecture et l'assimilation des informations. Prévoyez des espaces blancs et concentrez-vous sur l'essentiel en utilisant un style clair et concis. Privilégiez la qualité plutôt que la quantité.

7. Liens hypertextes et passerelles

La structure d'un site repose sur les liens hypertextes qui permettent de relier différents documents entre eux. D'autres liens peuvent être prévus pour orienter les utilisateurs vers d'autres sites susceptibles de les intéresser. Il s'agit généralement de sites fournissant des informations complémentaires sur un sujet spécifique ou sur une activité similaire (voir l'exemple de lien dans le site *(e)-business: la lettre du commerce électronique* au chapitre précédent).

8. Participation des utilisateurs

Vous pouvez inviter les utilisateurs qui consultent votre site à:

- faire part de leurs commentaires, suggestions ou critiques;
- participer à la conception ou aux tests du produit;
- prendre part à des séances interactives visant à améliorer un produit ou un service

Sachez toutefois que toute réponse demandant une présentation plus élaborée qu'un simple message électronique entraîne du travail supplémentaire au niveau de la programmation et de la conception.

9. Sécurité

Les informations publiées sur le Web s'adressent à un public très vaste, réparti dans le monde entier. À moins de protéger vos documents, il est impossible d'en garder la trace et de savoir ce qu'ils deviennent une fois qu'ils ont été téléchargés par l'un des millions d'ordinateurs connectés. Et ce, malgré les lois internationales en matière de protection des droits d'auteur.

Vous pouvez, si vous le souhaitez, limiter l'accès de certaines sections de votre site à une catégorie spécifique d'utilisateurs ou de clients, en formant un groupe fermé d'utilisateurs dont l'accès est protégé par un mot de passe.

Si vous souhaitez relier votre site Web à des informations très confidentielles, par exemple une base de données clients dont l'accès doit être strictement contrôlé, vous pouvez installer un système de protection appelé *mur coupe-feu* ("firewall"). Ce système, de plus en plus répandu, consiste à utiliser un autre ordinateur pour filtrer les demandes d'accès. Tout demande ne correspondant pas aux critères définis est ainsi rejetée.

business@harrap.fr

10. Promotion du site

Un utilisateur qui ne connaît pas l'URL de votre site, c'est-à-dire son adresse, peut le trouver de différentes façons:

- par l'intermédiaire d'un lien hypertexte dans un autre site;

- en utilisant un moteur de recherche;

- par le bouche-à-oreille;

- dans une publicité;

- par hasard.

Il est donc essentiel que les moteurs de recherche puissent localiser votre site. Ces moteurs utilisent la page d'accueil pour l'indexation du site. Cette page doit donc contenir tous les termes et les concepts que les utilisateurs sont susceptibles d'utiliser pour vous localiser. Ces termes peuvent être cachés, si leur usage est réservé aux moteurs de recherche, ou visibles à l'écran.

Vous pouvez également recourir aux méthodes traditionnelles pour faire connaître votre site: cartes de visite, brochures de vente, rapports d'activité ou campagnes de presse. Un site Web correspondant toutefois à une stratégie marketing, il est conseillé de ne pas abuser de la publicité. En effet, ce n'est pas tant la promotion d'un site que l'intérêt qu'il suscite parmi les utilisateurs qui est garant de son succès.

Au milieu des années quatre-vingt-dix, le président Bill Clinton déclara que l'Internet allait devenir une zone planétaire de libre-échange favorable aux transactions commerciales. Ce jugement s'appuyait sur les nombreuses prévisions du chiffre d'affaires réalisé sur l'Internet, un billion de dollars d'ici 2010 pour certains. Toutes les prévisions ne sont pas si optimistes, mais la plupart s'accordent à prévoir un chiffre d'affaires brut pouvant aller jusqu'à 300 milliards de dollars à l'échelle mondiale, avec plus de 200 milliards de dollars pour les États-Unis et plus de 60 milliards de dollars pour l'Europe, et ceci d'ici l'année 2001 (Source: Forrester Research).

Cependant, nombreux sont ceux qui restent sceptiques quant aux possibilités commerciales de l'Internet. Il y a à cela plusieurs raisons :

- À moins d'être bien informé et de s'armer de patience, on peut encore avoir l'impression que la confusion règne sur l'Internet. Les informations ou les résultats sont souvent longs à obtenir. Le téléchargement des graphiques de certains sites Web peut être lent et les liens ne marchent pas toujours car certains sites peuvent être «en cours de développement». L'encombrement des réseaux peut ralentir les temps de réponse et, dans les cas extrêmes, provoquer des interruptions.

- Des essais réalisés très tôt ont montré que les consommateurs hésitaient à faire leurs achats sur l'Internet. Les raisons avancées étaient qu'ils ne pouvaient pas voir, toucher ou goûter les produits et que le fait de ne pas pouvoir être «sur place» les gênait.

- Les consommateurs hésitent à communiquer leur numéro de carte de crédit sur le Web. En effet, il est impossible de réellement vérifier l'identité du vendeur et de s'assurer que le numéro de la carte ne se retrouvera pas entre les mains d'un escroc. Les transactions commerciales sur le Web dépendent de la vérification de l'identité de l'acheteur et du vendeur.

- Certains produits sont moins adaptés à la vente sur l'Internet que d'autres. Il est ainsi beaucoup plus facile de vendre des services et des produits culturels que des biens matériels. Ceci est dû en partie à la nature de la distribution. Les entreprises qui commercialisent des produits pour lesquels la présence de l'acheteur n'est pas indispensable, tels que des livres, des disques ou des logiciels, sont celles qui actuellement tirent le meilleur parti de l'Internet. Ce type de vente se rapproche de la vente par correspondance.

Cependant, cette situation évolue rapidement, et ce pour plusieurs raisons :

• Le Web se professionnalise grâce à la présence de grands noms et à l'idée qui fait son chemin que le marketing sur l'Internet doit cibler des groupes spécifiques, tout comme pour les autres médias. L'Internet compte de plus en plus d'utilisateurs familiarisés avec le réseau. Les consommateurs savent de mieux en mieux comment trouver les sites qui les intéressent et ce qu'ils vont y trouver. On commence à constater que les sites Web peuvent apporter un plus par rapport aux réseaux traditionnels de la vente.

Figure 8: La librairie Amazon, qui fonctionne uniquement par l'Internet, serait d'après ses dirigeants la plus grande librairie du monde. Cet écran renseigne les utilisateurs qui consultent le site pour la première fois, et notamment ceux qui désirent en savoir plus sur les méthodes de paiement.

business@harrap.fr

- Au fur et à mesure du développement de l'infrastructure de l'Internet, les télécommunications s'améliorent et les prix baissent. Des universités américaines testent actuellement Internet2, qui laisse entrevoir des taux de transmission de données 1000 fois plus rapides.

- Les institutions financières du monde entier ont beaucoup investi dans les systèmes de paiement électronique. En Europe et aux États-Unis, les principales sociétés de cartes de crédit, dont Visa et MasterCard, mettent au point des moyens de paiement sûrs, en étroite collaboration avec des éditeurs de logiciels. L'infrastructure nécessaire est encore chère, mais les prix baisseront au fur et à mesure que les entreprises adopteront le système et que les banques amortiront leur investissement.

- L'Internet qui ne connaît pas de contraintes géographiques ou temporelles offre un avantage considérable sur les moyens de vente traditionnels. En effet, la possibilité de demander un produit adapté à ses besoins, de négocier le prix et la livraison, à domicile, 24 heures sur 24, sept jours sur sept, représente un gain de temps et d'argent considérable pour le client comme pour le fabricant.

Le paiement électronique

Le développement du commerce électronique a été freiné par les pirates informatiques qui ont réussi à pénétrer dans certains systèmes qui pourtant promettaient confidentialité et sécurité. Bien que le piratage informatique reste rare, quelques affaires très médiatisées ont souvent suffi à marquer les esprits.

La monnaie électronique

De nombreux petits achats anonymes pour lesquels on n'utilise pas sa carte de crédit, par exemple l'achat de journaux et de magazines, représentent autant de transactions potentielles sur l'Internet. Plusieurs entreprises innovatrices, en collaboration avec des banques et des éditeurs de logiciels, ont mis en place un système de monnaie électronique ("e-cash") pour l'Internet dans le but de sécuriser les transactions.

Le fonctionnement d'un compte électronique est simple. Il suffit d'ouvrir un compte auprès d'une banque électronique, telle que First Virtual, DigiCash ou CyberCash. L'argent électronique est ensuite conservé sur le disque dur du client ou sur l'ordinateur de la banque et l'utilisateur autorise les paiements au moyen de son mot de passe.

Ce système fait encore peu d'adeptes en dehors des particuliers et des vendeurs qui ont pris part aux tests. Il est possible que les consommateurs s'attendent à la gratuité des informations sur le Web ou qu'ils n'aiment pas le système du paiement à la consultation, même pour de petites sommes. Parmi les autres raisons avancées devant le manque de succès de la monnaie électronique, on trouve le peu de publicité fait autour de ces systèmes ainsi que l'hésitation des consommateurs à faire des achats en ligne.

Les paiements par carte de crédit et le cryptage

Le cryptage ("encryption"), c'est-à-dire le codage des informations afin que seul le destinataire puisse les lire, est probablement la solution la plus prometteuse pour payer par carte de crédit en toute sécurité. C'est en tout cas celle qui a reçu le plus de publicité et d'investissements.

Visa et MasterCard ont mis au point conjointement un système de cryptage, SET (Secure Electronic Transaction), qui propose de sécuriser les transactions électroniques par carte de crédit à l'aide d'un cryptage pratiquement inviolable. L'expéditeur et le destinataire doivent être en possession d'un logiciel permettant de vérifier leur identité et fourni par l'organisme de carte de crédit. Le système vérifie que le vendeur est habilité à recevoir des paiements par carte de crédit, sans jamais transmettre le numéro de la carte. Les informations restent cryptées jusqu'à ce qu'elles parviennent à la banque, garantissant ainsi une sécurité maximale pour le vendeur et le client.

Une icône dorée, clef ou cadenas, apparaît en bas et à gauche de l'écran du navigateur. Lorsque l'icône est affichée en surbrillance, toute information sur la carte de crédit est cryptée avant d'être transmise. Seuls le commerçant ou la banque autorisés détiennent la clef pour décoder le message.

Figure 9: L'icône représentant un cadenas ouvert indique que l e cryptage est impossible sur le site.

Selon des estimations, 80% des banques européennes offriront leurs services sur l'Internet d'ici l'an 2000. Le commerce électronique a cependant encore besoin de gagner la confiance du public pour prendre son essor et ne plus être uniquement le domaine réservé de quelques pionniers.

Une stratégie commerciale sur le Web

Le nombre de sociétés réalisant des transactions et gagnant de l'argent sur le Web ne cesse de croître. Les banques pourront bientôt sécuriser les paiements électroniques. Mais avant de vendre ou d'acheter sur le Web, il est important d'effectuer un certain nombre de démarches :

- Renseignez-vous sur les préférences de vos clients pour le paiement ainsi que sur leur comportement d'achat. Vérifiez s'ils sont équipés ou non pour le commerce électronique.

- Demandez-vous si vos produits ou vos services sont bien adaptés au commerce électronique et à la vente par correspondance. Si ce n'est pas le cas, sachez qu'une vitrine virtuelle sur le Web est un bon moyen de faire connaître ses produits et d'élargir sa clientèle.

- Vérifiez que vous pouvez vous permettre l'infrastructure nécessaire au commerce électronique. Ceci est particulièrement important lorsque les prix de vente ne sont pas très élevés. Surveillez les coûts d'installation car ils vont certainement baisser.

- Consultez d'autres sites. On assiste, à la fin des années 90, au développement du commerce électronique. De nombreuses organisations sont sans cesse à la recherche de nouveaux moyens de communication interactif; c'est pourquoi certains sites créés il y a seulement deux ans paraissent déjà vieillots aujourd'hui.

- Si vous optez pour le commerce électronique, pensez aux stratégies que vous devrez développer pour créer une communauté commerciale. Pensez aux moyens de rassurer vos clients sur la sécurité des transactions électroniques. En cas de doute, réfléchissez avant de vous lancer ou demandez à vos clients d'utiliser les moyens de paiement traditionnels.

- Consultez votre banque et votre fournisseur d'accès à l'Internet pour connaître leurs projets en matière de commerce électronique et voir comment ils peuvent vous aider. Sans leur aide, mieux vaut vous contenter d'une vitrine virtuelle, que ce soit pour l'achat ou la vente.

L'Internet n'est pas hors du droit, mais sa spécificité rend difficile l'application des lois existantes. Une entreprise désirant créer un site Web doit tenir compte de la législation relative à la publicité mensongère, aux obligations des vendeurs, aux droits des consommateurs et à la propriété intellectuelle. En fonction de la complexité du site, il peut être nécessaire de faire appel à un juriste.

Publicité et vente

Toute organisation qui publie des informations sur le Web, en tant que stratégie marketing ou à des fins publicitaires, doit respecter les codes de conduite en vigueur et vérifier que les informations publiées sont correctes et à jour. Il est dans l'intérêt des entreprises de faire du Web un endroit où les consommateurs peuvent acheter en toute confiance.

En règle générale, la publicité sur le Web est soumise aux lois et à la réglementation du pays d'où se fait l'accès au site. Les entreprises doivent donc respecter les lois nationales. La compagnie aérienne Virgin a dû ainsi payer une amende, conformément à la réglementation de la publicité aux États-Unis, pour avoir affiché sur son site Web des prix qui n'étaient plus actuels. En 1996, un tribunal américain a engagé des poursuites contre une société italienne pour l'utilisation non autorisée d'une marque américaine, simplement parce que l'accès de son site Web était permis aux utilisateurs américains.

Les codes et standards du Bureau de Vérification de Publicité (BVP) en France et ceux de l'Advertising Standards Authority (ASA) au Royaume-Uni, sont valables pour le Web comme pour les autres médias. Bien que ces codes n'aient pas force de loi, la plupart des organisations obtempèrent lorsqu'elles sont rappelées à l'ordre. La loi en France punit d'autre part tout auteur de publicité mensongère. Alors que de plus en plus de sociétés utilisent le Web comme support publicitaire, le débat continue sur la question de la réglementation.

Protection des consommateurs

Au sein de l'Union européenne, les consommateurs sont couverts par la convention de Bruxelles lors de leurs transactions avec des pays membres. Bien que ce soit au consommateur de fournir les preuves, tout citoyen de l'Union européenne peut engager des poursuites dans tout pays membre contre une société située dans tout autre pays membre. Il n'existe pas à l'heure actuelle de réelle protection du consommateur lorsqu'il achète à partir d'un pays membre un bien en provenance d'un pays situé en dehors de l'Union européenne.

La directive européenne pour la vente à distance, adoptée en février 1997 par la Commission européenne, entrera certainement en vigueur avant l'an 2000. Tous les vendeurs sur le Web devront s'assurer que les termes et conditions de la vente sont facilement accessibles à l'écran. Les termes et conditions devront préciser le pays sous la juridiction duquel la vente s'effectue. Les informations suivantes devront être également obligatoirement fournies:

- le nom et l'adresse du vendeur;

- des informations détaillées sur le produit;

- les accords pour la livraison et le paiement;

- la date de livraison et la procédure à suivre en cas de retard;

- à qui incombe la responsabilité en cas de perte ou de dommages.

Pour de nombreux produits, à l'exception des produits d'information tels que des logiciels ou des magazines électroniques, le client aura le droit de résilier tout contrat de vente, à condition de respecter un délai d'une semaine après l'achat. Si un vendeur pense avoir du mal à respecter les conditions de livraison, il devra peut-être préciser clairement sur son site Web que son entreprise n'offre pas des produits en vente mais que le client est invité à faire une offre d'achat.

Taxes

L'emplacement géographique d'une société et le type de produit ou de service vendu déterminent les taxes à payer. Mais l'Internet, qui ne connaît pas de frontières temporelles ou spatiales, est en train de modifier cette conception. La notion de produit ou de service est également en pleine mutation: il ne s'agit plus nécessairement de quelque chose que l'on peut toucher ou sentir.

Le droit fiscal repose en outre sur une distinction entre les biens et les services. Mais cette distinction est loin d'être simple lorsque l'Internet est également le moyen de livraison du produit, lors par exemple du téléchargement d'un film, d'une musique ou d'un livre. Le problème devient encore plus délicat lorsde transactions impliquant plusieurs pays puisqu'il faut prendre en considération différentes façons d'appliquer les taxes à l'achat et les taxes sur la valeur ajoutée.

À l'heure actuelle cependant, les responsables de l'Union européenne et des États-Unis s'accordent à vouloir faire de l'Internet une zone de libre-échange. Si l'OMC donne son accord, il n'y aura plus de droits à payer sur les transmissions électroniques.

Une autre solution consisterait à créer une taxe calculée sur le nombre de bits pour toutes les transmissions électroniques, qu'il s'agisse d'une télécopie, d'un appel téléphonique ou d'un message électronique. Une taxe portant sur toute unité numérique transmise sur l'Internet, quel qu'en soit le contenu, représenterait un changement important, en passant d'une taxe sur la valeur ajoutée à une taxe sur la quantité de données transmises.

Droits d'auteur

Suite aux progrès technologiques, la législation sur les droits d'auteur ne suffit plus pour assurer la protection de la propriété intellectuelle. Les juristes de l'Union européenne et des États-Unis continuent de réfléchir à la question, car les droits d'auteur couvrent aussi bien la transmission des documents que leur reproduction.

Dès qu'un produit culturel, qu'il s'agisse de texte, d'images, de graphiques, de vidéo ou de musique, est disponible sur l'Internet, sa valeur est menacée. Lorsqu'un client reçoit par l'intermédiaire de l'Internet un document qu'il a payé, rien à part la législation sur les droits d'auteur ne s'oppose à ce qu'il le reproduise ou le modifie sur le champ. Un document électronique peut ainsi être retransmis à des centaines, voire des milliers, d'autres destinataires par l'intermédiaire du courrier électronique ou d'un site Web. La protection des droits d'auteur, difficile dans le monde réel, est pratiquement impossible sur l'Internet. Les autorités ne peuvent donc que compter sur la bonne volonté des utilisateurs.

Bien que l'on entende généralement par édition la publication d'écrits dans des livres et des magazines, cette vision est bien trop étroite. On peut considérer que toute personne qui envoie un message électronique ou qui publie des informations dans un site Web fait également de l'édition. Par conséquent, toute information ne peut être publiée sans l'accord préalable de l'auteur.

Pour certains la législation sur les droits d'auteur va être transformée par l'Internet, pour d'autres c'est la nature des transactions sur l'Internet qui changera en fonction de la législation sur les droits d'auteur. Le débat reste ouvert.

Respect de la vie privée

En France, la loi du 6 janvier 1978 relative à l'informatique, aux fichiers et aux libertés a pour objectif la protection des droits et des libertés de la personne par rapport à la création et à l'exploitation de fichiers informatiques contenant des données personnelles. Toute personne ou entreprise désirant créer un fichier informatique qui contient des données personnelles doit obligatoirement en faire la déclaration préalable auprès de la Commission nationale de l'informatique et des libertés (CNIL) et s'engager à respecter la loi.

En 1998, une nouvelle directive de l'Union européenne renforce les normes de sécurité concernant l'accessibilité des informations sur les personnes sur tout le territoire de l'UE. Par voie de conséquence, toute information transférée à l'extérieur de l'UE bénéficie du même niveau de protection qu'à l'intérieur, et ceci même lorsque le transfert d'informations s'effectue au sein d'une même organisation.

L'un des principaux avantages du Web est que le propriétaire du site peut obtenir des informations sur les préférences de ses clients et sur leur comportement d'achat. En effet, lorsque quelqu'un consulte un site Web, il laisse son adresse Internet comme carte de visite. La pratique qui consiste à relever les adresses est parfois vue comme une intrusion dans la vie privée. Elle est cependant indissociable du fonctionnement de l'Internet: en effet, le site doit connaître le nom de domaine du visiteur pour pouvoir transmettre les informations requises. Il existe d'autres moyens d'obtenir des informations sur les personnes qui consultent le site, tels que les cartes d'enregistrement ou l'utilisation, controversée, de *cookies*.

Les cookies sont des informations relevées par le site Web et copiées sur le disque dur de l'utilisateur, souvent à son insu. Ces informations qui portent sur les habitudes d'utilisation de l'Internet et sur les activités du client, peuvent ensuite être récupérées par le serveur lors d'une consultation ultérieure du site. Certains navigateurs peuvent être configurés pour avertir de l'envoi d'un cookie et les programmes les plus récents donnent la possibilité de les rejeter. Il existe également des programmes, tels que Cookie Crusher et Cookie Crumbler, qui rejettent automatiquement tous les cookies. Certains sites Web précisent qu'ils n'utilisent pas de cookies.

Propositions pour le commerce électronique mondial

En juillet 1997, le président des États-Unis a exposé les principales règles du commerce électronique international dans un document intitulé *"A Framework for Global Electronic Commerce"*. Ces propositions qui incluent la nécessité de faire de l'Internet une zone de libre-échange pour le commerce électronique, s'organisent autour de cinq principes et neuf thèmes.

Principes

1. La priorité doit être donnée au secteur privé.

2. Les gouvernements doivent s'abstenir de prendre des mesures qui freinent de façon excessive le libre-échange sur l'Internet.

3. Lorsqu'une aide gouvernementale est nécessaire, son objectif devra être de définir un cadre juridique simple, prévisible et cohérent.

4. Les gouvernements doivent reconnaître les qualités propres à l'Internet.

5. Le commerce électronique sur l'Internet doit être facilité au niveau mondial.

Thèmes

1. Douanes et taxes

2. Systèmes de paiement électronique

3. "Code commercial uniforme" pour le commerce électronique

4. Protection de la propriété intellectuelle

5. Respect de la vie privée

6. Sécurité

7. Infrastructure des télécommunications et de l'informatique

8. Contenu: publicité et fraude

9. Normes techniques.

Le document original complet (A Framework for Global Electronic Commerce, The White House, July 1, 1997) peut être consulté à l'adresse suivante:

http://www.ecommerce.gov.framewrk.htm

6: L'INTERNET ET STRATEGIE COMMERCIALE

L'intégration de l'Internet dans la stratégie de l'entreprise nécessite une analyse des opportunités et des limites du réseau, des objectifs fixés et du meilleur moyen de les atteindre ainsi que des forces et des faiblesses de l'entreprise. Une gestion efficace repose sur une vision stratégique de l'avenir.

Les limites de l'Internet

Les objectifs à atteindre dépendent en grande partie de la vision que l'entreprise a de l'Internet et des bénéfices qu'elle pense en tirer.

Le nombre de nouveaux utilisateurs, la quantité de nouvelles pages Web et les ventes de produits et de services continuent d'augmenter de plus de 100% par an.

Pour beaucoup cependant l'Internet, encore entouré de mystère, ne signifie pas grand-chose ou reste trop compliqué et confus. Les critiques portent essentiellement sur les aspects suivants:

• le développement anarchique du réseau, où informations sérieuses et sites pornographiques se côtoient;

• la confusion et la surcharge d'information, ainsi que la prédominance d'informations peu intéressantes;

• la lenteur des temps de réponse et des transmissions aux heures de pointe;

• les fréquentes interruptions, dues à la saturation des lignes, dont on entend beaucoup parler;

• la rapidité d'évolution des technologies, trop difficile à suivre pour beaucoup;

• l'absence de preuves réelles de la rentabilité de l'Internet;

• la préférence de la télévision, par câble ou par satellite, en raison de la complexité et des incohérences du Web.

Les opportunités offertes par l'Internet

Cette vision négative ne tient pas compte des nombreux signes d'évolution:

1. La croissance continuelle de l'Internet et sa présence à l'échelle planétaire.

2. Les développements technologiques constants, tels que Internet2, pour répondre aux besoins des entreprises.

3. Les investissements faits par les principales banques et éditeurs de logiciels pour développer le commerce électronique sur le Web.

4. Le succès commercial rapide que de nombreuses entreprises ont connu.

5. La promotion, les injections de fonds publics et les efforts législatifs réalisés par l'Union européenne et les États-Unis ainsi que par différents États.

6. La prédominance de l'esprit d'entreprise qui refuse de construire l'avenir avec les recettes du passé.

D'autres signes vont dans le sens de ce scénario positif:

- La confiance grandissante des consommateurs grâce à la mise en place de systèmes de paiement sécurisés.

- L'adoption de mesures efficaces pour la protection des droits d'auteur.

- L'apparition de standards adoptés par les grands groupes de télécom-munications, les éditeurs de logiciels et les sociétés commerciales.

- L'installation de moyens de télécommunication très performants, chez les particuliers et dans les entreprises, suites aux subventions des gouvernements, aux investis-sements des sociétés de télécommunication et des particuliers.

- La possibilité, pour ceux qui préfèrent payer plus pour un service de qualité, de se connecter à l'Internet par l'intermédiaire de réseaux privés, plus importants et plus fiables.

- La baisse des prix de connexion et d'accès à l'Internet en raison de la concurrence.

- L'intégration progressive de l'Internet dans la vie profes-sionnelle et privée, au même titre que la presse et la télévision.

Modèles économiques

Une entreprise a en gros le choix entre cinq modèles économiques différents pour offrir des services sur l'Internet:

1. *Communication* – L'Internet est dans ce cas principalement utilisé pour bénéficier de la rapidité et de l'efficacité du courrier électronique.

2. *Publicité* – L'entreprise peut utiliser son site Web comme une vitrine commerciale. Elle peut également, moyennant paiement, afficher des bandeaux publicitaires dans d'autres sites Web et dans des moteurs de recherche.

3. *Abonnement* – Il est possible de proposer l'accès illimité à un service ou à un produit, par exemple, un journal, un magazine ou un service de mise à jour, sur abonnement, généralement payable annuellement. Pour être viable, ce modèle nécessite un changement de comportement des utilisateurs du Web, qui jusqu'à présent hésitent à utiliser des services payants.

4. *Marketing* – L'entreprise peut fournir des informations générales ou personnalisées ainsi que des attractions. Dans ce cas, le site Web peut, grâce à son interactivité, offrir aux groupes d'utilisateurs sélectionnés, les communautés, un service supérieur à celui de la télévision.

5. *Cybermagasin* – Une entreprise peut faire de la vente sur le Web. Le commerce électronique doit cependant auparavant surmonter certains obstacles majeurs et gagner la confiance du grand public.

Principes stratégiques

1. Il est essentiel de bien comprendre le fonctionnement de l'Internet et son potentiel, en lisant la presse et les ouvrages spécialisés, en faisant des essais et en discutant avec d'autres utilisateurs.

2. Une vue d'ensemble de l'entreprise et de ses objectifs est indispensable pour comprendre ce que l'Internet peut apporter à l'organisation et à ses clients.

3. L'entreprise doit chercher à connaître ses clients, en analysant les comportements d'achat et le niveau d'interactivité requis. Cette analyse doit également tenir compte de l'attente des clients, des informations que l'entreprise souhaite obtenir sur sa clientèle, et de ce que l'Internet peut apporter aux produits et aux services proposés. Il peut s'agir d'une meilleure information, de nouvelles

méthodes de distribution ou bien d'un service personnalisé pour les particuliers et les groupes.

4. La participation de la direction et la contribution du plus grand nombre de personnes sont indispensables au succès de l'utilisation de l'Internet. Le personnel doit pour cela se familiariser avec le fonctionnement du réseau. Des compétences techniques, graphiques et juridiques sont nécessaires. Il est important de déterminer les ressources qu'il est possible, ou souhaitable, de dédier à l'Internet.

5. Mieux vaut ne pas voir trop grand au départ, l'essentiel est de commencer. Il est important de définir des objectifs précis et de prévoir des résultats rapides, sans s'attendre à des miracles. Sachez reconnaître les personnes qui peuvent aider à obtenir ces résultats et prouver ainsi le succès du projet.

6. Le succès d'un site Web ne se mesure pas uniquement au nombre de ventes réalisées. Il ne faut pas négliger toutes les activités qui, en suscitant l'intérêt et les questions d'éventuels clients, peuvent indirectement générer des ventes.

7. Pour la clientèle comme pour le personnel, les activités sur l'Internet doivent refléter les activités réelles de l'entreprise.

8. Des procédures devront être mises en place pour déterminer:

• Les personnes qui ont accès au Web et les critères d'attribution de l'accès.

• Le type d'informations qui pourront être importées du réseau.

• Les auteurs responsables des informations publiées sur le Web.

9. Il est important de suivre de près l'utilisation de l'Internet, en analysant certaines données : niveau d'utilisation du courrier électronique et du Web au sein de l'organisation, économies réalisées sur le temps du personnel, revenus directs ou indirects et réactions des clients.

10. Les services créés sur l'Internet doivent rester flexibles et pouvoir évoluer rapidement. Il est essentiel pour cela d'assurer une veille technologique, d'explorer les nouvelles possibilités et de ne pas hésiter à prendre des risques.

COURRIER ELECTRONIQUE

1. Comment rédiger un courrier électronique

- Une adresse électronique comprend deux parties. La première est constituée du nom du destinataire et la seconde du nom de domaine. Les deux parties sont séparées par une arrobase @ (que l'on prononce "at" en anglais). Il est essentiel de taper l'adresse exacte car la moindre faute de frappe empêcherait le message de parvenir à votre correspondant.

- Le courrier électronique étant un moyen de communication rapide, les messages sont souvent rédigés en style télégraphique en utilisant de nombreux acronymes et abréviations. La concision du style et l'utilisation de formes abrégées peuvent parfois créer des problèmes. Il convient de n'utiliser que les abréviations et les acronymes dont vous savez qu'ils seront compris par votre correspondant.

- Pour indiquer que l'on hausse le ton au cours d'un message, on passe des lettres minuscules aux lettres majuscules. Il est donc recommandé d'éviter d'écrire un message en n'utilisant que des lettres majuscules dans la mesure où votre correspondant interprèterait cela comme un signe de mauvaise humeur de votre part.

- La convivialité du courrier électronique encourage une certaine familiarité, que l'on peut parfois regretter après-coup. Cette caractéristique a répandu le sentiment que les messages électroniques sont peu fiables, non durables, voire même inexacts, et ne valent donc pas la peine d'être cités.

- Il faut savoir que le courrier électronique est une forme de publication qui est donc soumise en tant que telle à la législation relative aux droits d'auteur et à la diffamation. Un message électronique doit par conséquent être considéré de la même façon que toute autre forme de communication écrite.

```
Victoria Jones, Report on customer Intel, init          _ □ X
       Subject: Report on customer Intel, initial contact

To: Raymond Le Farge
From: Victoria Jones
Subject: Report on customer Intel, initial contact
Cc: Louise Gibbon, Malcolm Russell, Pierre Le Croin
Bcc:
X-Eudora-Signature: <Standard>

Raymond,
As requested, a few important points from my meeting with Intel on Thursday 17
May 99:

- Director impressed with the overall concept, would like to meet you to
discuss projected costs
- Account managers to present at next monthly meet on 27 June
- Creative dept to work toward initial mock-up and liaise with their team
before end of month

Recommendations:

1. We call all concerned with this account to meet before end week (I suggest
9.00 Wed)
2. We discuss our presentations and proposals at this meeting and relay
minutes to Intel by Monday pm

Look forward to your comments - good luck in HK!

Best wishes
Victoria
```

2. Abréviations et acronymes

On trouvera ci-dessous la liste des abréviations les plus couramment utilisées dans le courrier électronique et les groupes de discussion. Il est recommandé de n'employer ces abréviations que lorsque l'on est sûr que le destinataire connaît leur signification. Certaines d'entre elles appartiennent à un registre plus familier (elles sont suivies ici de la mention *Fam*) et doivent être réservées à une correspondance plus relâchée:

AAMOF	As A Matter of Fact (en fait)
Adv	Advice (conseil)
AFAICT *Fam*	As Far As I Can Tell (Pour autant que je sache)
AFAIK *Fam*	As Far As I Know (Pour autant que je sache)
AFK	Away From Keyboard (indique que l'on va quitter momentanément son poste)
AIIC *Fam*	As If I Care (ça m'est bien égal)
AISI *Fam*	As I See It (de mon point de vue)
AIUI *Fam*	As I Understand It (si j'ai bien compris)
B4 *Fam*	Before (avant)
BAK	Back At Keyboard (de retour devant l'écran)
BBFN *Fam*	Bye Bye For Now (à plus tard)
BBL *Fam*	Be Back Later (je reviens)
BCNU *Fam*	Be Seeing You (à plus tard)
BFN *Fam*	Bye For Now (à plus tard)
BOC *Fam*	But Of Course (mais certainement)
BRB *Fam*	Be Right Back (je reviens tout de suite)
BST *Fam*	But Seriously Though (blague à part)

BTW *Fam*	By The Way (à propos)
cld	could
CUL *Fam*	See You Later (à plus tard)
CYA *Fam*	See Ya (à plus)
Doc	Document (document)
DUCWIM *Fam*	Do You See What I Mean? (tu vois ce que je veux dire?)
DYJHIW *Fam*	Don't You Just Hate It When (c'est vraiment exaspérant quand)
EOD	End Of Discussion (fin de la discussion)
EOF	End Of File (fin de fichier)
ETLA	Extended Three Later Acronym (acronyme de plus de trois lettres)
F2F *Fam*	Face To Face (en face, face à face)
FAQ	Frequently Asked Questions (foire aux questions)
FOAF *Fam*	Friend Of A Friend (l'ami d'un ami)
FOC	Free Of Charge (gratuit, gratuitement)
Foll	following, to follow (suivant, à suivre)
FYA *Fam*	For Your Amusement (pour te distraire)
FYI	For Your Information (pour ton/ votre information)
GA *Fam*	Go Ahead (vas-y)
GAL *Fam*	Get A Life (tu n'as rien de mieux à faire?)
GGN *Fam*	Gotta Go Now (il faut que j'y aille)
HAND *Fam*	Have A Nice Day (bonne journée)
HHOJ *Fam*	Ha Ha, Only Joking (je plaisante)
HHOS *Fam*	Ha Ha, Only Serious (je suis sérieux)
HTH *Fam*	Hope This Helps (j'espère que cela te/vous sera utile)
IAC	In Any Case (en tout cas, de toute façon)
IAE	In Any Event (en tout cas, de toute façon)
IDTS	I Don't Think So (je ne crois pas)
IIRC *Fam*	If I Recall Correctly (si mes souvenirs sont bons)
IMHO *Fam*	In My Humble Opinion (à mon humble avis)
IMNSHO *Fam*	In My Not So Humble Opinion (à mon avis)
IMO *Fam*	In My Opinion (à mon avis)
IOW *Fam*	In Other Words (autrement dit)
ISTM *Fam*	It Seems To Me (il me semble que)
ISTR *Fam*	I Seem To Recall (si je me souviens bien)
ISWYM *Fam*	I See What You Mean (je comprends)
ITRO *Fam*	In The Region Of (environ)
IWBNI *Fam*	It Would Be Nice If (ce serait bien si)

JK *Fam*	Just Kidding (je plaisante)
L8R *Fam*	Later (à plus)
NBD *Fam*	No Big Deal (ce n'est pas grave)
NRN *Fam*	No Reply Necessary (réponse facultative)
NTL	Nevertheless (néanmoins)
NW! *Fam*	No Way! (sûrement pas !)
OBTW *Fam*	Oh, By The Way (à propos)
OIC *Fam*	Oh, I See (je comprends)
OMG *Fam*	Oh, My God (mon Dieu!)
OTOH *Fam*	On The Other Hand (d'un autre côté)
OTT *Fam*	Over The Top (excessif)
OTW *Fam*	On The Whole (dans l'ensemble)
PD	Public Domain (domaine public)
PITA *Fam*	Pain In The Arse (emmerdement, emmerdeur)
POD	Piece Of Data (information)
POV	Point Of View (point de vue)
prhps	perhaps (peut-être)
RSN *Fam*	Real Soon Now (très bientôt)
RTFM *Fam*	Read The Fucking Manual (regarde dans le manuel, nom de Dieu!)
RUOK *Fam*	Are You OK (ça va?)
TIA *Fam*	Thanks In Advance (merci d'avance)
TLA	Three Letter Acronym (acronyme de trois lettres)
TNX *Fam*	Thanks (merci)
TTYL *Fam*	Talk To You Later (à bientôt)
TTYRS *Fam*	Talk To You Real Soon (à très bientôt)
TVM *Fam*	Thanks Very Much (merci beaucoup)
VR	Virtual Reality (réalité virtuelle)
WBS *Fam*	Write Back Soon (réponds-moi vite)
WIBNI *Fam*	Wouldn't It Be Nice If (ce serait bien si)
WRT	With Regard To (en ce qui concerne)
YHM	You Have Mail (vous avez du courrier)

Souriants

Bien que quelques esprits chagrins en condamnent l'emploi, les souriants (c'est-à-dire des caractères du clavier qui, lorsque l'on penche la tête à gauche, forment des visages) sont fréquemment utilisés dans la correspondance électronique et, chaque jour ou presque, un nouveau souriant apparaît sur les écrans. Comme les abréviations, les souriants ne doivent être employés qu'à l'occasion d'une correspondance amicale. Les souriants les plus utilisés sont:

:-)	Content; je plaisante
:-))	Très content
:-D	Rire à gorge déployée
:-(	Triste
:-((	Très triste
:´-(	Pleurer
:-II	En colère
:-C	Très mécontent
:-O	Choqué
:-@	Crier
;-)	Clin d'œil
:-I	Froncer les sourcils
(:-)	Chauve
:-)»	Barbu
:-)X	Porter un nœud papillon
(I-)	Chinois
3:-)	Vache
8-)	Porter des lunettes
I-)	Dormir
:-i	Fumeur
:-?	Fumeur de pipe
:-/	Indécis
CI:-)	Porter un chapeau melon
d:-)	Porter une casquette
[:-)	Porter des écouteurs
I-O	Bâiller

Français-Anglais
French-English

abandon nm *(de programme)* abort

abandonner vt *(fichier, sous-programme)* to abort

abonné, -e **1** *adj* **être abonné au Minitel** to subscribe to Minitel
2 *nm,f* subscriber; *Tél* **un abonné du téléphone/d'Internet** a telephone/an Internet subscriber; **il n'y a pas d'abonné au numéro que vous avez demandé** ≃ the number you have dialled has not been recognized

abonnement nm **(a)** *(au téléphone)* line rental **(b)** *(à un fournisseur d'accés)* account, subscription (**auprès de** with); **abonnement à un service en ligne** on-line subscription

abonner **s'abonner** *vpr* **(a)** **s'abonner au téléphone** to have a telephone installed **(b)** *(à un fournisseur d'accés)* to subscribe; **s'abonner auprès de qn** to set up an account with sb

accéder **accéder à** *vt ind (données)* to access

accélérateur nm accelerator
◇ **accélérateur graphique** graphic(s) accelerator

accent nm accent
◇ *accent aigu* acute accent
◇ *accent circonflexe* circumflex accent; *(utilisé seul)* caret
◇ *accent grave* grave accent

accès nm access; *Internet (à une page Web)* hit; **avoir accès à qch** to be able to access sth; **à accès multiple** multi-access; **accès refusé** access denied
◇ *accès aléatoire* random access
◇ *accès non autorisé* unauthorized access
◇ *Internet* **accès commuté** dial-up access
◇ *accès à distance* remote access
◇ *Internet* **accès par ligne commutée** dial-up access
◇ *accès sécurisé par mot de passe* password-protected access
◇ *accès séquentiel* sequential access

accessoire de bureau nm desk accessory

accolade nf (curly) bracket

accusé de réception nm acknowledgement

acquisition de données nf data acquisition

actif, -ive *adj (fichier, fenêtre)* active

activé, -e *adj (fichier, fenêtre)* active; *(option)* enabled

activer *vt* to activate; **activer une option** to enable an option

actualisation *nf* (a) *(d'écran)* refresh (b) *(d'un logiciel)* update

actualiser *vt* (a) *(écran)* to refresh (b) *(logiciel)* to update

adaptateur *nm* adapter

additionnel, -elle *adj (option, extension)* add-on

administrateur, -trice *nm,f*
◇ **administrateur de réseau** network manager *or* administrator
◇ **administrateur de serveur** server administrator

administration de réseau *nf* network management

adresse *nf* address
◇ *Can* **adresse de courriel** e-mail address
◇ **adresse électronique** e-mail address
◇ **adresse Internet** Internet address
◇ **adresse IP** IP address
◇ *Internet* **adresse URL** URL

adresser *vt* to address

affichage *nm* (screen) display
◇ **affichage couleur** colour display
◇ **affichage à cristaux liquides** liquid crystal display
◇ **affichage graphique** graphics display
◇ **affichage numérique** digital display
◇ **affichage tel écran-tel écrit, affichage tel-tel, affichage Wysiwyg** WYSIWYG display

afficher 1 *vt (message)* to display; *(fichiers, articles)* to show; **l'écran affiche** the on-screen message reads, the screen displays the message
 2 **s'afficher** *vpr (sur un écran)* to be displayed

afficheur *nm* visual display unit, VDU, display
◇ **afficheur LCD** LCD display

agenda *nm (ordinateur portable)* notebook
◇ **agenda électronique** personal organizer

agrandir *vt* to enlarge, to magnify; *(fenêtre)* to maximize

aide *nf* help
◇ **aide contextuelle** context-sensitive help
◇ **aide en ligne** on-line help

ajout de mémoire *nm* memory upgrade

ajouter *vt (à une base de données)* to append

album *nm (sur Macintosh)* scrapbook

algol *nm (abrév Algorithmic Oriented Language)* ALGOL

algorithme *nm* algorithm

alias *nm (de courrier électronique, de bureau)* alias

aliassage *nm PAO* aliasing

alignement *nm (de caractères)* alignment

aligner vt (caractères) to align

alimentation nf

◇ **alimentation feuille à feuille** cut sheet feed, single sheet feed

◇ **alimentation page par page** cut sheet feed, single sheet feed

◇ **alimentation papier** sheet-feed, paper feed

alimenter vt (imprimante) to feed

alinéa nm indentation

allumer vt & vi to power up

alphanumérique adj alphanumeric

alt pour e accent aigu, il faut taper alt 130 e acute is alt 130

altéré, -e adj (disque, fichier) corrupt

altérer 1 vt (disque, fichier) to corrupt
  2 s'altérer vpr (disque, fichier) to corrupt

amélioration nf (d'image, de qualité) enhancement

améliorer vt (logiciel) to upgrade; (image, qualité) to enhance

amorçage nm (d'ordinateur) booting

amorcer 1 vt (ordinateur) to boot (up); amorcer de nouveau to reboot
  2 s'amorcer vpr (ordinateur) to boot (up)

amovible adj (disque dur) removable

analogique adj analog

analyse nf

◇ **analyse de données** data analysis

◇ **analyse des systèmes, analyse systémique** systems analysis

analyste nmf computer analyst

analyste-programmeur, -euse nm,f systems analyst

ancrage nm (de texte) justification; ancrage à droite/gauche right/left justification

ancre nf Internet anchor

animation nf (computer) animation

animer vt to animate

anneau à jeton nm token ring

annuaire nm telephone directory

◇ **annuaire électronique** electronic telephone directory (on Minitel)

◇ **annuaire du téléphone, annuaire téléphonique** telephone directory

annulation nf cancel

◇ **annulation d'entrée** (commande) cancel entry

annuler 1 vt to cancel; (opération) to undo; annuler les révisions (commande) undo changes
  2 s'annuler vpr to cancel

antémémoire nf cache (memory); mettre en antémémoire to cache

anti-aliassage nm PAO anti-aliasing

anti-crénelage *nm PAO* anti-aliasing

anti-reflet *adj* non-reflecting, anti-glare

antivirus *nm* antivirus *m*

aperçu avant impression *nm* print preview

apostrophe *nm* apostrophe

appareil *nm* (a) *(téléphone)* telephone; **qui est à l'appareil?** who's speaking? (b) *(machine)* apparatus, appliance

◇ *appareil à dicter* Dictaphone®

◇ *appareil photo numérique* digital camera

appel *nm* appel (téléphonique) (telephone) call, phone call; **prendre un appel** to take a (telephone) call; **recevoir un appel** to receive a (telephone) call; **il y a eu un appel pour vous** there was a (telephone) call for you

◇ *appel automatique* automatic dial

◇ *appel gratuit Br* Freefone® call, *Am* toll-free call

◇ *appel en PCV Br* reverse-charge call, *Am* collect call

appeler *vt* (a) appeler qn (au téléphone) to ring sb (up), to call sb; **appeler en PCV** *Br* to reverse the charges, *Am* to call collect
(b) *(fichier)* to call up

appelette *nf Internet* applet

application *nf* application

◇ *application bureautique* business application

◇ *application graphique* graphics application

◇ *application en service* current application

appuyer *vi* appuyer sur *(touche)* to hit, to press

araignée *nf Internet* crawler

arborescence *nf (structure)* tree diagram, directory structure; *(chemin)* directory path

arbre *nm (organisation des données)* tree

Archie *nm Internet* Archie

architecture *nf* architecture

archive *nf* archive

◇ *archive autodécompactable* self-extracting archive

archiver *vt* to archive

ardoise électronique *nf* notepad computer

argent *nm*

◇ *argent électronique* e-cash, electronic money

◇ *argent virtuel* e-cash, electronic money

arrêt de fin de session *nm* shutdown

arrêter s'arrêter *vpr (système)* to shut down

arrière-plan *nm* background

arrobas *nm* at sign; **gdurand, arrobas, transex, point, fr** gdurand at transex, dot, fr

ART *nm (abrev* **Autorité de régulation des télécommunications**) = French telecommunications and Internet watchdog

art ASCII *nm* ASCII art

article *nm* (a) *(d'un menu)* command

(**b**) *Internet (dans des groupes de discussion)* article

(**c**) *(dans une base de données)* record

ascenseur *nm (d'une fenêtre)* scroll box

ASCII *nm (abrév* **American Standard Code for Information Interchange)** ASCII

assembleur *nm (programme)* assembler

assistance *nf*
◇ *assistance technique* technical support
◇ *assistance technique téléphonique* support line
◇ *assistance à l'utilisateur* user support

assistant *nm (programme)* assistant
◇ *assistant numérique* personal digital assistant, PDA

assisté, -e *adj* **assisté par ordinateur** *(conception, enseignement, fabrication, production)* computer-aided, computer-assisted

astérisque *nm* asterisk

asynchrone *adj* asynchronous

attente *nf* **mettre qn en attente** *(au téléphone)* to put sb on hold; **être en attente** *(au téléphone)* to be on hold; **liste de fichiers à imprimer en attente** print queue

attribuer *vt (mémoire)* to allocate

attribution *nf (de mémoire)* allocation

augmentation de puissance *nf* upgrade, upgrading

authentification *nf* authentication

authentifier *vt* to authenticate

automatique *adj* automatic

automatisation *nf* automation

autorisation *nf*
◇ *autorisation d'accès* access authorization

autoroute *nf* superhighway
◇ *autoroute de l'information* information superhighway

autotest *nm* self-test

autotester s'autotester *vpr* to self-test

avance automatique *nf* automatic feed

avancement *nm*
◇ *avancement par friction* friction feed
◇ *avancement du papier* sheetfeed

avatar *nm Internet* avatar

avertissement *nm*
◇ *avertissement de réception (de message)* acknowledgement
◇ *avertissement à réception d'un courrier* mail received message

babillard *nm* JO *Internet* bulletin board system, BBS

bac *nm*
◇ *bac d'alimentation papier* sheet feeder
◇ *bac de ou à feuilles* paper tray
◇ *bac de ou à papier* paper tray

badaud, -e *nm,f Internet* lurker

baie *nf (pour unité de disque)* bay

balise *nf* tag
◇ *balise de début* opening tag
◇ *balise de fin* closing tag

baliser *vt* to tag

banc *nm* bank
◇ *banc de mémoire* memory bank

bancatique *nf* electronic banking

bande *nf* tape
◇ *bande audionumérique* digital audio tape, DAT
◇ *bande de défilement* scroll bar
◇ *bande magnétique* magnetic tape

bandeau *nm Internet* banner
◇ *bandeau publicitaire* advertising banner

bannière *nf Internet* banner

banque *nf* **(a)** *(activité)*
◇ *banque à distance* remote banking
◇ *banque à domicile* tele-banking, home banking
  (b) *(pour l'archivage)*
◇ *banque de données* data bank
◇ *banque d'images* image bank

barre *nf (barre de menu)* bar
◇ *barre de défilement* scroll bar
◇ *barre d'espacement* space bar
◇ *barre d'état* status bar
◇ *barre d'icônes* icon bar
◇ *barre de lancement rapide* quick launch bar
◇ *barre de menu* menu bar; *Internet*
◇ *barre de navigation* navigation bar
◇ *barre oblique* oblique, slash
◇ *barre oblique inversée* backslash, reverse slash
◇ *barre d'outils* tool bar
◇ *barre de sélection* menu bar
◇ *barre des tâches* taskbar
◇ *barre de titre* title bar

bas *nm*
◇ *bas de casse* lower-case
◇ *PAO bas de page* footer

bascule *nf (entre applications)* toggle

basculer *vi (entre applications)* to toggle

basculeur *nm (touche)* toggle (key)

base *nf*
◇ *base de données* database; **mettre qch dans une base de données** to enter sth into a database
◇ *base de données client-serveur* client-server database
◇ *base de données relationnelle* relational database

Basic *nm* BASIC

baud *nm* baud; **à (une vitesse de) 28,800 bauds** at 28,800 baud

bavardage *nm Internet* chat

bavarder *vi Internet* to chat

bavardoir *nm Can Internet* chat room

BBS *nm Internet (abrév* **bulletin board system)** BBS

BD *nf (abrév* **base de données)** dbase

bibliothèque *nf (de programmes)* library
◇ *bibliothèque de programmes* program library

biclic *nm* double click

bicliquer *vi* to double-click

bidirectionnel, -elle *adj* bidirectional; *Tél* **bidirectionnel simultané** full duplex

bidouilleur, -euse *nm,f* hacker, expert user

billétique *nf* cash dispenser technology

binaire *adj* binary

binette *nf Can Internet* smiley, emoticon

BinHex (*abrév* **Binary Hexadecimal**) BinHex

BIOS *nm* (*abrév* **Basic Input/Output System**) BIOS

bisynchrone *adj* bisynchronous, bisync

bit *nm* bit; **bits par seconde** bits per second

bitmap *adj & nm* bitmap

bloc *nm (de texte)* block

blocage majuscule *nm* caps lock

bloc-notes *nm* notepad, memo pad, *Am* scratchpad; *(pour texte supprimé)* clipboard
◇ *bloc-notes électronique* electronic notepad

bloqué, -e *adj (écran)* frozen

bogue *nf* bug; **exempt de bogues** bug-free
◇ *bogue de l'an 2000* millennium bug
◇ *bogue de logiciel* software bug

bogué, -e *adj* bug-ridden

boîte *nf*
◇ *boîte de dialogue* dialogue box, message box
◇ *boîte à disquettes* disk box
◇ *boîte à ou aux lettres électronique* (electronic) mailbox
◇ *boîte à outils* toolbox

boîtier *nm* case
◇ *boîtier de commande* command box
◇ *boîtier vertical* tower

booléen, -enne *adj* Boolean

bordure *nf (d'un paragraphe, d'une cellule)* border

borne interactive *nf* kiosk

boucler se boucler *vpr (lignes)* to wrap

boule de commande *nf* trackball

bourrage papier *nm* paper jam

bouton *nm* button
◇ *bouton de défilement* scroll button
◇ *bouton Démarrer* start button
◇ *Internet* **bouton de navigation** navigation button
◇ *bouton d'option, bouton radio* radio button
◇ *bouton de réinitialisation* reset button
◇ *bouton de souris* mouse button

bpp *nmpl (abrév* **bits par pouce**) bpi

bps *nmpl (abrév* **bits par seconde**) bps

branchement *nm (d'appareils)* connection

broche *nf* pin

brouteur *nm* JO *Internet* browser

brut, -e *adj (données, chiffres statistiques)* raw

bug *nm* bug

bureau *nm* (a) office (b) *(écran)* desktop
◇ *bureau actif* active desktop
◇ *bureau électronique* electronic desktop
◇ *bureau informatisé* electronic office, paperless office

bureautique *nf* office IT *or* automation

bus *nm* bus
◇ *bus d'adresses* address bus
◇ *bus de données* data bus

butineur *nm* JO *Internet* browser

Le bureau Mac
The Mac desktop

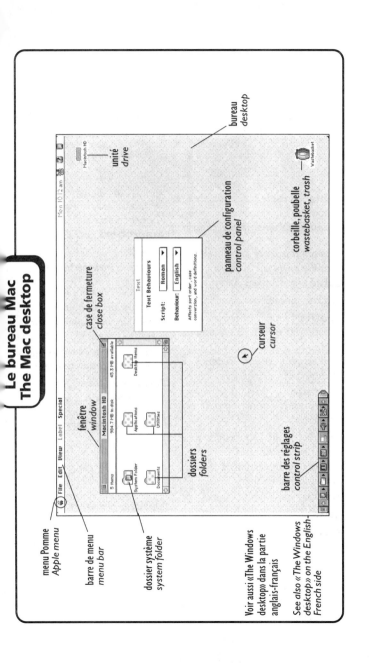

menu Pomme
Apple menu

barre de menu
menu bar

dossier système
system folder

Voir aussi «The Windows desktop» dans la partie anglais-français

See also «The Windows desktop» on the English-French side

fenêtre
window

case de fermeture
close box

panneau de configuration
control panel

unité
drive

bureau
desktop

dossiers
folders

curseur
cursor

barre des réglages
control strip

corbeille, poubelle
wastebasket, trash

File Edit View Label Special

Macintosh HD

5 items   994.7 MB in disk   45.3 MB available

System Folder

Documents

Applications

Utilities

Desktop Items

Text

Text Behaviours

Script: Roman

Behaviour: English

Affects sort order, case conversion, and word definitions

Mon 10:12 am

Macintosh HD

Wastebasket

C++ *nm* C++

câble *nm* cable; **câbles** cabling, cables

◇ *câble d'imprimante* printer cable

◇ *câble parallèle* parallel cable

◇ *câble série* serial cable

câblé, -e *adj* hard-wired

cache *nm* cache

caddie *nm Internet Br* shopping basket, *Am* shopping cart

cadencé, -e *adj* **cadencé à** running at

cadrage *nm (d'objets)* positioning; *(de caractères)* alignment

cadre *nm* (**a**) *(pour graphique)* box (**b**) *Internet* frame

cadrer *vt (objets)* to position; *(caractères)* to align

cafteur *nm Internet* cookie

cage *nf (d'une fenêtre)* scroll box

calculateur *nm* (desktop) calculator

◇ *calculateur électronique* electronic computer

calculatrice *nf* calculator

◇ *calculatrice de bureau* desktop calculator

◇ *calculatrice imprimante* print-out calculator

◇ *calculatrice de poche* pocket calculator

camembert *nm Fam* pie chart

caméra *nf*

◇ *caméra Internet* web cam, live cam

◇ *caméra vidéo numérique* digital video camera

canal *nm (de communication, pour IRC)* channel

CAO *nf (abrév* **conception assistée par ordinateur)** CAD

capacité *nf* capacity

◇ *capacité de disque/disquette* disk capacity

◇ *capacité de mémoire* memory capacity

◇ *capacité de stockage* storage capacity

◇ *capacité de traitement* throughput

capture d'écran *nf* screen capture, screen dump, screen shot

caractère *nm* character

◇ *caractères alphanumériques* alphanumeric characters

◇ *caractère de contrôle* control character

◊ *caractère d'interruption* break character

◊ *caractère joker* wildcard character

◊ *caractère majuscule* upper-case character

◊ *caractère minuscule* lower-case character

◊ *caractères par pouce* characters per inch

◊ *caractères par seconde* characters per second

carnet d'adresses *nm (pour courrier électronique)* address book

carte *nf* (a) *(magnétique)* card (b) *(d'ordinateur)* card, board

◊ *carte accélérateur graphique* graphics accelerator card *or* board

◊ *carte accélératrice* accelerator card *or* board

◊ *carte d'affichage* display card

◊ *carte bancaire à puce* smart card *(used as a bank card)*

◊ *carte bus* bus board

◊ *carte de circuits* circuit board

◊ *carte de circuit(s) intégré(s)* integrated circuit board, IC board

◊ *carte contrôleur de disque* disk controller card

◊ *carte d'extension* expansion card *or* board

◊ *carte d'extension mémoire* memory expansion card *or* board

◊ *carte fax* fax card

◊ *carte graphique* graphics card

◊ *carte magnétique* magnetic card

◊ *carte mémoire* memory card

◊ *carte à mémoire* smart card

◊ *carte mère* motherboard

◊ *carte modem* modem card

◊ *Tél carte Pastel* phone card *(use of which is debited to one's own phone number)*

◊ *carte à puce* smart card

◊ *carte réseau* network card

◊ *carte RNIS* ISDN card

◊ *carte SCSI* SCSI card

◊ *carte son* sound card

◊ *carte de télécopie* fax card

◊ *carte de téléphone* phone-card

◊ *carte unité centrale* CPU board

◊ *carte vidéo* video board, video card

◊ *carte vidéo accélératrice* video accelerator card

carte-adaptateur *nf* adapter card

cartouche *nf* cartridge

◊ *cartouche Bernoulli*® Bernoulli® disk

◊ *cartouche DAT* DAT cartridge

◊ *cartouche d'encre* ink cartridge

◊ *cartouche d'enregistrement sur bande audionumérique* DAT cartridge

◊ *cartouche Jaz*® Jaz® disk

◊ *cartouche de toner* toner cartridge

◊ *cartouche Zip*® Zip® disk

case *nf (bouton)* button; *(en forme de boîte)* box

◊ *case d'aide* help button

◊ *case 'annuler'* cancel button

◊ *case de dimensionnement* size box

◊ *case de fermeture* close box

◇ *case d'option* ou *de pointage* check box, option box

◇ *case de redimensionnement* size box

◇ *case de saisie* input box

◇ *case zoom* zoom box

cassette *nf*

◇ *cassette d'alimentation (de copieuse, imprimante)* paper tray

◇ *cassette numérique* digital audio tape

catalogue en ligne *nm* electronic catalogue

cavalier *nm (broche)* jumper

CD *nm (abrév* **compact disc***)* CD

◇ *CD réinscriptible* CD-RW

CD-I *nm (abrév* **compact disc interactif***)* CDI, interactive CD

CD-Photo *nm* photo CD

CD-R *nm (abrév* **compact disc recordable***)* CD-R

CD-ROM *nm (abrév* **compact disc read only memory***)* CD-ROM

◇ *CD-ROM d'installation* setup CD-ROM

cédérom *nm* JO CD-ROM

◇ *cédérom d'installation* setup CD-ROM

cédille *nf* cedilla

cellule *nf (dans un tableur)* cell

central téléphonique *nm* telephone exchange

centre *nm*

◇ *centre de calcul* computing centre

◇ *centre de traitement de l'information* data processing centre

certificat *nm*

◇ *certificat de garantie* warranty ou guarantee certificate

◇ *Internet* **certificat de sécurité** security certificate

césure *nf* break, hyphenation

CFAO *nf (abrév* **conception et fabrication assistées par ordinateur***)* CAD/CAM

CGA *nm (abrév* **colour graphics adaptor***)* CGA

CGI *nf (abrév* **common gateway interface***)* CGI

chaîne *nf* string

◇ *chaîne de caractères* character string

chaîner *vt* to chain; *(commandes)* to pipe

champ *nm (dans une base de données)* field

◇ *champ mémo* memo field

◇ *champ numérique* numeric field

◇ *champ de texte* text field

changement *nm*

◇ *changement de ligne* line feed

◇ *changement de page* page break

charger **1** *vi (disque, programme)* to load up

2 se charger *vpr (disque, programme)* to load; **se charger automatiquement** to load automatically, to autoload

chargeur *nm (pour imprimante, scanner, photocopieuse)* feeder

chat *nm Internet* chat

chatter *vi Internet* to chat

chef des traitements *nm* data processing manager

chemin *nm* path

◊ *chemin d'accès* path, pathname

◊ *chemin d'accès aux données* data path

◊ *chemin du courrier électronique* mail path

chiffre *nm* digit, figure

◊ *chiffre ASCII* ASCII value *or* number

◊ *chiffres numériques* numerics

chiffrement *nm (de message)* encoding, encryption

◊ *chiffrement de données* data encryption

chiffrer *vt* encrypt

chiffreur *nm* encoder, encrypter

ci-joint *adj* attached; **veuillez trouver ci-joint...** please find attached...

circuit *nm* circuit

◊ *circuit ET* AND circuit

◊ *circuit logique* logic circuit

citation *nf (dans un courrier électronique)* quote

citer *vt (dans un courrier électronique)* to quote

classeur *nm* filer

clavier *nm (d'ordinateur, de machine à écrire)* keyboard; **introduire des données par clavier** to key (in) data

◊ *clavier alphanumérique* alphanumeric keypad

◊ *clavier AZERTY* AZERTY keyboard

◊ *clavier étendu* expanded keyboard, extended keyboard

◊ *clavier multi-fonction* multifunctional keyboard

◊ *clavier numérique* numeric keypad

◊ *clavier QWERTY* QWERTY keyboard

claviste *nmf* keyboarder

clé *nf* key; *(du DOS)* switch *Internet*

◊ *clé de chiffrement* encryption key

◊ *clé gigogne* dongle

clic *nm* click; **faire un clic (sur)** to click (on)

cliché mémoire *nm* dump

client *nm (d'un réseau)* client

◊ *client de messagerie électronique* e-mail client, mail reader

clipart *nm* clip art

cliquer *vi* to click (**sur** on); **cliquer deux fois** to double-click; **cliquer avec le bouton gauche/droit de la souris (sur)** to left-click/right-click (on); **cliquer et glisser** to click and drag

clone *nm* clone

clore *vt* **clore une session** to log off, to log out

clôture *nf* close

◊ *clôture de session* logging off

CMJN *PAO (abrév* **cyan, magenta, jaune, noir)** CMYK

cobol *nm* COBOL

codage *nm* encoding, coding

◊ *codage de données* data encryption

La disposition du clavier anglais

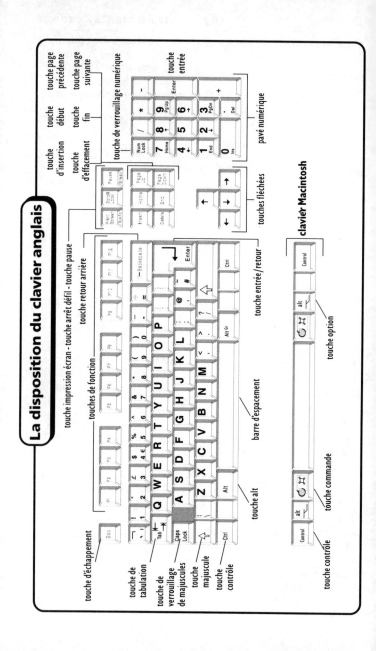

touche d'échappement

touche de tabulation

touche de verrouillage de majuscules

touche majuscule

touche contrôle

touche alt

touche impression écran - touche arrêt défil - touche pause

touches de fonction

touche retour arrière

touche d'insertion

touche d'effacement

touche page précédente

touche page suivante

touche début

touche fin

touche de verrouillage numérique

touche entrée

pavé numérique

touches fléchées

touche entrée / retour

clavier Macintosh

barre d'espacement

touche contrôle

touche commande

touche option

code *nm* code
◇ *code d'accès* access code
◇ *code alphanumérique* alphanumeric code
◇ *code ASCII* ASCII code
◇ *code à barres* bar code
◇ *code binaire* binary code
◇ *code de caractère* character code
◇ *code de commande* command code
◇ *code d'identification* identification code
◇ *code machine* machine code

coder *vt* to encode, to code

collecte de données *nf* data collection

coller *vt* to paste

colonne *nf (dans une table, un tableur)* column

combinaison de touches *nf* key combination

commande *nf* command; à **commande vocale** voice-activated
◇ *commande d'annulation* undo command
◇ *commande à bascule* toggle switch
◇ *commande binaire* bit command
◇ *commande du DOS* DOS command
◇ *commande d'effacement* delete command
◇ *commande erronée (message d'erreur)* bad command
◇ *commande d'insertion* insert command
◇ *commande de recherche* find command
◇ *commande système d'exploitation* operating system command
◇ *commande téléphonique, commande par téléphone* telephone order

commander *vt* to drive; **commandé par menu** menu-driven; **commandé à la voix** voice-activated

commerce électronique *nm* electronic commerce, e-commerce

communication *nf* (a) *(de données)* communication
(b) *Tél* communication (téléphonique) telephone call; **mettez-moi en communication avec M. Martin** put me through to Mr Martin; **je vous passe la communication** I'll put you through; **vous avez la communication** you're through; **la communication est mauvaise** the line *or* connection is bad

◇ *communication de données* data communications, datacomms
◇ *communication internationale* international call
◇ *communication interurbaine* toll call
◇ *communication en ligne* online communication
◇ *communication locale* local call
◇ *communication longue distance* long-distance call
◇ *communication en PCV* *Br* reverse-charge call, *Am* collect call
◇ *communication télématique* datacommunications, datacomms

commutation *nf*
◇ *commutation temporelle asynchrone* asynchronous transfer mode
◇ *Internet* **commutation de paquets** packet switching

compacter *vt (base de données)* to pack

compatibilité *nf* compatibility

compatible *adj* compatible; **ces deux applications ne sont pas compatibles** these two applications are incompatible *or* not compatible; **compatible vers le haut/vers le bas** upward/downward compatible; **compatible avec les versions antérieures** backward compatible; **compatible IBM** IBM-compatible; **compatible Mac** Mac-compatible

compilateur *nm* compiler

compiler *vt* to compile

composant *nm* component

composer *vt (numéro de téléphone)* to dial

composition *nf* dialling
◇ *composition automatique* automatic dialling

compresser *vt (fichier)* to compact, to compress, to zip

compresseur de données *nm* data compressor

compression *nf (de données)* compression; *(d'un fichier)* compacting, compression

comprimer *vt (données)* to compress; *(fichier)* to compact, to compress

compte *nm* account
◇ *compte d'accès par ligne commutée* dial-up account
◇ *compte de courrier électronique* e-mail account
◇ *compte Internet* Internet account

compteur *nm* counter

concaténé, -e *adj* concatenated

concentrateur *nm* hub

concepteur, -trice *nm,f* designer
◇ *Internet* **concepteur de sites Web** web designer

conception *nf* design
◇ *conception assistée par ordinateur* computer-aided *or* computer-assisted design
◇ *conception des produits* product design

condenser *vt (base de données)* to pack

confidentialité *nf* confidentiality
◇ *confidentialité des données* data privacy

configurable *adj* configurable

configuration *nf* configuration
◇ *configuration par défaut* default setting
◇ *configuration matérielle* hardware configuration

configurer *vt* to configure

conforme *adj* compliant (à with); **conforme à l'an 2000** year 2000 compliant

connaissances informatiques *nfpl* computer literacy; **avoir des connaissances informatiques** to be computer-literate

connecté, -e *adj* **être connecté** to be connected

connecter 1 *vt* to connect; **connecté en anneau/bus/étoile** in a ring/bus/star configuration; **connecté en série** series-connected; **connecter en boucle** to daisy-chain
2 se connecter *vpr* **se connecter à un système** to log on to a system; **se connecter à l'Internet** to connect to the Internet

connecteur *nm* connector

connectivité *nf* connectivity

connexion *nf* connection; **connexion en boucle** daisy-chaining

console *nf* console

◊ *console de visualisation* visual display unit, VDU

consommables *nmpl* consumables

contact de page *nm Internet* hit

contaminé, -e *adj* **contaminé par un virus** virus-infected

continuer *vi* (*dans boîte de dialogue*) to proceed

contrôle *nm* control

◊ *contrôle d'accès* access control

◊ *contrôle du curseur* cursor control

contrôler *vt* **contrôlé par le logiciel** software-controlled; **contrôlé par menu** menu-driven, menu-controlled; **contrôlé par ordinateur** computer-controlled

contrôleur *nm* controller

◊ *contrôleur d'affichage* display *or* screen controller

◊ *contrôleur de bus* bus controller

◊ *contrôleur de disque* disk controller

conversion *nf* (*de données*) conversion

◊ *conversion de fichier* file conversion

convertir *vt* (*données*) to convert; **convertir un système en numérique** to digitize a system

convertisseur analogique numérique *nm* digitizer

convivial, -e *adj* (*ordinateur, machine*) user-friendly

convivialité *nf* (*d'un ordinateur, d'une machine*) user-friendliness

cookie *nm Internet* cookie

copie *nf* (*de document, lettre*) copy; **faire une copie de qch** to make a copy of sth

◊ *copie archivée* archive (copy)

◊ *copie de bloc* copy block

◊ *copie en clair* hard copy, printout

◊ *copie de disquette* (*commande DOS*) disk copy

◊ *copie d'écran* print screen

◊ *copie sur papier* hard copy, printout

◇ *PAO* *copie prête pour la reproduction* CRC, camera-ready copy

◇ *copie de sauvegarde* backup copy

◇ *copie de sûreté* backup copy

copier *vt (document, lettre)* to copy; **copier qch sur le disque dur** to copy sth onto hard disk; **copier qch sur disquette** to copy sth to disk

copier-coller *nm* copy-and-paste; **faire un copier-coller (sur qch)** to copy and paste (sth)

coprocesseur *nm* co-processor

◇ *coprocesseur arithmétique* maths co-processor

corbeille *nf (de Mac)* wastebasket, *Am* trash; *(dans Windows)* recycle bin

◇ *corbeille d'arrivée (pour courrier électronique)* in box

◇ *corbeille de départ (pour courrier électronique)* out box

corps *nm* (a) *(d'un document, d'un courrier électronique)* body (b) *(de police de caracteres)* point size, type size, font size

correcteur *nm* checker

◇ *correcteur grammatical* grammar checker

◇ *correcteur d'orthographe, correcteur orthographique* spellchecker

correction *nf* (a) *(à une lettre, un document)* correction (b) *(logiciel)* patch

◇ *correction d'orthographe, correction orthographique* spellcheck

corriger *vt* to correct; **corriger automatiquement** to auto-correct

couche *nf* layer

couleur Pantone® *nf PAO* Pantone® colour, spot colour

coup de téléphone *nm* telephone call

couper *vt (texte)* to cut

couper-coller *nm* cut-and-paste; **faire un couper-coller (sur qch)** to cut and paste (sth)

courant *nm (électricité)* electricity, power

courbe *nf* curve

◇ *courbe de Bézier* Bézier curve

courriel *nm Can* e-mail

courrier *nm*

◇ *courrier électronique* e-mail, electronic mail; **envoyer un courrier électronique à qn** to e-mail sb; **envoyer qch par courrier électronique** to send sth by e-mail; **contacter qn par courrier électronique** to contact sb by e-mail

◇ *courrier escargot* snail mail

cpp *(abrév* **caractères par pouce)** cpi

cps *(abrév* **caractères par seconde)** cps

craquer *vt* to crack

crayon *nm*

◇ *crayon lumineux, crayon optique* light pen

création *nf*

◇ *création de pages Web* web authoring

crénage *nm PAO* kerning

crénelage *nm PAO* aliasing

crochet *nm* square bracket; **entre crochets** in square brackets

cryptage *nm* encryption

crypter *vt & vi* to encrypt

cryptographie *nf* encryption

curseur *nm* cursor

cyber *nm* cyber

cybercafé *nm* cybercafé, Internet café

cybercrime *nm* cybercrime

cyberculture *nf* cyberculture

cyberespace *nm* cyberspace; **dans le cyberespace** in cyberspace

cyberjargon *nm Internet* netspeak

cybernaute *nm* cybernaut

cybernétique **1** *adj* cybernetic
     2 *nf* cybernertics

cyberpunk *nm* cyberpunk

cybersexe *nm* cybersex

DAT nm (abrév **digital audio tape**) DAT

DD 1 adj (abrév **double densité**) DD

  2 nm (abrév **disque dur**) HD

DDE nm (abrév **dynamic data exchange**) DDE

débit nm rate

◇ **débit en bauds** baud rate

◇ **débit binaire** bit rate

◇ **débit de données** data throughput

débogage nm debugging

déboguer vt to debug

débogueur nm debugger

débrayer vt to disconnect

déchiffrement nm decryption

◇ **déchiffrement de données** data decryption

déchiffrer vt to decrypt

déclarer vt (valeur) to define

décodage nm decoding

décoder vt to decode

décodeur nm decoder

décompresser vt (fichier) to decompress

déconnecté, -e adj (imprimante) off-line

déconnecter se déconnecter vpr to go off-line

découpage nm (de fichier, d'image) splitting

découper vt (fichier, image) to split

décrocher vt (combiné téléphonique) to pick or lift up; **décrocher le téléphone** (pour ne pas être dérangé) to take the phone off the hook; (pour répondre) to pick up the phone

dédié, -e adj (serveur, ligne téléphonique) dedicated

défaire vt (opération) to undo

défaut nm default; **par défaut** by default; **sélectionner qch par défaut** to default to sth; **lecteur par défaut** default drive

défilement nm scroll, scrolling

défiler vi **faire défiler un document** to scroll through a document; **défiler vers le bas, faire défiler de haut en bas** to scroll down; **défiler vers le haut, faire défiler de bas en haut** to scroll up

défini, -e adj **défini par l'utilisateur** user-defined

définissable adj **définissable par l'utilisateur** user-definable

défragmentation *nf* defragmentation

défragmenter *vt* to defragment

dégradé *nm PAO* blend

DEL *nf (abrév* **diode émettrice de lueur)** LED

délimiter *vt (champ)* to delimit

délimiteur *nm (d'un champ)* delimiter

démarrage *nm* start-up
◦ *démarrage automatique* autostart
◦ *démarrage à chaud* warm start, warm boot
◦ *démarrage à froid* cold start, cold boot

démarrer *vt (ordinateur)* to boot (up), to start up

demi-tente *nf PAO* half-tone

démodulateur *nm* demodulator

densité *nf* **à double densité** double-density

dépannage *nm* troubleshooting

dépassement de capacité *nm* overflow

déplacement *nm (de curseur)* movement

déplacer *vt* to move

déplombage *nm* decoding, decrypting

déplomber *vt* to decode, to decrypt, to crack

dépouillement *nm (des données)* processing

dépouiller *vt (données)* to process

dérangement *nm Tél (panne)* **la ligne est en dérangement** the line is out of order, there's a fault on the line

dérouler *vt (menu)* to pull down

désactivation *nf* deactivation

désactivé, -e *adj* disabled

désactiver *vt* to deactivate, to disable, to deselect

descripteur *nm* descriptor

désembrayer *vt* to disconnect

désinstallateur *nm* deinstaller

désinstallation *nf* deinstallation

désinstaller *vt* to deinstall, to uninstall

dessin *nm* design
◦ *dessin assisté par ordinateur* computer-aided design

destinataire *nmf (d'un message électronique)* recipient

détecteur de virus *nm* virus detector

détection *nf*
◦ *détection d'erreurs* error detection
◦ *détection virale, détection de virus* virus detection

deux-points *nm* colon

développeur, -euse *nm,f* software developer

déverrouiller *vt (fichier, disquette)* to unlock; *(majus-*

cules) to lock off; **déverrouiller un fichier en écriture** to unlock a file, to remove the read-only lock on a file

dézipper *vt (fichier)* to unzip

diagnostic d'autotest *nm* self-test diagnosis

dialogue *nm* dialogue

◇ *dialogue d'établissement de liaison* handshaking

dialoguer *vi* to interact

diaporama *nm* slide show

didacticiel *nm* tutorial, courseware

dièse *nf* hash

différé *nm* **en différé** *(traitement)* off-line

dimensionner *vt (objets)* to size

direction systématisée *nf* systems management

disponible *adj* available; **disponible pour Mac/PC** available for the Mac/PC

dispositif *nm* device

◇ *dispositif d'alimentation* power unit; *(pour papier)* sheet feed

◇ *dispositif d'alimentation feuille à feuille* cut sheet feeder

◇ *dispositif d'alimentation papier* sheet feed, paper feed

◇ *dispositif externe* external device

◇ *dispositif de sortie* output device

◇ *dispositif de stockage* storage device

◇ *Tél dispositif de redirection*

d'appel call forwarding device

disposition *nf*

◇ *disposition de clavier* keyboard layout

◇ *disposition de texte* text layout

disque *nm* disk

◇ *disque amovible* removable disk

◇ *disque cible* target disk

◇ *disque compact* compact disk, CD

◇ *disque compact interactif* interactive CD, CD-I

◇ *disque de démarrage* boot disk

◇ *disque de destination* destination disk

◇ *disque dur* hard disk

◇ *disque fixe* fixed disk

◇ *disque laser* laser disk

◇ *disque magnétique* magnetic disk

◇ *disque maître* master disk

◇ *disque optique* optical disk

◇ *disque optique compact* CD-ROM

◇ *disque souple* floppy disk

◇ *disque source* source disk

◇ *disque système* system disk

◇ *disque vidéo numérique* digital video disk, digital versatile disk

disquette *nf* diskette, floppy (disk); **sur disquette** on diskette, on floppy

◇ *disquette cible* target disk

◇ *disquette de copie* copy disk

◇ *disquette de démarrage* boot disk, start-up disk

◇ *disquette de démonstration* demo disk

◇ **disquette de destination** destination disk
◇ **disquette de diagnostic** diagnostic disk
◇ **disquette (à) double densité** double density disk
◇ **disquette d'installation** installation disk, installer
◇ **disquette magnétique** magnetic disk
◇ **disquette optique** optical disk, floptical disk
◇ **disquette pour PC** PC disk
◇ **disquette programme** program disk
◇ **disquette (à) simple densité** single density disk
◇ **disquette source** source disk
◇ **disquette système** system disk
◇ **disquette vierge** blank unformatted disk

distance *nf* à distance remote

DNS *nm Internet* (*abrév* **Domain Name System**) DNS

DOC *nm* (*abrév* **disque optique compact**) CD-ROM

document *nm* document
◇ **document de base** source document
◇ **document source** source document
◇ **document transmissible** transferable document
◇ **document type** standard document

domaine *nm Internet* domain
◇ **domaine public** public domain

donnée *nf* piece of data; **données** data

◇ **données de base** background data
◇ **données brutes** raw data
◇ **données numériques** digital data

DOS *nm* DOS

dossier *nm* (*répertoire*) folder; (*fichier*) file
◇ **dossier actif** active file
◇ **dossier archivé** archive file
◇ **dossier clos** closed file
◇ **dossier ouvert** open file
◇ **dossier sauvegardé** saved file
◇ **dossier système** system file

double 1 *adj* double
2 *nm* (*de données*) backup
◇ **double densité** double density

double-clic *nm* double-click; **faire un double-clic (sur)** to double-click (on)

double-cliquer *vi* to double-click

doubleur de fréquence (d'horloge) *nm* clock speed doubler

dpi (*abrév* **dots per inch**) dpi

DRAM *nf* (*abrév* **dynamic random access memory**) DRAM

droits d'accès *nmpl* privileges, access privileges

durée de connexion *nf* on-line time, connect time

DVD *nm* (*abrév* **Digital Video Disk, Digital Versatile Disk**) DVD

EAO nm (abrév **enseignement assisté par ordinateur**) CAL

échange nm
◇ *échange de données* data exchange
◇ *échange de données informatisé* electronic data exchange
◇ *échange dynamique de données* dynamic data exchange

échappement nm (touche) escape

échelle des gris nf PAO levels of grey

écluse nf [JO] *Internet* firewall

économiseur d'écran nm screen saver

écran nm screen, display; **à l'écran** on screen; **travailler sur écran** to work on screen
◇ *écran d'accueil* start-up screen
◇ *écran d'aide* help screen
◇ *écran antireflet* antiglare screen
◇ *écran couleur* colour screen or display
◇ *écran à cristaux liquides, écran LCD* LCD screen, liquid crystal screen
◇ *écran divisé* split screen
◇ *écran à haute définition, écran à haute résolution* high-resolution screen
◇ *écran à matrice active* active matrix screen
◇ *écran pleine page* full page display
◇ *écran plat* flat screen
◇ *écran tactile* touch or touch-sensitive screen
◇ *écran de visualisation* visual display unit, VDU

écraser vt (fichier) to zap, to overwrite

écrire vt to write; (noter) to write down; **écrire à qn** to write to sb; **écrire une lettre à la machine** to type a letter; **écrire qch sur disque** to write sth to disk

EDI nm (abrév **échange de données informatisé**) EDE

éditer vt (texte) to edit; **non édité** unedited

éditeur nm (de programme) editor
◇ *éditeur d'icônes* icon editor
◇ *éditeur de liens* linker, link editor
◇ *éditeur de logiciels* software company
◇ *éditeur de texte* text editor

édition *nf (de données)* editing; *(de menu)* edit

◇ *édition électronique* electronic publishing

éditique *nf* [JO] electronic publishing

effaçable *adj (mémoire)* erasable

effacement *nm* deletion

effacer 1 *vt (données)* to erase, to delete; *(écran)* to clear
  2 *vi* to delete

effleurement *nm* à effleurement *(clavier)* touch-sensitive

EGA *nm (abrév* **enhanced graphics adaptor)** EGA

électronique 1 *adj (réservation, traitement de données, point de vente, argent)* electronic
  2 *nf* electronics

élément *nm (d'un menu)* item

◇ *elément ET* AND element

émoticon *nm Internet* smiley, emoticon

emplacement *nm* slot

◇ *emplacement pour carte* card slot

◇ *emplacement pour carte d'extension* expansion slot

◇ *emplacement d'évolutivité* upgrade slot

émulateur de terminal *nm* terminal emulator

émulation *nf* emulation

◇ *émulation de terminal* terminal emulation

émuler *vt* emulate

enchaînement *nm* concatenation

encodage *nm* encoding

encoder *vt* to encode

encodeur *nm* encoder

endommager *vt (disque, fichier)* to corrupt

enregistrement *nm (de données)* logging, recording; *(article de base de données)* record

enregistrer *vt* (a) *(données, programme)* to store
  (b) *(sauvegarder) (changements, ajouts)* to save; **voulez-vous enregistrer les modifications?** do you want to save changes?; **enregistrer sous...** save as
  (c) *(CD-ROM)* to write

enseignement assisté par ordinateur *nm* computer-aided learning, computer-based training

ensemble *nm (de caractères, d'informations)* set

◇ *ensemble de données* data set

◇ *ensemble logiciel* software suite

en-tête *nm* header

entraînement du papier *nm (d'une imprimante)* paper advance

entrée *nf (processus)* input, entry; *(information)* entry; *(touche)* enter (key)

◇ *entrée de données* data entry

entrée/sortie *nf* input/output

entrer 1 *vt (données)* to enter,

to input; *(au clavier)* to key in
2 *vi (utilisateur)* to log in *or* on

environnement *nm* environment

envoi multiple *nm Internet*
crossposting; **faire un envoi
multiple de qch** to cross-post
sth

épine dorsale *nf Internet*
backbone

EPS *nm (abrév* **encapsulated
PostScript)** EPS

équipement *nm* equipment

◇ *équipement informatique*
computer equipment

ergonomie *nf* ergonomics

ergonomique *adj* ergonomic

erreur *nf* error

◇ *erreur aléatoire* random error
◇ *erreur de codage* coding error
◇ *erreur disque* disk error
◇ *erreur fatale* fatal error
◇ *erreur de logiciel* software
error
◇ *erreur de syntaxe* syntax
error
◇ *erreur système* system error

E/S *nf (abrév* **entrée/sortie)** I/O

espace *nm (dans un texte)*
space

◇ *espace disque* disk space
◇ *espace insécable* hard space
◇ *espace mémoire* memory
space
◇ *Internet* **espace Web** Web
space

espacement *nm* spacing

◇ *espacement arrière* backspace

◇ *espacement de caractères*
character spacing

esperluette *nf* ampersand

essai *nm* test

◇ *essai de performance*
benchmark

établissement d'appel *nm*
Tél call connection

état *nm (d'une base de données)*
report

◇ *état du projet* status report

éteindre *vt* to power down, to
shut down

étendre *vt (mémoire)* to
upgrade, to expand

Ethernet *nm* Ethernet®

évolué, -e *adj (langage)* high-
level

évoluer *vi* **faire évoluer qch** to
upgrade sth

évolutif, -ive *adj (matériel,
système)* upgradable

évolutivité *nf (de matériel,
système)* upgradability

exécutable *adj (programme)*
executable

exécuter *vt (programme)* to
execute, to run; *(commande)*
to execute, to carry out

exécution *nf (d'un programme)* execution, running;
(d'une commande) execution,
carrying out

export *nm* export

◇ *export de données* data
export

exportation *nf (d'un fichier)*
exporting; *(données exportées)*
exported data

exporter *vt (fichier)* to export (**vers** to)

extensible *adj (matériel, système)* upgradeable; *(mémoire)* expandable, upgradeable

extension *nf* (**a**) *(augmentation)* expansion

(**b**) *(dispositif)* add-on

◇ *extension mémoire* memory expansion *or* upgrade

◇ *extension de nom de fichier* file name extension

extractible *adj (disque)* removable

fabrication *nf*

◇ *fabrication assistée par ordinateur* computer-assisted manufacture

◇ *fabrication intégrée par ordinateur* computer-integrated manufacturing

facilité d'emploi *nf (d'un ordinateur)* user-friendliness, ease of use

fac-similé *nm* facsimile, exact copy

facture *nf* bill

◇ *facture de téléphone* telephone bill

FAO *nf (abrév* **fabrication assistée par ordinateur)** CAM

FAQ *Internet (abrév* **frequently asked questions, foire aux questions)** FAQ

faute *nf* error

◇ *faute de frappe* keying error

favoris *nmpl Internet* favorites

fax *nm (appareil)* fax (machine); *(message)* fax; **envoyer qch par fax** to send sth by fax, to fax sth

◇ *fax modem* fax modem

faxer *vt (message, document)* to fax

fenêtre *nf (sur écran)* window

◇ *fenêtre activée* active window

◇ *fenêtre d'aide* help window

◇ *fenêtre de dialogue* dialogue window

◇ *fenêtre flottante* floating window

◇ *fenêtre graphique* graphics window

fermer *vt (fichier, fenêtre)* to close; *(commande)* to end

fermeture *nf (d'un fichier, d'une fenêtre)* closing; *(d'une commande)* ending; *(d'un ordinateur)* shutdown

ferret *nm* tag

feuille *nf* sheet

◇ *feuille de calcul* spreadsheet

◇ *feuille de style* style sheet

feuilleter *vi* **feuilleter en arrière** page down; **feuilleter en avant** page up

fibre *nf* **câble en fibres optiques** fibre optic cable

fiche *nf* pin

◇ *fiche gigogne* dongle

◇ *fiche de pointage* clocking-in card

fichier *nm* file

◇ *fichier actif* active file

◇ *fichier d'adresses* mailing list, address file

◇ *fichier ASCII* ASCII file
◇ *fichier autoexec.bat* auto-exec.bat (file)
◇ *fichier binaire* binary file
◇ *fichier de commande* command file
◇ *fichier compte-rendu* log file
◇ *fichier config.sys* config.sys (file)
◇ *Internet fichier de cookies* cookie file
◇ *fichier disque* disk file
◇ *fichier document* document file
◇ *fichier exécutable* executable file
◇ *Internet fichier FAQ* FAQ file
◇ *fichier à imprimer* print job
◇ *fichier joint (de courrier électronique)* attachment
◇ *fichier lisez-moi* read-me file
◇ *fichier maître* master file
◇ *fichier principal* master file
◇ *fichier de sauvegarde* back-up file
◇ *fichier source* source file
◇ *fichier système* system file
◇ *Can Internet fichier de témoins* cookie file
◇ *fichier temporaire* temporary file
◇ *fichier texte* text file

fil *nm* cord; **sans fil** cordless
◇ *fil de discussion (d'un groupe de discussion)* thread

file d'attente *nf (d'une imprimante)* print queue *or* list; **mettre en file d'attente** to spool, to queue

filtre *nm* filter
◇ *filtre anti-reflet* glare screen

fin *nf*
◇ *fin de ligne* line end
◇ *fin de page* page break
◇ *fin de page obligatoire* hard page break
◇ *fin de paragraphe* paragraph break
◇ *fin de session* logoff

finaud, -e *nm,f* [JO] hacker

firmware *nm* firmware

flèche *nf* pointer, arrow
◇ *flèche vers le bas* down arrow
◇ *flèche vers la droite* right arrow
◇ *flèche vers la gauche* left arrow
◇ *flèche vers le haut* up arrow

foire aux questions *nf Internet* FAQ

fonction *nf*
◇ *fonction de comptage de mots* word count facility
◇ *fonction couper-coller* cut-and-paste facility
◇ *fonction de répétition* repeat function
◇ *fonction de sauvegarde* save function

fonctionnement *nm* running, working
◇ *fonctionnement en réseau* networking

fonctionner *vi (logiciel)* to run

fond perdu *nm PAO* bleed

fonte *nf* font
◇ *fonte d'imprimante* printer font

format *nm* format

⬦ *format ASCII* ASCII format

⬦ *format de fichier* file format

⬦ *format graphique* image format

⬦ *format d'impression* print format

⬦ *format de page* page format or setup

⬦ *format de paragraphe* paragraph format

⬦ *format TIFF* TIFF

formatage *nm (de disque)* formatting

formater *vt (disque)* to format; **non formaté** unformatted

formulaire *nm* form

⬦ *formulaire de saisie* input form

forum de discussion *nm* Internet forum

fournisseur *nm* vendor

⬦ Internet *fournisseur d'accès* access provider.

⬦ Internet *fournisseur de contenu* content provider

fragmentation *nf* fragmentation

⬦ *fragmentation de disque* disk fragmentation

frais *nmpl*

⬦ *frais d'inscription* setup charge, setup fee

⬦ *frais d'interurbain* toll

frappe *nf (dactylographie)* typing; *(sur un clavier d'ordinateur)* keying

⬦ *frappe en continu* type-ahead

⬦ *frappe au kilomètre* continuous input

⬦ *frappe de touche* keystroke

freeware *nm* freeware; **freewares** freeware programs

fréquence *nf*

⬦ *fréquence d'horloge* clock speed

⬦ *fréquence de rafraîchissement* refresh rate

fusion *nf* merge

⬦ *fusion de fichiers* file merge

fusionner *vt (fichiers)* to merge

gabarit *nm* PAO *(pour un document)* template

gamme *nf* **un ordinateur d'entrée de gamme** an entry level computer

garantie *nf* warranty, guarantee

◇ **garantie retour atelier** return-to-base warranty *or* guarantee

◇ **garantie sur site** on-site warranty *or* guarantee

garantir *vt* to guarantee; **cet ordinateur est garanti cinq ans** this computer is guaranteed for five years

garde-barrière *nf Internet* firewall

générateur *nm* generator

◇ **générateur de caractères** character generator

générer *vt* to generate; **généré par ordinateur** computer-generated

gestion *nf* management

◇ **gestion de bases de données** database management

◇ **gestion de données** data management

◇ **gestion de fichiers** file management

◇ **gestion de parc réseau** network management

◇ **gestion des systèmes d'information** informations systems management

gestionnaire *nm (de disques)* manager, driver

◇ **gestionnaire de fichiers** file manager

◇ **gestionnaire de fichiers et de répertoires** filer

◇ **gestionnaire de mémoire** memory manager

◇ **gestionnaire de projets** project management package

◇ **gestionnaire de réseau** network manager

GIF *nm (abrév* **Graphics Interchange Format)** GIF

◇ *Internet* **GIF animé** animated GIF

gigaoctet *nm* gigabyte

glisser *vi* **faire glisser** *(pointeur)* to drag

◇ **glisser d'icônes** icon drag

glisser-lâcher *nm* drag and drop

◇ **glisser-lâcher d'icônes** icon drag and drop

Go *nm* (*abrév* **gigaoctet**) GB

gopher *nm Internet* gopher

GPAO *nf* (*abrév* **gestion de production assistée par ordinateur**) computer-aided production management

grand réseau *nm* wide area network

grapheur *nm* graphics package

graphique *nm* (**a**) *(diagramme)* chart (**b**) **graphiques** graphics

◇ *graphique en barres* bar chart

◇ *graphiques de gestion* business graphics

◇ *graphiques de présentation* presentation graphics

graphisme *nm* graphics

◇ *graphisme en couleur* colour graphics

grappe *nf* (*de terminaux*) cluster

gras 1 *nm* bold; **en gras** in bold **2** *adj* bold

graticiel, gratuiciel *nm* JO freeware

graver *vt* (*CD-ROM*) to write, to burn

graveur *nm* (*de CD-ROM*) writer, burner

◇ *graveur de disque compact* compact disc recorder, CD-R

grille *nf* grid

gros système *nm* mainframe

groupe *nm*

◇ *Internet* **groupe de discussion** discussion group

◇ *Internet* **groupe de nouvelles** newsgroup

guide de l'utilisateur *nm* instruction manual, user manual

guillemets *nm* inverted commas

habillage du texte *nm* text wrap

hardware *nm* hardware

haut, -e *adj*
◇ *haute densité* high density
◇ *haut de gamme* high-end
◇ *haute resolution* high-resolution; **de haute vitesse** high-speed

haut-parleur *nm* speaker

hexadécimal, -e *adj* hexadecimal

HD *adj* (*abrév* **haute densité**) HD

hébergement *nm* *Internet (de site Web)* hosting; **hébergement de sites Web** web hosting

héberger *vt* *Internet (site Web)* to host

histogramme *nm* histogram, column graph

historique *nm* (*de document*) log; *Internet (dans un logiciel de navigation)* history list

horloge *nf* clock
◇ *horloge du système* system clock

hub *nm* hub

hybride *adj (CD-ROM)* hybrid

hyperlien *nm* hyperlink

hypermédia *nm* hypermedia

hypertexte *adj & nm* hypertext

hypertoile *nf* [JO] *Internet* World Wide Web

IA *nf* (*abrév* **intelligence artificielle**) AI

icône *nf* icon

iconographie *nf* PAO artwork

identificateur *nm* identifier

identification *nf* identification

◇ *identification de l'utilisateur* user identification

illisible *adj* (*fichier, données*) unreadable

illustration *nf* illustration; *PAO* **illustrations** artwork, illustrations

image *nf* image

◇ *Internet* **image cliquable** clickable image

◇ *image digitalisée* digitized image

◇ *image intégrée* inline image

◇ *images de synthèse* computer-generated images, CGI

◇ *image vectorielle* vector graphics

import *nm* import

◇ *import de données* data import

importer *vt* to import (**depuis** from)

impression *nf* printing

◇ *impression en arrière-plan* background (mode) printing

◇ *impression couleur* colour printing

◇ *impression écran* screen dump

◇ *impression ombrée* shadow printing

◇ *PAO* **impression en quadrichomie** process colours

◇ *impression en qualité brouillon* draft quality printing

imprimante *nf* printer

◇ *imprimante à bulles* bubble-jet printer

◇ *imprimante couleur* colour printer

◇ *imprimante feuille à feuille* sheet-fed printer

◇ *imprimante à jet d'encre* inkjet printer

◇ *imprimante à impact* impact printer

◇ *imprimante (à) laser* laser printer

◇ *imprimante à marguerite* daisy-wheel printer

◇ *imprimante matricielle* dot-matrix printer

◇ *imprimante parallèle* parallel printer

Différents types d'imprimantes

Imprimante matricielle

▷ l'impression se fait grâce à un
  ruban-encreur
▷ capable d'imprimer plusieurs
  feuillets à la fois ainsi que du
  papier en continu
▷ coût par page imprimée peu
  élevé
▷ assez bruyante
▷ qualité d'impression médiocre

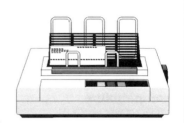

Imprimante à jet d'encre

▷ les caractères sont formés
  sur le papier grâce à un fin
  jet d'encre
▷ impression en couleurs à
  coût réduit
▷ coût par page imprimée
  assez élevé
▷ peu bruyante

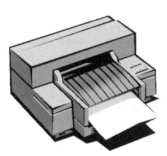

Imprimante laser

▷ l'impression se fait grâce à
  un rayon laser
▷ coût par page imprimée peu
  élevé
▷ peu bruyante
▷ rapide
▷ les imprimantes laser
  couleur reviennent cher à
  l'achat

◇ *imprimante série* serial printer

◇ *imprimante thermique, imprimante thermoélectrique* thermal printer

imprimer 1 *vt* to print (out) **2 s'imprimer** *vpr (document)* to print

impulsion *nf Tél* pulse

incompatibilité *nf* incompatibility (**avec** with)

incompatible *adj* incompatible (**avec** with)

index *nm (d'une base de données)* index

indexer *vt (base de données)* to index

indicatif *nm* (**a**) *Tél* indicatif (**téléphonique**) *Br* dialling code, *Am* dial code (**b**) *(de DOS)* prompt

◇ *indicatif du pays* international *Br* dialling code *or Am* dial code

◇ *indicatif (du) DOS* DOS prompt

infecter *vt (fichier, disque)* to infect

infographie *nf* computer graphics

informaticien, -enne *nm,f* computer scientist

information *nf* data, information

informatique *nf* information technology, IT, computing; *(science)* computer science, computing; **elle travaille dans l'informatique** she works in computing

◇ *informatique d'entreprise* business data processing

◇ *informatique de gestion* business computing

◇ *informatique individuelle* personal computing

informatisation *nf* computerization

informatiser *vt* to computerize

inforoute *nf Can* information superhighway, infohighway

infrarouge *nm* infrared

ingénierie *nf*

◇ *ingénierie assistée par ordinateur* computer-aided engineering, CAE

◇ *ingénierie des systèmes assistée par ordinateur* computer-aided software engineering, CASE

initialisation *nf (d'ordinateur, modem, imprimante)* initialization

initialiser *vt (ordinateur, modem, imprimante)* to initialize; **non initialisé** uninitialized

inscription *nf* registration

◇ *inscription en ligne* on-line registration

inscrire *vt (logiciel)* to register

insérer *vt* to insert

insertion *nf* insertion

◇ *insertion de caractères* character insert

installer *vt (logiciel, matériel)* to install

instruction *nf* instruction

intégration *nf* integration

◇ *intégration de bases de données* database integration

intégré, -e *adj (fax, modem)* integrated

intelligence artificielle *nf* artificial intelligence

interactif, -ive *adj* interactive

interdit, -e *adj* interdit **d'écriture** *(disquette)* write-protected

interface *nf* interface

◇ Internet **interface commune de passerelle** common gateway interface, CGI

◇ *interface graphique* graphic interface

◇ *interface parallèle* parallel interface

◇ *interface série* serial interface

◇ *interface utilisateur* user interface

◇ *interface utilisateur graphique* graphical user interface

◇ *interface WIMP* WIMP

interlignage *nm PAO* line spacing, leading

interligne *nm PAO* spacing

internaute *nmf* Internet user; **internaute novice** newbie

Internet *nm* Internet; **Internet 2** Internet 2; **naviguer sur l'Internet** to surf the Internet

interpolation *nf* interpolation

interpréteur *nm* interpreter

interrogation *nf (d'une base de données)* inquiry, query; *(activité)* interrogation

◇ *interrogation à distance* remote access

interrogeable à distance *adj Tél (répondeur)* with a remote-access facility

In French, should one write **"l'Internet"** with a capital "i" and the definite article, or **"internet"** with a lower-case "i" and no definite article, or either of the two other possible permutations? No definitive spelling has yet prevailed but the trend does seem to be towards the use of a capital "i", the argument being that even though it is not a proper noun, the Internet is a unique thing and so follows the model of "la Terre", "le Soleil".

Whereas in English we always say "*the* Internet", there is much more flexibility in the use or not of the article in French. A pattern is hard to detect because of its use in constructions where the article is not required grammatically ("par Internet", like "par fax") but it seems that the form **"l'Internet"** is winning out, perhaps under the influence of English.

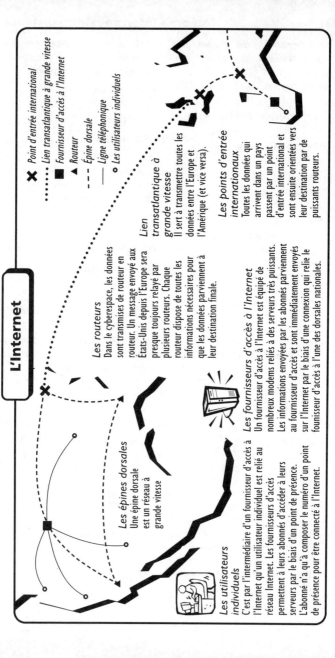

L'Internet

Légende:
- ✕ Point d'entrée international
- •••• Lien transatlantique à grande vitesse
- ■ Fournisseur d'accès à l'Internet
- ▲ Routeur
- – – – Épine dorsale
- —— Ligne téléphonique
- ○ Les utilisateurs individuels

Les routeurs
Dans le cyberespace, les données sont transmises de routeur en routeur. Un message envoyé aux États-Unis depuis l'Europe sera presque toujours relayé par plusieurs routeurs. Chaque routeur dispose de toutes les informations nécessaires pour que les données parviennent à leur destination finale.

Lien transatlantique à grande vitesse
Il sert à transmettre toutes les données entre l'Europe et l'Amérique (et vice versa).

Les points d'entrée internationaux
Toutes les données qui arrivent dans un pays passent par un point d'entrée international et sont ensuite orientées vers leur destination par de puissants routeurs.

Les fournisseurs d'accès à l'Internet
Un fournisseur d'accès à l'Internet est équipé de nombreux modems reliés à des serveurs très puissants. Les informations envoyées par les abonnés parviennent au fournisseur d'accès et sont immédiatement envoyées sur l'Internet par le biais d'une connexion qui relie le fournisseur d'accès à l'une des dorsales nationales.

Les épines dorsales
Une épine dorsale est un réseau à grande vitesse

Les utilisateurs individuels
C'est par l'intermédiaire d'un fournisseur d'accès à l'Internet qu'un utilisateur individuel est relié au réseau Internet. Les fournisseurs d'accès permettent à leurs abonnés d'accéder à leurs serveurs par le biais d'un point de présence. L'abonné n'a qu'à composer le numéro d'un point de présence pour être connecté à l'Internet.

interroger *vt (base de données)* to query, to interrogate

interrupteur *nm* switch

◊ *interrupteur DIP* DIP switch

Intranet *nm* Intranet

introduction de données *nf* data input

introduire **1** *vt* **introduire des données** to input *or* enter data
2 s'introduire *vpr* **s'introduire en fraude dans un réseau** to hack into a network

intrus, -e *nm,f (dans un réseau, dans un système)* intruder

invalide *adj (mot de passe, nom du fichier)* invalid

inversion vidéo *nf* reverse mode

invite *nf* prompt

◊ *invite du DOS* DOS prompt

italique *adj & nm* italic

Java *nm Internet* Java

jeu *nm (de caractères, d'instructions)* set

◊ *jeu de caractères* character set

◊ *jeu de fiches* card index

◊ *jeu informatique* computer game

joker *nm* wildcard

joindre *vt (document, fichier)* to append, to attach (**à** to)

journal *nm (fichier)* log

◊ *journal sur CD-ROM* CD-ROM newspaper

◊ *journal en ligne* electronic newspaper

justification *nf (de texte)* justification

◊ *justification à droite* right justification

◊ *justification à gauche* left justification

◊ *justification verticale* vertical justification

justifier *vt (de texte)* to justify; **justifié à gauche/à droite** left/right justified

Kb *nm (abrév* **kilobit**) Kb

kilobaud *nm* kilobaud

kilobit *nm* kilobit

kilo-octet *nm* kilobyte

kit *nm* kit

◊ *Internet* **kit d'accès, kit de connexion** connection kit, starter pack

◊ **kit d'évolution, kit d'extension** upgrade kit

KO *nm (abrév* **kilo-octet**) K, KB; **une disquette de 720 KO** a 720K disquette

ko/s *(abrév* **kilo-octets par seconde**) kbps

label de volume *nm* volume label

lâcher *vt (icône)* to drop
◇ *lâcher d'icônes* icon drop

lancement *nm (d'impression)* start; *(de programme)* running

lancer *vt (impression)* to start; *(programme)* to run, to start (up)

langage *nm* language
◇ *langage assembleur ou d'assemblage* assembly language
◇ *langage auteur* authoring language
◇ *langage de commande* command language
◇ *Internet langage Javascript* Java script
◇ *langage machine* machine language
◇ *langage de programmation* programming language
◇ *langage utilisateur* user language

languette *nf* slider

largeur de bande *nf* bandwidth

lecteur *nm* reader; *(de disque, de disquettes)* drive

◇ *lecteur de bande audio-numérique* DAT drive
◇ *lecteur Bernoulli®* Bernoulli® drive
◇ *lecteur de cartes magnétiques* magnetic card reader
◇ *lecteur de carte à mémoire* smart card reader, card reader
◇ *lecteur de carte à puce* smart card reader
◇ *lecteur de CD-ROM ou* [JO] *cédérom* CD-ROM drive
◇ *lecteur de CD-ROM ou* [JO] *cédérom double vitesse* double-speed CD-ROM drive
◇ *lecteur de courrier* mail reader
◇ *lecteur DAT* DAT drive
◇ *lecteur par défaut* default drive
◇ *lecteur de destination* destination drive
◇ *lecteur de disque dur* hard disk drive
◇ *lecteur de disque optique* CD-ROM drive
◇ *lecteur de disquettes* disk drive, floppy (disk) drive
◇ *lecteur de documents* document reader
◇ *lecteur Jaz®* Jaz® drive
◇ *lecteur OCR* OCR reader

◇ *lecteur optique de carac-tères* optical character reader

◇ *lecteur de pages* page scanner

◇ *lecteur Zip®* Zip® drive

lecture *nf* read; **en lecture seule** in read-only mode; **mettre un fichier en lecture seule** to make a file read-only

◇ *lecture optique* optical reading

◇ *lecture au scanneur* scan

lecture-écriture *nf* read-write (mode)

lettrine *nf PAO* drop cap

libertel *nf Internet* freenet

licence *nf* licence (agreement)

◇ *licence individuelle d'utilisa-tion* single user licence

lien *nm (hyperlien)* link

◇ *lien hypertexte* hypertext link

lier *vt* to link (**à** to)

ligne *nf* (a) *Tél* line; **être en ligne** to be on a call; **la ligne est occupée** the line is *Br* engaged or *Am* busy; **la ligne a été coupée** I've/we've/*etc* been cut off; **il y a quelqu'un sur la ligne** there's someone on the line; **vous êtes en ligne** you're connected, you're through; **il est déjà en ligne** he's on another line; **la ligne est en dérangement** the line is out of order

  (b) **en ligne** on line; **sur ligne** on line; **hors ligne** off line

  (c) *(de texte)* line

  (d) *(d'un tableur)* row

◇ *PAO* **ligne de base** baseline

◇ *ligne de commande* com-mand line

◇ *ligne directe* direct line

◇ *ligne directe accessible 24 heures sur 24* 24-hour hotline

◇ *ligne d'état* status line

◇ *ligne extérieure* outside line

◇ *ligne louée* leased line

◇ *PAO* **ligne orpheline** orphan

◇ *ligne ouverte* open line

◇ *ligne privée* private line

◇ *ligne RNIS* ISDN line

◇ *ligne spécialisé* dedicated line

◇ *ligne téléphonique* tele-phone line

◇ *PAO* **ligne veuve** widow

lire *vt (disquette)* to read; **lire au scanneur** to scan

lisible *adj* **lisible par ordinateur** machine-readable

lissage de caractères *nm* character smoothing

liste *nf* **être sur la liste rouge** to be *Br* ex-directory or *Am* unlisted

◇ *Internet* **liste de diffusion** distribution or discussion list, mailing list

◇ *liste de fichiers à imprimer* print list, print queue

◇ *liste de publipostage* mailing list

◇ *liste à puces* bulleted list

◇ *liste rapide* draft

◇ *Internet* **liste de signets** bookmark list, hot list

listing *nm* listing, printout

livre d'or *nm (de page Web)* guestbook

localisation *nf* localization

localiser *vt* to localize

logiciel *nm* software; **un logiciel** a software package; *(programme)* a piece of software

◇ *logiciel d'application* application software

◇ *logiciel auteur* authoring software

◇ *logiciel de bureautique* business software

◇ *logiciel client* client software

◇ *logiciel de communication* communications software, datacomms software

◇ *logiciel de comptabilité* accounting program

◇ *logiciel de conception assistée par ordinateur* computer-aided design package

◇ *logiciel contributif* shareware

◇ *logiciel de conversion* conversion software

◇ *logiciel convivial* user-friendly software

◇ *logiciel de courrier électronique* e-mail software

◇ *logiciel de dessin* art package, drawing program

◇ *logiciel du domaine public* public domain software

◇ *logiciel d'exploitation* system software

◇ *Internet logiciel de filtrage* filtering software, blocking software

◇ *logiciel grapheur, logiciel graphique* graphics software, illustration software

◇ *logiciel intégré* integrated software

◇ *Internet logiciel de lecture de nouvelles* news reader

◇ *logiciel de mise en page* desktop publishing package

◇ *logiciel multi-utilisateur* multi-user software

◇ *Internet logiciel de navigation* browser

◇ *logiciel de PAO* DTP software

◇ *logiciel de planification* scheduler

◇ *logiciel de présentation* presentation software

◇ *logiciel public* public domain software

◇ *logiciel de reconnaissance vocale* voice recognition software

◇ *logiciel de réseau* network software

◇ *logiciel système* system software

◇ *logiciel de système d'exploitation* operating system software

◇ *logiciel de télémaintenance* remote-access software

◇ *logiciel de traitement de texte* word-processing software, word-processing packages

◇ *logiciel utilisateur* user software

◇ *logiciel utilitaire* utility program

longue distance *adj (appel)* long-distance

machine *nf* machine; **écrire** *ou* **taper une lettre à la machine** to type a letter

◇ *machine à additionner* adding machine

◇ *machine à affranchir* *Br* franking machine, *Am* postal meter

◇ *machine à calculer* calculator

◇ *machine à écrire* typewriter

◇ *machine de traitement d'information* data processor

◇ *machine de traitement de texte(s)* word processor

macro-commande *nf* macro (command)

macro-instruction *nf* macro instruction

macrolangage *nm* macro language

magnéto-optique *adj* magneto-optical

maître de poste *nm Internet* postmaster

majuscule **1** *adj* upper-case **2** *nf* upper case

manche à balai *nf* joystick

mandataire *nm Internet* proxy

manette de jeu *nf* joystick

manuel d'utilisation *nm* user manual

marger **1** *vt (page)* to set the margin(s) for **2** *vi* to set the margin(s); **marger à droite/à gauche** to set the right/left margin

marque *nf (code)* marker, flag, tag

◇ *marque d'insertion* insertion marker

◇ *marque de paragraphe* paragraph mark

marquer *vt (texte)* to mark, to flag, to tag

marqueur *nm (code)* marker, flag, tag

◇ *marqueur de fin de texte* end-of-text marker

masse *nf (d'informations)* bulk

matériel *nm* hardware

◇ *matériel informatique* computer hardware

matrice *nf* matrix; *(de données)* array

Mb *nm (abrév mégabit)* Mb

Mbps *(abrév mégabits par seconde)* Mbps

méga *nm* megabyte, meg

mégabit *nm* megabit; **mégabits par seconde** megabits per second

mégahertz *nm* megahertz

mégaoctet *nm* megabyte

mél *nm* *Internet* e-mail

mémoire *nf* memory; **cet ordinateur possède 32 mégaoctets de mémoire RAM** this computer has 32 megabytes of RAM; **mettre un dossier en mémoire** to write a file to memory; **extraire des données de la mémoire** to read out data

◊ *mémoire bloc-notes* scratchpad memory

◊ *mémoire à bulles* bubble memory

◊ *mémoire centrale* main memory

◊ *mémoire conventionnelle* conventional memory

◊ *mémoire disponible* available memory

◊ *mémoire à disque* disk memory

◊ *mémoire haute* high memory

◊ *mémoire intermédiaire* buffer memory

◊ *mémoire de masse* mass storage

◊ *mémoire morte* read-only memory

◊ *mémoire RAM dynamique* dynamic RAM

◊ *mémoire tampon de texte* text buffer

◊ *mémoire tampon* buffer memory

◊ *mémoire vive* random access memory

◊ *mémoire vive dynamique* dynamic random access memory

mémoire-cache *nf* cache (memory); **mettre en mémoire-cache** to cache

mémorisation *nf* writing to memory

mémoriser *vt* to write to memory

menu *nm* menu

◊ *menu d'aide* help menu

◊ *menu en cascade* cascading menu

◊ *menu déroulant* pull-down menu, drop-down menu

◊ *menu flottant* tear-off menu

◊ *menu hiérarchique* hierarchical menu

◊ *menu d'impression* print menu

◊ *menu local* pop-up menu

◊ *menu pomme* Apple menu

◊ *menu principal* main menu

message *nm* (**a**) *(communication)* message (**b**) *(à l'écran)* message

Note that although the Journal Officiel recommmends the use of the term **mél.** only as a written abbreviation(on the same model as **tél.**), it is commonly used as a noun (eg "envoyer/recevoir un mél").

L'itinéraire d'un Courrier Électronique

1 Votre ordinateur

Votre voyage dans l'Internet commence dans votre ordinateur. On utilise un **logiciel de courrier électronique** pour composer et envoyer des messages. Depuis votre ordinateur, votre message est transmis au serveur de votre **fournisseur d'accès** grâce à un **modem** ou à une connexion **RNIS**.

2 Votre fournisseur d'accès

Votre fournisseur d'accès vous sert d'intermédiaire pour accéder à l'Internet. Quand vous envoyer un message, il est tout d'abord transmis à votre fournisseur d'accès; de là, un **routeur** l'aiguille vers un réseau national d'interconnexion (ou **dorsale**) et c'est là qu'il commence véritablement son trajet sur l'autoroute de l'information.

3 Sur l'Internet

Sur l'Internet, les données sont transmises de routeur en routeur grâce à un système de maillage. Chaque fois que votre message parvient à un routeur, il est expédié vers un autre routeur, et ainsi de suite jusqu'à ce qu'il atteigne sa destination. Le nombre de routeurs par lequel votre message est retransmis dépend de la distance que votre message doit couvrir.

4 La fin du voyage

En fin de trajet, votre message est reçu par le routeur du fournisseur d'accès de votre correspondant. Un message de réception de courrier électronique est alors envoyé à votre correspondant par son fournisseur d'accès.

◊ *message d'accueil* welcome message

◊ *message d'aide* help message

◊ *message d'alerte* warning message, alert box

◊ *message d'attente (du système)* (system) prompt

◊ *message électronique* e-mail; **envoyer un message électronique à qn** to e-mail sb

◊ *message enregistré* recorded message

◊ *message d'erreur* error message

◊ *message d'invite* prompt

◊ *message système* broadcast message

◊ *message téléphonique* telephone message

◊ *message télex* telex (message)

messagerie *nf*

◊ *Internet* **messagerie de dialogue en direct** chat

◊ *messagerie électronique* electronic mail service, e-mail

◊ *messagerie vocale* voice mail

mettre *vt* **mettre en forme** to format; **mettre à jour** *(logiciel)* to update; **mettre en ligne** to put on-line

micro 1 *nm* (a) *(abrév* **micro-ordinateur**) micro(computer) (b) *(abrév* **microphone**) mike
2 *nf (abrév* **micro-informatique**) microcomputing

microédition *nf* desktop publishing, DTP

micro-informatique *nf* microcomputing, microprocessing

micro-ordinateur *nm* micro (computer)

◊ *micro-ordinateur de bureau* desktop computer

◊ *micro-ordinateur portable* laptop (computer)

microprocesseur *nm* microprocessor

microprogramme *nm* [JO] firmware

MIME *nm (abrév* **Multipurpose Internet Mail Extensions**) MIME

MiniDisc *nm* MiniDisc®

mini-ordinateur *nm* minicomputer

mini-tour *nf* mini tower

minuscule *adj & nf* lower-case

MIPS *nm (abrév* **million d'instructions par seconde**) mips

mise *nf*

◊ *mise en attente d'appels* call holding

◊ *mise en attente des fichiers à imprimer* printer spooling

◊ *mise en forme* formatting

◊ *mise à jour (de logiciel)* update

◊ *Internet* **mise en ligne** putting on-line

◊ *mise en mémoire* saving

◊ *mise à niveau* upgrade

◊ *mise en page* page design, page layout

◊ *mise sur pied* setting up

◊ *mise en relation (avec un service)* log-on

◊ *mise en réseau* networking

◊ *mise hors tension* power-down

◊ *mise sous tension* power-up

Mo *nm (abrév* **mégaoctet**) MB

mode *nm* mode; **en mode point** *(image)* bit-mapped, bitmap

◇ *mode autonome* off-line mode

◇ *mode brouillon* draft mode

◇ *mode connecté* on-line mode

◇ *mode continu* continuous mode

◇ *mode (de) dialogue* dialogue mode

◇ *mode édition* edit mode

◇ *mode graphique* graphics mode

◇ *mode d'impression rapide* draft mode

◇ *mode d'insertion* insert mode

◇ *mode paysage* landscape mode

◇ *mode portrait* portrait mode

◇ *mode rapide* draft mode

◇ *mode réponse (d'un modem)* answer mode

◇ *mode de superposition* overwrite mode

◇ *mode survol* browse mode

◇ *mode texte* text mode

modèle *nm* model; *(pour un programme)* template

◇ *modèle client-serveur* client-server model

modem *nm* modem; **envoyer qch à qn par modem** to modem sth to sb, to send sth to sb by modem

◇ *modem externe* external modem

◇ *modem fax* fax-modem

◇ *modem interne* internal modem

◇ *modem RNIS* ISDN modem

modem-câble *nm* cable modem

modérateur *nm Internet* moderator

module d'extension *nm* plug-in

moniteur *nm* monitor

◇ *moniteur couleur* colour monitor

◇ *moniteur à écran plat* flat screen monitor

◇ *moniteur SVGA* SVGA monitor

◇ *moniteur à tube cathodique* cathode ray tube monitor

monnaie électronique *nf* electronic money, e-cash

monoposte *nm* standalone

monotâche *adj & nm* single-tasking

mops *nmpl (abrév mégaoctets par seconde)* MBps

mosaïque *nf* **afficher en mosaïque** *(fenêtres)* to tile

mot *nm* word

◇ *mot clé* keyword

◇ *mot de passe* password

moteur de recherche *nm Internet* search engine

MS-DOS *nm (abrév Microsoft Disk Operating System)* MS-DOS

multidiffusion *nf Internet* multicast

multi-écran *nm* split screen

multimédia *adj & nm* multimedia

multiplateforme *adj* cross-platform

multiposte *adj* multi-station

L'ordinateur multimédia

unité centrale

lecteur de CD-ROM

baie

lecteur de disque

moniteur

haut-parleur

clavier

souris

tablette graphique

microphone

appareil photo numérique

manette de jeu

scanner

modem-fax

imprimante à jet d'encre

multiprocesseur *nm* multi-processor

multitâche *adj & nm* multi-tasking

multitraitement *nm* multi-processing, multithreading

multi-utilisateur *adj* multi-user

mûr coupe-feu *nm* *Internet* firewall

navigateur *nm* *Internet* browser

navigation *nf* *Internet* browsing, navigation; **navigation sur l'Internet** Internet surfing; **navigation rapide/sécurisée** rapid/secure browsing

naviguer *vi* to navigate; **naviguer sur l'Internet** to surf the Net, to browse the Web, to navigate the Net

Net *nm* **le Net** the Net

netiquette *nf* (*sur l'Internet*) netiquette

newsgroup *nm* *Internet* newsgroup

niveau *nm*
◇ *niveau d'accès* (*dans un réseau*) access level
◇ *niveaux de gris* shades of grey
◇ *niveau de sécurité* security level

nœud *nm* node

nom *nm*
◇ *nom de champ* field name
◇ *Internet* **nom de domaine** domain name
◇ *nom de fichier* file name

◇ *nom de fichier erroné* (*message d'erreur*) bad file name
◇ *nom de l'utilisateur* user name

non-autorisé, -e *adj* (*nom de fichier*) illegal

non-connecté, -e *adj* offline

non-formaté, -e *adj* (*disque*) unformatted

non-initialisé, -e *adj* uninitialized

non-récupérable *adj* nonrecoverable

norme USB *nf* USB

note de fin de document *nf* end note

notebook *nm* notebook

numérique *adj* (*calculateur, ordinateur*) digital; (*données, pavé*) numerical

numériquement *adv* digitally

numérisation *nf* digitization

numériser *vt* to digitize

numériseur *nm* digitizer
◇ *numériseur d'image* image digitizer

numéro *nm* *Tél* number; **composer** *ou* **faire un numéro** to dial a number

◊ **numéro d'accès** *(à un fournisseur d'accès)* access number

◊ **numéro azur** = special telephone number for which users are charged at the local rate irrespective of the actual distance of the call

◊ **numéro de fax** fax number

◊ **numéro de licence** registration number

◊ **numéro Internet** Internet number

◊ **numéro IP** IP number

◊ **numéro de poste** extension number

◊ **numéro de téléphone** telephone number

◊ **numéro d'urgence** hot-line, emergency number

◊ **numéro vert** *Br* ≃ Freefone® number, 0800 number, *Am* ≃ toll-free number, 800 number

numérotation *nf* **(a)** *(attribution d'un numéro)* numbering **(b)** *Tél* dialling

◊ **numérotation abrégée** speed dial

◊ **numérotation groupée** group dialling

objet nm (dans un document) object; (de courrier électronique) subject

occupé, -e adj (téléphone) busy, Br engaged; **la ligne est occupée** the line or number is busy or Br engaged; **ça sonnait occupé** I got the busy or Br engaged signal

occurence nf (lors d'une recherche) hit

octet nm (eight-bit) byte

off-line adj off-line

ombre nf (dans un texte, dans un encadré) shade

onduleur nm UPS

opérateur, -trice 1 nm,f Tél operator 2 nm (a) (commande) operator (b) (pour signal) carrier

◇ **opérateur booléen** Boolean operator

◇ **opérateur de publication assistée par ordinateur** desktop publishing operator

◇ **opérateur de saisie** keyboard operator, keyboarder

◇ **opérateur système** systems operator, SYSOP

opération nf operation

optimiser vt (matériel, système) to upgrade

optimiseur nm optimizer

option nf option

◇ **option d'impression** print option

◇ **option de menu** menu option

◇ **option de sauvegarde** save option

optique adj optical

ordinateur nm computer; **mettre qch sur ordinateur** to put sth on computer

◇ **ordinateur autonome** stand-alone (computer)

◇ **ordinateur bloc-notes** notebook (computer)

◇ **ordinateur de bureau** desktop computer

◇ **ordinateur central** mainframe (computer)

◇ **ordinateur compatible** compatible computer

◇ **ordinateur familial** home computer

◇ **ordinateur frontal** front-end computer

◇ **ordinateur de gestion** business computer

◇ **ordinateur individuel** personal computer

◇ *ordinateur multimédia* multimedia computer

◇ *ordinateur de poche* palmtop (computer)

◇ *ordinateur portable* laptop (computer)

ordinogramme *nm* flowchart

ordre *nm* order

◇ *ordre croissant* ascending order

◇ *ordre décroissant* descending order

organigramme *nm* (data) flow chart, flow diagram

organisation *nf* organization

◇ *organisation des données* data organization

organiseur *nm* *(logiciel)* organizer

orienté objet *adj* object-orientated

orpheline *nf PAO* orphan

outil *nm* tool

◇ *outil auteur* authoring tool

◇ *outil de création de pages Web* web authoring tool

◇ *outil de navigation sur le Web* web browser

ouverture de session *nf* log-on

ouvrir *vt (fichier, répertoire)* to open; **ouvrir une session** to log on

package *nm* package

page *nf* page
◇ *Internet* **page d'accueil** home page
◇ **page de garde** *(d'un fax)* cover sheet, cover page
◇ *Tél* **les pages jaunes** the Yellow Pages®
◇ *Internet* **page perso, page personnelle** personal home page
◇ **page précédente** page up
◇ **pages en regard** facing pages
◇ **page suivante** page down
◇ *Internet* **page Web** web page

page-écran *nf* screen page

pagination *nf* pagination

paginer *vt* to paginate

palette *nf* palette
◇ **palette graphique** graphics palette
◇ **palette d'outils** tool palette

panne *nf (d'ordinateur)* failure, crash
◇ **panne logicielle** software failure
◇ **panne matérielle** hardware crash
◇ **panne du système** system crash

panneau *nm*
◇ **panneau d'affichage** bulletin board
◇ **panneau de configuration** control panel

PAO *nf (abrév* **publication assistée par ordinateur**) DTP

papier *nm* paper
◇ **papier à bandes perforées** perforated paper
◇ **papier (en) continu** continuous paper *or* stationery, listing paper
◇ **papier couché** coated paper
◇ **papier à étiquettes** sheets of labels
◇ **papier d'impression** printer paper
◇ **papier listing** listing paper
◇ **papier multiple** multi-part stationery
◇ **papier peint** wallpaper
◇ **papier thermique, papier thermosensible** thermal paper

paquet *nm (de données)* packet

parallèle *adj (imprimante, interface)* parallel

paramétrable *adj* configurable; **paramétrable par l'utilisateur** user-definable

paramétrage *nm* configuration

paramètre *nm* parameter, setting; *(du DOS)* switch

paramétrer *vt* to configure

parc d'ordinateurs *nm* computer population, total number of computers in service

parcage *nm (de disque dur)* parking; **effectuer le parcage d'un disque** to park a disk

parcourir *vt (document)* to scroll through

parenthèse *nm* (round) bracket; **entre parenthèses** in (round) brackets

parité *nf* parity

parquer *vt (disque dur)* to park

partage *nm*
◊ *partage des données* data sharing
◊ *partage de fichiers* file sharing
◊ *partage d'imprimantes* printer sharing

partagiciel *nm* JO shareware

partition *nf (d'un disque dur)* partition; **diviser un disque dur en partitions** to partition a hard disk

PASCAL *nm* PASCAL

passage *nm* **passage automatique à la ligne (suivante)** autoflow, wordwrap

passerelle *nf Internet* **passerelle (de connexion) (avec)** gateway (to)

patienter *vi* to wait; **faire patienter qn** *(au téléphone)* to ask sb to hold; **est-ce que vous désirez patienter?** would you like to hold?

pause *nf* pause

pavé *nm* keypad
◊ *pavé numérique* numeric keypad

paysage *nm* **(mode) paysage** landscape (mode); **imprimer qch en paysage** to print sth in landscape

PC *nm* *(abrév* **personal computer)** PC

PCI *nm (abrév* **peripheral component interface)** PCI

PCMCIA *nm (abrév* **PC memory card international association)** PCMCIA

PCV *nm Tél (abrév* **payable chez vous) (appel en) PCV** *Br* reverse-charge call, *Am* collect call; **appeler en PCV, faire un appel en PCV** *Br* to reverse the charges, *Am* to call collect

PDF *nm (abrév* **portable document format)** PDF

perfectionner *vt (logiciel)* to upgrade

périphérique **1** *adj* peripheral
2 *nm* peripheral, device
◊ *périphérique d'entrée* input device
◊ *périphérique d'entrée-sortie* input/output device
◊ *périphérique externe* external device
◊ *périphérique de sortie* output device

personnaliser *vt (menu, programme)* to customize

perte *nf*
◊ **perte de données** data loss
◊ **perte de données irréparable** irretrievable data loss

petites capitales *nfpl* small caps

Photo-CD *nm* photo CD

photocomposeuse *nf PAO (machine)* typesetter, imagesetter

photocopie *nf* (photo)copy

photocopier *vt* to (photo)copy

photocopieur *nm* photocopier, photocopying machine

photocopieuse *nf* photocopier, photocopying machine

photostyle *nm* light pen

pilote *nm (logiciel)* driver
◊ **pilote de mise en file d'attente** spooler

piloter *vt* to drive; **piloté par menu** menu-driven

piratage *nm*
◊ **piratage informatique** (computer) hacking
◊ **piratage de logiciels** software piracy

pirate *nm*
◊ **pirate informatique** cracker, hacker
◊ **pirate du téléphone** phreaker

piste *nf (de disque)* track
◊ **piste magnétique** *(sur carte)* magnetic strip

pixel *nm* pixel

pixélisé, -e *adj* bit-mapped, bitmap

planté, -e *adj Fam* **être planté** *(réseau, ordinateur)* to be down

planter *vi Fam (réseau, logiciel)* to go down, to crash

plaquette *nf* circuit board

plate-forme *nf* platform

plug and play *nm* plug & play

plugiciel *nm* [JO] plug-in

pochette d'expédition de disquette *nf* disk mailer

poignée *nf* handle

point *nm* (a) *(signe de ponctuation)* dot, *Am* period (b) *PAO (tailles des caractères)* point
◊ *Internet* **point d'accès** POP, point of presence
◊ **point de césure** breakpoint, hyphenation point
◊ **point d'exclamation** *Br* exclamation mark, *Am* exclamation point
◊ **point final** *Br* full stop, *Am* period
◊ **point d'interrogation** *Br* question mark, *Am* query mark
◊ *Internet* **point de présence** POP, point of presence
◊ **point de vente électronique** electronic point of sale

point-virgule *nm* semicolon

pointer 1 *vt (curseur)* to position (**sur** on); **le mot pointé** the word where the cursor is
2 *vi (à l'arrivée)* to clock in; *(à la sortie)* to clock out

pointeur *nm* pointer

police ▸ prise

58

police *nf* police (de caractères) (character) font

◇ *police bitmap* bitmap font

◇ *police par défaut* default font

◇ *police pixelisée* bitmap font

◇ *police téléchargeable* uploadable font

pont *nm* (d'un réseau) bridge

port *nm* port; *Internet* socket

◇ *port de communication* comms port, communications port

◇ *port d'imprimante* printer port

◇ *port modem* modem port

◇ *port parallèle* parallel port

◇ *port série* serial port

◇ *port série universel* universal serial bus, USB

◇ *port souris* mouse port

portable **1** *adj* (ordinateur) laptop; (téléphone) mobile
2 *nm* (ordinateur) laptop; (téléphone) mobile (phone)

portail *nm Internet* portal

portatif, -ive **1** *adj* (ordinateur) laptop
2 *nm* (ordinateur) laptop

porte-documents *nm* (de Windows) briefcase

porteuse *nf Tél* carrier

portrait *nm* (mode ou format) portrait portrait (mode); **imprimer qch en portrait** to print sth in portrait

poser *vt* (format) to set

positionner *vt* (curseur, graphique) to position

possibilité *nf*

◇ *possibilités d'extension* upgradability

poste *nm* (a) *Tél* extension; **poste 106** extension 106; **le poste est occupé** the extension is *Br* engaged *or Am* busy; **je vous passe le poste** I'm putting you through
(b) (appareil)

◇ *poste autonome* stand-alone

◇ *poste terminal* terminal

◇ *poste de travail* workstation

PostScript *nm* PostScript

poubelle *nf* wastebasket, *Am* trash

ppp (abrév **points par pouce**) dpi

PréAO *nf* (abrév **présentation assistée par ordinateur**) computer-assisted presentation

préformaté, -e *adj* preformatted

préformater *vt* to preformat

préinstallé, -e *adj* preinstalled

préinstaller *vt* to preinstall

premiere plan *nm* foreground

prépresse *nm PAO* prepress

préprogrammé, -e *adj* preprogrammed

préprogrammer *vt* to preprogram

presse-papiers *nm* (pour texte supprimé) clipboard

prévisualisation *nf* print preview

prise *nf* (électrique) (femelle) socket; (mâle) plug

problème *nm* problem

◇ **problème de logiciel** software problem

procédé *nm* process

procédure *nf* procedure

◇ **procédure de chargement** loading procedure

processeur *nm* processor

◇ **processeur central** central processing unit, CPU

◇ **processeur de données** data processor

progiciel *nm* software package

◇ **progiciel de communication** comms package

◇ **progiciel de comptabilité** accounting package

◇ **progiciel intégré** integrated package

programmateur, -trice *nm,f* programmer

programmation *nf* (computer) programming

◇ **programmation par objets, programmation orientée objet** object-oriented programming

programme *nm* program

◇ **programme antivirus** anti-virus program

◇ **programme d'application** application program

◇ **programme de commande d'impression** printer driver

◇ **programme de commande de la souris** mouse driver

◇ **programme de conversion** conversion program

◇ **programme en cours d'éxécution** active program

◇ **programme de courrier électronique** e-mail program

◇ **programme de création de pages Web** web authoring program

◇ **programme de dessin** drawing program, paint program

◇ **programme de diagnostic** diagnostic program

◇ **programme de gestion** driver

◇ **programme informatique** computer program

◇ **programme d'installation** setup program, installer

◇ **programme sentinelle** watchdog program

◇ **programme utilitaire** utility program

◇ **programme virus** virus program

programmé, -e *adj* programmed

programmer 1 *vt* to program; **programmer en assembleur** to program in assembly language
2 *vi* to program

programmeur, -euse *nm,f* (computer) programmer

projection de diapositives *nf* (sur écran d'ordinateur) slide show

promener se promener *vpr* to browse; **se promener dans** to browse through

protection *nf* protection

◇ **protection contre la copie** copy protection

◇ **protection contre l'écriture** *ou* **en écriture** write protection

◇ *protection de fichiers* file protection

◇ *protection de l'information* data protection

◇ *protection par mot de passe* password protection

protégé, -e *adj* protégé contre la copie copy-protected; protégé contre l'écriture *ou* en écriture write-protected; protégé par mot de passe password-protected

protéger *vt* protéger contre l'écriture *ou* en écriture to write-protect; protéger contre la copie to copy-protect

protocole *nm* protocol; *(de réseau)* frame format; *(de traitement)* procedure

◇ *protocole HTTP sécurisé* secure HTTP

◇ *protocole Internet* Internet protocol

◇ *Internet protocole MIME* MIME

◇ *Internet protocole point à point* point-to-point protocol

◇ *Internet protocole POP* post office protocol, POP

◇ *Internet protocole PPP* PPP

◇ *Internet protocole SLIP* SLIP

◇ *Internet protocole SMTP* SMPT

◇ *Internet protocole de téléchargement* download protocol

◇ *Internet protocole de transfert anonyme* anonymous FTP

◇ *Internet protocole de transfert de fichiers* file transfer protocol

◇ *protocole de transmission* transmission protocol

publication assistée par ordinateur *nf* desktop publishing

publiciel *nm Can* public domain software

publier *vt (document, page Web)* to publish

puce *nf* (**a**) *(composant)* (micro)chip (**b**) *(symbole)* bullet

◇ *puce à mémoire* memory chip

pupitre *nm*

◇ *pupitre (de commande)* console (desk)

◇ *pupitre de visualisation* visual display unit

quadrichromie *nf PAO* four-colour process

quadrillage *nm* gridline

qualité *nf* quality

◇ *qualité brouillon* draft quality

◇ *qualité courrier* (near) letter quality

◇ *qualité d'impression* print quality

quitter *vt* (**a**) *(base de données, programme)* to quit; **quitter le système** to quit

(**b**) *(au téléphone)* **ne quittez pas** hold on, hold the line

raccordement *nm* link

raccorder 1 *vt (câble, appareils)* to connect
  2 se raccorder *vpr* **se raccorder à** *(câble, appareils)* to link up to

raccourci *nm* shortcut
◇ *raccourci clavier* keyboard shortcut

raccrocher *vi (au téléphone)* to hang up

racine *nf* root directory

rafraîchir *vt* to refresh

rafraîchissement *nm* refresh

RAM *nf* RAM
◇ *RAM sur carte* on board RAM

ranger *vt* **ranger en mémoire** to store

rapidité *nf* speed
◇ *rapidité d'impression* print speed
◇ *rapidité de traitement* processing speed

rappel *nm*
◇ *Tél* **rappel du dernier numéro** redial feature

rappeler *vt (faire revenir)* to call up

rassemblement *nm (de données)* gathering

rassembler *vt (données)* to gather; *(documents)* to collate

réacheminement *nm (de message)* redirecting

réacheminer *vt (message)* to redirect

réalité virtuelle *nf* virtual reality

réamorcer 1 *vt* to reboot
  2 se réamorcer *vpr* to reboot

recharger *vt* to reload

recherche *nf* search; *(de données, d'un fichier)* retrieval; **faire une recherche** to do a search
◇ *recherche arrière* backward search
◇ *recherche avant, recherche vers le bas* forward search
◇ *recherche binaire* binary search
◇ *recherche booléenne* Boolean search
◇ *recherche dichotomique* binary search
◇ *recherche documentaire* information retrieval
◇ *recherche de données* data retrieval

◇ *recherche globale* global search

◇ *recherche vers le haut* backward search

◇ *recherche et remplacement* search and replace

◇ *recherche et remplacement global* global search and replace

rechercher *vt (données, fichier)* to search, to do a search for; **rechercher et remplacer qch** to search and replace sth; **rechercher en arrière** *ou* **vers le haut** to search backwards; **rechercher en avant** *ou* **vers le bas** to search forwards

recomposer *vt (numéro de téléphone)* to redial

reconfigurer *vt* to reconfigure

reconnaissance *nf*

◇ *reconnaissance des caractères* character recognition

◇ *reconnaissance optique des caractères* optical character recognition

◇ *reconnaissance de la parole*, *reconnaissance vocale* speech recognition

rectangle de sélection *nm* selection box

recueil de données *nm* data collection

récupération *nf (d'un fichier, de données)* retrieval, recovery

récupérer *vt (fichier, données)* to retrieve, to recover

redéfinir *vt (touche)* to redefine

redémarrage *nm* reboot, restart

◇ *redémarrage à chaud* warm boot, warm start

redémarrer *vi* to reboot, to restart

redimensionnement *nm* resizing

redimensionner *vt* to resize

réduire *vt* to reduce; *(fenêtre)* to minimize

réessayer *vi* to retry

refaire *vt* (a) *(opération, commande)* to redo (b) *Tél (numéro)* to redial; **refaire le numéro** to redial

référence *nf (lors de comparaisons entre produits)* benchmark

référencer *vt* to reference

reformatage *nm* reformatting

reformater *vt* to reformat

régénération *nf*

◇ *régénération de l'écran* screen refresh

régional *nm Tél* area telephone system

registre *nm (de mémoire)* register; *(de Windows)* registry

◇ *registre d'accès mémoire* memory access register

réglages *nmpl* settings

règle *nf* (a) *(sur écran)* ruler (line) (b) *PAO* ruler

réglette *nf (pour un clavier)* template

réinitialisation *nf* reset; *(de la mémoire)* reinitialization

réinitialiser *vt* to reset; *(mémoire)* to reinitialize

réinscriptible *adj (support)* rewritable

réinsérer *vt (bloc)* to reinsert

réinstaller *vt* to reinstall

relancer *vt (programme)* to rerun; *(logiciel)* to restart

relief *nm* highlight; **mettre en relief** to highlight

relier se relier *vpr* to link up

remplacement à chaud *nm (of devices)* hot swap

remplacer *vt* to replace; **tout remplacer** replace all

rendement *nm (d'un ordinateur)* throughput

rendu *nm PAO* rendering

renommer *vt (fichier)* to rename

renseignements *nmpl Tél Br* directory enquiries, *Am* information

renvoi *nm* cross-reference

renvoyer *vt* to cross-refer

repaginer *vt* to repaginate

répertoire *nm* directory, folder

◊ **répertoire central, répertoire principal** main directory, root directory

répondeur *nm* répondeur (téléphonique) answering machine, answerphone

repose-poignets *nm* wrist rest

reprendre *vt (programme)* to restart, to resume

reprise *nf (d'un programme)* restart

reprogrammable *adj (touche)* reprogrammable

reprogrammer *vt* to reprogram

requête *nf* query

réseau *nm (d'ordinateurs)* network; **mettre en réseau** to network

◊ **réseau en anneau** ring network

◊ **réseau de communication** communications network

◊ **réseau de communication de données** datacomms network

◊ **réseau de données** data network

◊ **réseau en étoile** star network

◊ **réseau informatique** computer network

◊ **réseau local** local area network, LAN

◊ **réseau longue distance** wide area network, WAN

◊ **réseau neuronal** neural network

◊ **réseau numérique à intégration de services** integrated services digital network

◊ **réseau de télématique** datacomms network

◊ **réseau d'utilisateurs** user network

résolution *nf (d'image)* resolution

restauration *nf (de fichier, texte, données)* restore

restaurer *vt (fichier, texte, données)* to restore

Topologies de réseaux

Réseau centralisé
Un ordinateur central contrôle l'accès au réseau

Réseau en étoile
Sa configuration rappelle
la forme d'une étoile.
Il possède un serveur de
réseau en son centre.

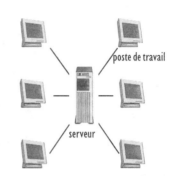

poste de travail

serveur

Réseau décentralisé
Chaque poste de travail peut accéder au réseau et communiquer avec d'autres postes de travail de façon indépendante

poste de travail

serveur

poste de travail

serveur

Réseau en bus
Un seul câble (le bus) déssert un certain
nombre de nœuds, parmi lesquels se
trouvent les postes de travail et les
imprimantes partagées

Réseau en anneau
Un certain nombre de nœuds sont disposés
autour d'un câble boucle fermée

restriction *nf*

◊ *restriction d'accès* access restriction

rétablir *vt* to redo

retouche d'images *nf* photo editing

retoucher *vt (image)* to retouch

retour *nm (sur clavier)* return

◊ *retour arrière* backspace

retrait *nm* **mettre en retrait** to indent

rétroéclairage *nm (d'écran)* backlight

rétro-éclairé, -e *adj (écran)* backlit

RISC *adj (abrév* **reduced instruction set chip** *ou* **computer)** RISC

RNIS *nm (abrév* **réseau numérique à intégration de services)** ISDN; **envoyer qch par RNIS** to ISDN sth, to send sth by ISDN

ROC *nf (abrév* **reconnaissance optique des caractères)** OCR

rôder *vi Internet* to lurk

rôdeur, -euse *nm,f Internet* lurker

rogner *vt PAO (image)* to crop

ROM *nf (abrév* **read only memory)** ROM

routeur *nm Internet* router

ruban *nm (sous la barre de menu)* ribbon

RVB *nm (abrév* **rouge, vert et bleu)** RGB

saisie *nf (de données)* capture

◊ *saisie automatique* automatic input

◊ *saisie de données* data capture, keyboarding

◊ *saisie manuelle* manual input

saisir *vt (données)* to capture

saut *nm*

◊ *saut de ligne* line break

◊ *saut de ligne manuel* hard return

◊ *saut de page* page break

sauter **1** *vt (commande)* to skip **2** *vi (réseau)* to crash

sauvegarde *nf (de données)* backup; **faire la sauvegarde d'un fichier** to save a file

◊ *sauvegarde automatique* autosave, automatic backup

◊ *sauvegarde sur bande* tape backup

sauvegarder *vt (fichier)* to save, to back up; **sauvegarder un fichier sur disquette** to save a file to disk; **sauvegarder automatiquement** to autosave

scanner¹, ⃞JO⃞ **scanneur** *nm* scanner; **passer qch au scanner** to scan sth; **insérer qch par scanner, capturer qch au scanner** to scan sth in

◊ *scanner à main* hand-held scanner

◊ *scanner optique* optical scanner

◊ *scanner à plat* flatbed scanner

◊ *scanner à tambour* drum scanner

scanner² *vt* to scan

scannérisation *nf* scanning

scanneur *nm* ⃞JO⃞ = scanner

schéma *nm* diagram

◊ *schéma de clavier* keyboard map

SCSI *nf (abrév small computer systems interface)* SCSI

SDRAM *nf (abrév synchronous dynamic random access memory)* SDRAM

secours *nm* de secours *(copie, fichier, disquette)* backup

secteur *nm (d'un disque)* sector

◊ *secteur endommagé* bad sector

◊ *secteur d'initialisation* boot sector

sécurité *nf* security

◊ *sécurité des données* data security

sélecteur *m* chooser

sélection *nf* selection

sélectionner *vt (texte)* to block, to select; **sélectionner qch par défaut** to default to sth

séparateur *nm* separator

séparation *nf*

◇ **séparation automatique des pages** automatic pagination

◇ *PAO* **séparation des couleurs** colour separation

◇ *PAO* **séparation quadrichromique** four-colour separation

séquence *nf* sequence

◇ **séquence de caractères** character string, sequence of characters

◇ **séquence de commandes** command sequence

séquentiel, -elle *adj* sequential

série *adj* serial

serveur *nm* server

◇ **serveur de courrier** mail server

◇ **serveur distant** remote server

◇ **serveur de fichiers** file server

◇ *Internet* **serveur FTP** FTP server

◇ **serveur mandataire** proxy server

◇ **serveur Minitel®** Minitel service provider

◇ **serveur de nouvelles** news server

◇ **serveur de procuration, serveur proxy** proxy server

◇ **serveur de réseau** network server

◇ **serveur sécurisé** secure server

◇ *Internet* **serveur télématique** bulletin board (system)

◇ **serveur de terminaux** terminal server

◇ *Internet* **serveur Web** web server

service *nm*

◇ **service après-vente** after-sales service, backup service

◇ **service d'assistance** *(téléphonique)* help desk, help line

◇ **service de bavardage Internet** Internet Relay Chat, IRC

◇ *Internet* **service de courrier électronique anonyme** anonymous remailer

◇ **service informatique** computer department

session *nf (sur l'Internet)* session

SET® *nf Internet (abrév* **secure electronic transaction)** SET®

SGAO *nm (abrév* **système de gestion assisté par ordinateur)** computer-assisted management system

SGBD *nm (abrév* **système de gestion de base de données)** DBMS

SGDBR *nm (abrév* **système de gestion de bases de données relationnelles)** RDBMS

SGML *nm (abrév* **Standard Generated Markup Language)** SGML

shareware *nm* shareware

signal *nm* signal

◇ *Tél* **signal d'appel** call waiting service

◇ *signal de détection de porteuse* carrier (detect) signal

◇ *signal numérique* digital signal

signaler *vt (marquer)* to flag up

signature *nf (dans un courrier électronique)* signature

◇ *signature numérique* digital signature

signe *nm*

◇ *signe égal* equal sign, equals sign

◇ *signe moins* minus sign

◇ *signe plus* plus sign

signet *nm (pour une page Web)* bookmark; **créer un signet sur une page** to bookmark a page

SIMM *nm (abrév single in-line memory module)* SIMM

simulateur *nm* simulator

◇ *simulateur de réalité virtuelle* virtual reality simulator

simulation *nf* simulation

◇ *simulation sur ordinateur* computer simulation

simuler *vt* to simulate

site *nm Internet* site

◇ *site FTP* FTP site

◇ *site marchand* e-commerce site

◇ *site miroir* mirror site

◇ *site Web* web site

société *nf*

◇ *société de traitement à façon* service bureau

socket *nf Internet* socket

software *nm* software

sommaire *nm PAO* para-graphe en **sommaire** hanging paragraph; **présentation en sommaire** hanging indent

son 3D *nm* surround sound

sortant, -e *adj (appel télé-phonique)* outgoing

sortie *nf* exit; *(information)* output

◇ *sortie (sur) imprimante* printout

◇ *sortie (sur) papier* (com-puter) printout

◇ *sortie parallèle* parallel output

◇ *sortie série* serial output

sortir 1 *vt (données)* to output **2** *vi (d'un programme)* to exit, to quit; **sortir d'un programme** to exit a program; **sortir d'un document** to come out of *or* quit a document

source *nf* source

◇ *source de données* data source

souriant *nm Internet* smiley

souris *nf* mouse

◇ *souris à infrarouge* infrared mouse

◇ *souris optique* optical mouse

◇ *souris sans fil* cordless mouse, wireless mouse

◇ *souris à trois boutons* three-button mouse

sous-menu *nm* submenu

sous-programme *nm* sub-routine, subprogram

sous-répertoire *nm* subdi-rectory

soutien *nm (aide)* support, backup

spécialisé, -e adj (terminal, ligne) dedicated

spécifications nfpl specification

spouleur nm spooler

standard nm Tél switchboard

standardiste nmf Tél (switchboard) operator

station nf (d'un réseau) station, node

◊ *station d'accueil* docking station

◊ *station de travail* workstation

stockage nm (de données) storage

◊ *stockage de données* data storage

stocker vt (informations) to store

structure nf structure

◊ *structure arborescente* directory or tree structure

◊ *structure en arbre* tree structure

◊ *structure en étoile* star structure

◊ *structure de fichier* file structure

stylo optique nm light pen

suite logicielle nf suite

suivi d'article nm (dans des groupes de discussion) follow-up message

suivre vt faire suivre qch (courrier électronique) to re-address sth, to redirect sth

super-ordinateur nm super-computer

superposer vt superposer une écriture to overwrite

support nm medium, support

◊ *support de données* data carrier

◊ *support de stockage* storage medium

◊ *support technique* technical support

supporter vt (format de fichier, périphérique, technologie) to support

supprimer vt to delete

surface d'affichage nf display area

surfer vi surfer sur l'Internet to surf the Net

surnom nm nickname

survoler vt to browse through

suspendre vt suspendre l'exécution d'un programme to abort a program

suspension nf suspension d'exécution (d'un programme) abort, aborting

SVGA nm (abrév **Super Video Graphics Array**) SVGA

symbole nm symbol

◊ *symbole Dingbat* dingbat

syntaxe nf syntax

synthèse nf Internet (de groupe de discussion) digest

synthétiseur de paroles nm voice synthesizer

sysop nm (abrév **Systems Operator**) SYSOP

système nm system

◊ *système à boîtier vertical* tower system

◇ **système expert** expert system

◇ **système d'exploitation** operating system

◇ **système d'exploitation de** ou **à disques** disk operating system

◇ **système de fichiers hiérarchique** hierarchical file system

◇ **système de gestion de bases de données** database management system

◇ **système de gestion de fichiers** file management system

◇ **système informatique** computer system

◇ **système informatisé** computerized information system

◇ **système intégré de gestion** integrated management system, management information system

◇ **système multi-utilisateur** multi-user system

◇ *Internet* **système de nom de domaine** domain name system, DNS

◇ **système de sauvegarde** backup system

◇ **système de sauvegarde sur bande** tape backup system

◇ **système de secours** backup system

◇ **système à tour** tower system

◇ **système de traitement de l'information** data processing system

table *nf* table

◇ *table de recherche, table de référence* look-up table

tableau *nm* (**a**) *(panneau de configuration)* control panel (**b**) *(de données)* table

tablette *nf*

◇ *tablette graphique* graphics tablet

◇ *tablette tactile* trackpad

tableur *nm* spreadsheet

◇ *tableur de graphiques* graphics spreadsheet

tabulation *nf* tab, tabulator; **délimité par des tabulations** tab-delimited

tâche *nf* task

◇ *tâche d'arrière-plan* background task

◇ *tâche de fond* background task or job

taille *nf (de fichier, de police de caractères)* size

taper **1** *vt* (**a**) *(sur un clavier)* to key; **tapez entrée ou retour** select enter or return (**b**) *(dactylographier)* **taper qch (à la machine)** to type sth

2 *vi* **taper (à la machine)** to type

tapis de souris *nm* mouse mat *or* pad

taux *nm (vitesse)* rate

◇ *taux d'actualisation* refresh rate

◇ *taux de compression* compression rate

◇ *taux de rafraîchissement* refresh rate

◇ *taux de transfert* transfer rate

taxer *vt Tél (appel)* to charge for

TCP-IP *Internet (abrév* **transmission control protocol/Internet protocol)** TCP-IP

technicien, -enne *nm,f* technician

◇ *technicien en informatique* computer technician

technologie *nf* technology

◇ *technologie de l'information* information technology, IT

◇ *Internet* **technologie du push de données** push technology

téléachat *nm* electronic shopping, home shopping

téléassistance *nf* remote help

téléchargeable *adj* downloadable

téléchargement *nm* download, downloading; *(vers un gros ordinateur)* upload, uploading

télécharger *vt* to download; *(vers un gros ordinateur)* to upload; **peut être téléchargé à partir de notre site Web** available to download from our web site

téléconférence *nf* conference call, teleconference; *(type de communication)* teleconferencing

télécopie *nf* fax (message)

télécopieur *nm* fax (machine)

tel écran-tel écrit *adj* WYSIWYG

télégestion *nf* teleprocessing, remote processing

téléinformatique *nf* teleprocessing

télématique **1** *adj (serveur, service, réseau)* data retrieval **2** *nf* telematics

téléphone *nm* telephone, phone
◇ *téléphone cellulaire* cellular phone, cellphone
◇ *téléphone sans fil* cordless telephone
◇ *téléphone Internet* Internet (tele)phone
◇ *téléphone mobile* mobile phone
◇ *téléphone portable* mobile phone

◇ *téléphone à touches* touch-tone telephone

téléphoner *vi* to call, to telephone; **téléphoner à qn** to call sb up, to telephone sb

téléphonie *nf* telephony
◇ *téléphonie sur l'Internet* Internet telephony

télétex *nm* teletex

télétraitement *nm* teleprocessing, remote data processing

Telnet *nm Internet* Telnet

tel-tel *nm* WYSIWYG

témoin *nm Can Internet* cookie

temps *nm*
◇ *temps d'accès* access time, seek time
◇ *temps d'accès disque* disk access time
◇ *temps réel* real time
◇ *temps de traitement* processing time

terminal *nm* terminal, VDU
◇ *terminal distant* remote terminal
◇ *terminal électronique de paiement* electronic payment terminal
◇ *terminal éloigné* remote terminal
◇ *terminal intelligent* smart terminal

terminateur *nm* terminator

tête *nf*
◇ *tête d'impression* print head
◇ *tête de lecture-écriture* read-write head

texte *nm* text

◇ *texte ASCII* ASCII text

◇ *texte de départ* source text

◇ *texte publicitaire* advertising copy

◇ *PAO texte simulé* Greek text

tierce partie de confiance *nf (pour le commerce électronique)* trusted third party

tirage *nm* hard copy

tiret *nm PAO* dash

◇ *tiret cadratin* em-dash

◇ *tiret demi-cadratin* en-dash

titre *nm* heading

Toile *nf* la Toile the Web

tomber *vi* tomber en panne *(ordinateur)* to crash

ton *nm*

◇ *tons de gris* shades of grey

tonalité *nf Tél Br* dialling *or Am* dial tone

◇ *tonalité d'appel* ringing tone

toner *nm* toner

touche *nf (de clavier)* key

◇ *touche d'aide* help key

◇ *touche d'alimentation* power-on key

◇ *touche Alt* Alt key

◇ *touche d'arrêt de défilement, touche Arrêt défil* scroll lock key

◇ *touche à bascule* toggle key

◇ *touche contrôle* control (key)

◇ *touche de curseur* cursor key

◇ *touche début* home (key)

◇ *touche de défilement* scroll key

◇ *touche de déplacement du curseur* cursor movement key

◇ *touche de déplacement vers le bas* down arrow key

◇ *touche de déplacement vers la droite* right arrow key

◇ *touche de déplacement vers le haut* up arrow key

◇ *touche de direction* arrow key

◇ *touche Echap* esc key

◇ *touche d'échappement* escape key

◇ *touche d'effacement* delete key

◇ *touche d'effacement arrière* backspace (key)

◇ *touche (d')entrée* enter (key)

◇ *touche d'espacement arrière* backspace (key)

◇ *touche fin* end (key)

◇ *touche fléchée, touche (à) flèche* arrow key

◇ *touche flèche vers le bas* down arrow key

◇ *touche flèche vers la droite* right arrow key

◇ *touche flèche vers la gauche* left arrow key

◇ *touche flèche vers le haut* up arrow key

◇ *touche (de) fonction* function key

◇ *touche Impr écran* print screen key

◇ *touche d'insertion* insert key

◇ *touche d'interruption* break key

◇ *touche majuscule* shift key

◇ *touche de modification* modifier key, edit key

◇ *touche multifonction* multifunctional key

◇ *touche numérique* number key

◇ *touche option* option key
◇ *touche page précédente* page up key
◇ *touche page suivante* page down key
◇ *touche Pause* pause key
◇ *touche personnalisée* hot key
◇ *touche de raccourci* shortcut key
◇ *touche de répétition* repeat-action key
◇ *touche retour* return key
◇ *touche de retour arrière* backspace key
◇ *touche de tabulation* tab key
◇ *touche de verrouillage du clavier numérique* num lock key
◇ *touche du verrouillage des majuscules* caps lock key

tour *nf (ordinateur)* tower

tourner *vi* **ce logiciel tourne sous DOS** this software runs on DOS; **faire tourner un programme** to run a program

TPC *nf (abrév* **tierce partie de confiance)** TTP

traceur *nm (périphérique)* plotter

trackball *nm ou nf* trackball

traducteur *nm (logiciel)* translator

traduction *nf*
◇ *traduction assistée par ordinateur* computer-assisted translation, machine translation
◇ *traduction automatique* machine translation

traduire *vt (logiciel)* to translate

trafic de réseau *nm* network traffic

trait *nm* line
◇ *PAO* **trait de coupe** crop mark
◇ *trait d'union* hyphen

traitement *nm (de données)* processing
◇ *traitement automatique de données* automatic data processing
◇ *traitement de données* data processing
◇ *traitement électronique de l'information* electronic data processing
◇ *traitement d'images* image processing
◇ *traitement de l'information* data processing
◇ *traitement par lots* batch processing
◇ *traitement séquentiel* sequential processing
◇ *traitement de texte* word processing; *(logiciel)* word processor, word processing software; **réaliser qch par traitement de texte** to word-process sth

traiter *vt (données)* to process

transférer *vt (données, appel téléphonique)* to transfer

transfert *nm (de données)* transfer
◇ *transfert de fichiers* file transfer
◇ *transfert de fonds électronique, transfert électronique de fonds* electronic funds transfer, EFT

◇ *transfert de fonds électronique sur point de vente* electronic funds transfer at point of sale, EFTPOS

transmission *nf (de données)* transfer, transmission

◇ *transmission par modem* modem transmission

tri *nm* sort; **effectuer un tri** to do a sort

◇ *tri alphabétique* alphasort

◇ *tri en ordre croissant* ascending sort

◇ *tri en ordre décroissant* descending sort, reverse sort

trier 1 *vt* to sort; **trier par ordre alphabétique** to sort in alphabetical order, to alphasort
2 **se trier** *vpr (fichier, données)* to sort

trouver *vt* **trouver et remplacer** to find and replace

tube *nm*

◇ *tube à rayons cathodiques, tube cathodique* cathode ray tube, CRT

ultraportatif *nm* mini laptop, palmtop

unité *nf* unit, module

◇ *unité d'affichage* display unit
◇ *unité arithmétique et logique* ALU, arithmetic logic unit
◇ *unité de bande* tape unit
◇ *unité centrale* central processing unit, CPU; *(de disque)* drive
◇ *unité de destination* destination drive
◇ *unité de disque* disk drive
◇ *unité de disque dur* hard drive
◇ *unité de disquettes* floppy drive
◇ *unité externe* external unit
◇ *unité interne* internal unit
◇ *unité périphérique* peripheral (device), device
◇ *unité de sauvegarde* backup device
◇ *unité de sauvegarde sur bande* tape backup unit
◇ *unité de sortie* output device
◇ *unité de stockage* storage device
◇ *unité de traitement de texte* text processor

UNIX *nm* Unix; **basé sur UNIX** Unix-based

URL *nm Internet* (*abrév* **uniform resource locator**) URL

Usenet *nm Internet* Usenet

utilitaire *nm (logiciel)* utility, utility program

utilisateur, -trice *nm,f* user; **pour utilisateurs multiples** multi-user

◇ *utilisateur final* end user

valeur *nf* value
- *valeur ASCII* ASCII value
- *valeur par défaut* default value

valider *vt (option)* to confirm; *(cellule, case)* to select

variable *nf* variable

veille *nf* standby mode, sleep mode; **en veille** in standby mode, in sleep mode

vente *nf*
- *vente et marketing assistés par ordinateur* computer-aided sales and marketing, CASM

vérificateur orthographique *nm* spellchecker

vérification *nf* check
- *vérification antivirale* anti-virus check
- *vérification orthographique* spellcheck

verr num *(abrév* **verrouillage numérique)** num lock

verrouillage *nm* lock
- *verrouillage des fichiers* file lock
- *verrouillage en lecture seule* read-only lock
- *verrouillage en majuscule(s)* caps lock
- *verrouillage du pavé numérique* num lock, numbers lock

verrouiller *vt (fichier, disquette)* to lock; **verrouiller en écriture** *(fichier)* to lock

version *nf (d'un logiciel)* version, release
- *version alpha* alpha version
- *version bêta* beta version
- *version brouillon* draft version

veuve *nf PAO* widow

VGA *nm (abrév* **Video Graphics Array)** VGA

vidage (de) mémoire *nm* memory dump

vide *adj (disquette, écran)* blank

vidéo *nm* video
- *vidéo numérique* digital video

vidéoconférence *nf* video-conference

vider *vt* **vider l'écran** to clear the screen; **vider la corbeille** to empty the wastebasket *or Am* the trash

vierge *adj (ligne, espace)* blank; *(disquette)* blank, un-formatted

vignette *nf* thumbnail

virgule *nf* comma

◇ *virgule flottante* floating point

virtuel, -elle *adj* virtual

virus *nm* virus; **désactiver un virus** to disable a virus

◇ *virus informatique* computer virus

◇ *virus de macro* macro virus

visioconférence *nf* videoconference

visualisation *nf* display

◇ *visualisation sur écran* soft copy

◇ *visualisation de la page à l'écran* page preview

visualiser *vt* to display; *(codes, document)* to view

visualiseur *nm* viewer

visuel *nm* visual display unit, VDU

vitesse *nf* speed

◇ *vitesse d'accès* access speed

◇ *vitesse de calcul* processing *or* computing speed

◇ *vitesse de clignotement* blink rate

◇ *vitesse de clignotement du curseur* cursor blink rate

◇ *vitesse d'écriture* write speed

◇ *vitesse de frappe (à la machine à écrire)* keying speed

◇ *vitesse de frappe à la minute/à l'heure* keystrokes per minute/hour

◇ *vitesse d'impression* print speed, printer speed

◇ *vitesse du processeur* processor speed

◇ *vitesse de traitement* processing speed

◇ *vitesse de transfert* transfer speed

voie *nf*

◇ *voie d'accès* path

◇ *voie de transmission de données* data link

volume *nm (d'informations)* bulk, volume

VRAM *nf (abrév* **video random access memory)** VRAM

VRML *nm (abrév* **virtual reality modelling language)** VRML

W3 nm (abrév **World Wide Web**) WWW, W3

Web nm le Web the Web

Webmaître, Webmaster, Webmestre nm web master

Word nm Word®; un **document/fichier Word** a Word docu-ment/file

World Wide Web nm le World Wide Web the World Wide Web

WORM (abrév **write once read many times**) WORM

WWW nm (abrév **World Wide Web**) WWW

Wysiwyg nm WYSIWYG

XML *nm* (*abrév* **Extensible Markup Language**) XML

zipper *vt* to zip

zone *nf*
◇ *zone d'affichage* display area, viewable area
◇ *zone d'amorçage* boot sector
◇ *zone de dialogue* dialogue box
◇ *zone tampon* (*en mémoire*) (memory) buffer
◇ *zone de travail* work area

DOING BUSINESS ON THE INTERNET

A guide to using the Internet as a business tool, with special reference to French

by Bob Norton and Cathy Smith

Bob Norton is Head of Information Services at the Institute of Management in Corby, England. Cathy Smith is Systems Controller in the Institute's Management Information Centre. They are responsible for managing the Institute's approach to the Internet and putting up its pages on the World Wide Web. Both have written widely on information management and are authors of the book *Understanding Business on the Internet*.

Contents

What is the Internet?

The Internet is an open, worldwide network of computer networks interconnected through a mix of private and public telephone lines. The individual networks are owned by various organizations, including government agencies, universities, commercial companies and voluntary bodies, all of which have decided to allow others to connect to their computers often referred to as servers – to share their information.

The most widely used Internet function is e-mail – an alternative to post, telephone and fax. Another is the Newsgroups and Discussion Lists which enable people who are remote from each other to come together on the Internet to debate common interests. The function which has captured the imagination is the World Wide Web, a program which links and retrieves data of all kinds, in various forms, such as text, graphics, video and sound, from the interconnected computers.

There is no one single owner of the Internet. The nearest thing to a governing body is a number of voluntary organizations such as The Internet Society or The Internet Engineering Taskforce, although neither of these bodies exercises control in a regulatory or legislative sense.

How did it start?

The origins of the Internet are in the Cold War in the early 1960s when the US government was searching for an effective communications system in the event of a nuclear attack. The theory was that if vital information was all held in one location, and that location was destroyed, the US defensive capability would be severely damaged. The Rand Corporation proposed that a decentralised network would continue to work even if some of its components were knocked out. Furthermore, information would be routed around the network, not as a complete package, but split into discrete packets that would find their own way through the network and re-assemble at the destination address.

In 1969 ARPANET was formed to put this theory into practice. It linked four universities together using high-speed transmission lines and modems, allowing government scientists and university researchers to communicate by e-mail. The fast telecommunications links proved successful, and other research organizations and companies in the USA and elsewhere began to connect up. The collective grouping became known as the Internet.

In the 1980s, large companies began to use the Internet for communication purposes, and in the 1990s, businesses of all kinds in countries all over the world began to get connected, as did individuals at home.

Recent estimates suggest that there are over 50 million subscribers in the USA, and that numbers are still rising rapidly. European usage is currently put at around 2-3% of all households. German usage is estimated to be higher than in the UK, where it is 3 million and rising, with Britain being closely followed by France, the Netherlands, Sweden, Italy and Spain. One estimate has suggested that there will be 250 million users by the year 2000; another that, at current growth rates, everyone on the planet will be connected up by the year 2003!

At the end of the 1990s, it is claimed that Internet traffic, particularly e-mail, is doubling every 100 days, and the World Wide Web is doubling in size every six months.

This massive growth in usage can be ascribed to four main factors:

- the convergence of the formerly separate technologies of computing and telecommunications

- the fall in the price, and rise in sales, of personal computers

- the discovery and promotion of the Internet by the media

- the growing user-friendliness of the Internet, especially the advent of the World Wide Web in 1993-4.

The early profile of the Internet user was that of a 35 year-old male described as literate and libertarian, believing in freedom of speech and the right of every group to be heard. By the mid 1990s this had changed to include the company manager, perhaps in his or her 40s, communicating with customers and suppliers in remote locations and using the Internet to search for and send

business@harrap.eng

information pertinent to the business.

Why is the Internet important?

There are tremendous benefits to be had in using the Internet for business: improved and cheaper communications, the opportunity to work more efficiently and effectively from a distance and the chance for companies of all sizes to promote themselves more easily and cheaply to a worldwide market.

In the early 1990s, however, many businesses fell for inflated promises of an effortless, electronic market where customers were there for the taking. Hype of another kind was fuelled by press articles creating fears that those who were not soon on the Internet would be out of touch and out of business.

Many companies jumped onto the Internet bandwagon, but they failed to look at the opportunity as a business project which, like any other, needed planning, resourcing, organizing and controlling. Many companies neglected to align and integrate their use of the Internet with their business needs and are now asking what they should do next to turn promise into reality, and how much resource they should put into their Internet operation.

Is the Internet just another passing fad, or is it something worthwhile which can improve the way we work and do business? The answer is that the Internet is here to stay, growing rapidly, and people's knowledge and use of it are becoming more sophisticated.

- The Internet is no longer the preserve of computer nerds. This is partly because the equipment you need – such as PC, modem and appropriate software – is increasingly being packaged as standard.

- It offers an alternative, often a much cheaper alternative, to obtaining, sending, receiving and storing information by traditional methods. We are all in the information business now.

- Many companies – small and large – are experimenting on the Internet to explore new ways of doing business, including the way they manage their workforce, the way they interact with other organizations, the way they promote their products or services, and the way they buy and sell. Others are using it in a more limited way because they can see no direct return on their investment. The promise of an electronic market, however, is now being reinforced by the investment of major banks and some businesses are beginning to derive some bottom-line value. Recent figures suggest that $3 billion worth – and growing – of Internet business transactions are carried out annually in the USA alone.

- The Internet impacts on both our personal and business lives even if we do not use it, and is central to current debates on:
  - the impact of technological progress on business, government and society
  - new forms of marketing and building relationships with customers
  - the social implications of the information 'haves' and 'have-nots' as information becomes a tradeable commodity worldwide and knowledge becomes the key to competitive advantage
  - the legal ramifications of the transfer of information across national borders.

The opportunities – and problems – of the Internet are the subject of debate in the US Senate and the European Parliament as governments struggle to get to grips with the challenges that the Internet poses. The Internet is government business now.

The Internet is evolving very rapidly but it takes time and effort to investigate its promise. It involves new ways of thinking out how best to take advantage of it. There is, at present, little substance for saying that those who leave it late will be out of business, but they will have a lot of learning and catching up to do while others will have stolen a march. The Internet – and Internet-type technology – is foreseen by many to be *the* business medium of the future.

Questions for Management

One of the most important factors is not to let the Internet dictate to your business; it is too easy to get carried away with the attraction of the technology rather than exploit it to help you. So it is important not to rush in, but keep key questions in mind.

Why use the Internet?

• A fear of getting left behind?
• To learn what it can offer?
• To explore its business potential?
• To assess what advantage it will offer our organization?

What are we trying to do on the Internet?

• Improve the external communications of the business?
• Search databases? Contact experts? Look at company and product information?
  • Exploit the marketing potential?
  • Gain a lead over the competition?
  • Deal better with existing customers, or attract new ones?

Who should be doing the Internet work?

• What Internet skills do we need?
• Should we hire new staff with Internet skills, or train ourselves and our staff to learn about the Internet and tackle it?
• Should we hire an expert consultant or contract the whole business out to a specialist?
• And when access is established, to whom shall we allow access?
• Who has the time to devote to the Internet?
• How do we make the time?

How should we set up access?

• Leased line, ISDN, or straightforward dial-up?
• How do we choose a service that provides us with the access that we need?

Communication

Electronic mail (e-mail) ["courrier électronique"] is the main use of the Internet with hundreds of millions of messages sent and received daily. Its huge appeal lies in its ease of use, its low cost to remote places (the price of a local call) and the facility to send electronic attachments (graphics, additional documents, even software) to text messages. E-mail overcomes time zone differences and inconvenience, as the recipient does not have to be "there" to receive it. One-to-many messaging is simple and cheap, and it enables you to exchange information with people unknown to you, through special interest groups, called *newsgroups* ["groupes de nouvelles"] or *discussion lists* ["listes de diffusion"].

An e-mail address usually takes this form:
yourname@organizationname.organizationtype.countryoforigin
e.g. jbloggs@inst-mgt.org.uk

Although there are many advantages to be gained, there are also several dangers to be aware of.

1. E-mail is not wholly secure, yet. Anyone can read and intercept your e-mail if they are determined to do so. Random surveys show that up to a quarter of the information packets, of which e-mail messages are composed, can fail to get to their destination, especially at peak periods when networks are heavily congested. Usually, in such cases, the messages are returned to the sender, so they are not actually lost.

2. E-mail is no guarantee of an immediate response. Some people prefer the telephone if information is needed for a deadline.

3. The ease and "friendliness" of e-mail might encourage off-the-cuff replies, which might be regretted later. This informality has generated a feeling that e-mail is an unreliable source, lacking permanence, possibly inaccurate, and not worthy of quoting. E-mail is in fact a form of publication, subject to the laws of libel and copyright. As such, e-mail should be treated in the same way as any other method of committing thoughts to print.

4. File attachments to e-mail can contain viruses. The problem is that it is difficult to know whether an attachment is "infected" or not until it is opened. Given that a virus can wreck the information stored on your computer, some organizations virus-check all attachments before opening them; others ban attachments

business@harrap.eng

altogether.

If you are going to use e-mail in your organization, you need to address some policy considerations such as:

1. Reducing the potential for inappropriate use, time-wasting and information overload.
2. Reaction—is e-mail to be regarded as more "urgent" than other forms of communications, and if so, how is it to be handled?
3. Responsibility for content—given the power of e-mail to reach so many so quickly and so cheaply.

Information Searching and Gathering

Information is available on a myriad of topics, in a variety of forms, and largely free of charge, on the *World Wide Web* (WWW) ["le Web"]. This is an application which allows users to view web sites ["sites Web"]—collections of files of text, graphics and other media—by means of a *browser* ["navigateur"] (a piece of software that sits on your PC) and move to other files by means of links established between them. These links are referred to as *hyperlinks* ["hyperliens"]. Each web site has an address, known as a *Uniform Resource Locator* or *URL* ["adresse URL"]. For example, http://www.renault.fr

http:// stands for HyperText Transfer Protocol; www.renault.fr gives us the name of the server and of the organization and the country code—in this case, France.

Figure 1: Renault's Home Page in French and English
(of their corporate site www.renault.com)

Every site has an entrance hall or main menu and this is known as the *home page* ["page d'accueil"]. Most addresses which you will see quoted are for the home page but some lead you to a specific section of a site. The part of the address which contains the name of the organization and the country code is referred to as the *domain name* ["nom de domaine"], such as renault.fr.

There are hundreds of thousands of sites of interest to business. Start with a site like The Institute of Management's Management Link at (http://www.inst-mgt.org.uk/external/mgt-link.html) which provides a list of, and links to, a wide selection of management and other business-related sites.

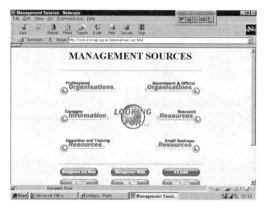

Figures 2 and 3: The Management Link is divided into Skills and Sources. Figure 2 looks at the options for sources, and Figure 3, some of the sites which enable you to explore company information in the UK

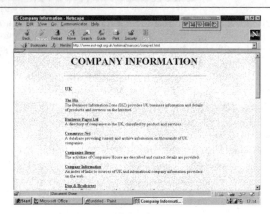

Figure 3

One of the most reliable ways to gather your own information is to pick it up by word of mouth, or tips in the press. Both major browsers (Netscape Navigator and Microsoft Internet Explorer) allow you to store frequently used addresses in their respective Bookmarks and Favorites options. If you don't know the address then the next best option is to use one of the many search tools which exist on the Web. Some of these are called directories which are constructed by people who select and apply index terms; others, called search engines, are software programs which trawl the Web at regular intervals for new information.

It is important to remember that you risk retrieving hundreds, maybe thousands, of information items (referred to as *hits* ["hits"]) simply because the Web is so vast and the search tools often do not distinguish between valuable, worthwhile information and trivia. Many of the search tools classify their information into categories such as business, sport, arts, current affairs, recreation, but be as specific as you can when typing in information requests.

Here are a few of the Web search tools:

Yahoo - (http://www.yahoo.fr) or (http://www.yahoo.co.uk)
Excite - (http://www.excite.fr) or (http://www.excite.co.uk)
Altavista - (http://www.altavista.com)
   AltaVista allows you to search for documents in English, French and many other languages.
Ecila - (http://ecila.ceic.com)

Eureka - (http://www.eureka-fr.com)
Lokace - (http://lokace.iplus.fr)
Francite - (http://francite.com)

Figure 4: The French version of Yahoo, and some of the main categories for information seaching

Marketing

Just as the Web is a source of information, it is also an arena for individuals and organizations to market their goods and services. Flowers, books and computer software have been early success stories. The WWW is a great leveller: the small business can stand alongside the large. Some marketing is very professional, other attempts are amateurish but all are experimental.

The Web is an interactive medium where the potential consumer chooses where they visit, when and for how long. It is open 24 hours a day, seven days a week and a Web site may receive visitors as easily from the other side of the world as from the person next-door.

Marketing on the WWW can be achieved by taking out advertisements on others' web sites. These appear in various forms:

• *Banners*: small rectangular graphics like roadside billboards. Once static, they are becoming increasingly animated and interactive.

- *Buttons*: similar to banners, but usually contain a corporate name, the brand, or even the industry. A click on the button will take you to the appropriate web site.
- *Keywords*: here advertisers can "buy" a term! For example, if Moet-Chandon were to buy the term "champagne', any time that someone does a search for "champagne" on a particular search engine, the name Moet-Chandon will pop up.

Marketing is primarily being tackled by building your own site. The success of a web site will depend on how attractive it is, how easy it is to find useful information, and how often the site is updated to offer the customer something new. Because the WWW is interactive it can offer great opportunities for discovering customer likes and dislikes and building up relationships. We look at designing a web site in the next section.

Figure 5: These 'button' advertisements are located at the foot of Ecila's Home Page. They have been paid by those companies to provide a direct link to their corporate web site. Look back to Figure 4 for an example of a 'banner' advertisement on Le Sicav.

Gaining Access to the Internet

There are basically two ways you can connect to the Internet:

Dial-up

Dial-up access requires a modem attached to your PC and a telephone line. You also need an account with a commercial Internet Access Provider ["fournisseur d'accès a l'Internet"].

Dial-up requires no major capital outlay and is therefore good for home use and for experimentation at work. On the other hand, it can be slow, especially at peak periods when the Internet is used by millions of people all over the world.

Increasingly, many businesses are installing ISDN (Integrated Services Digital Network) to provide faster and better-quality access than the existing telephone lines. It is more expensive but cheaper than leased lines (see below) and costs are falling.

> An efficient Internet connection depends on the whole chain which links the two computers — the power of the sending and receiving computers, the speed of the modem and the capacity of the telephone lines.

Leased line

A leased line is a physical cable, providing a fast and permanent connection to the Internet. This connection may be directly to one of the backbone networks on the Internet or made via an Internet Access Provider. A leased line is a much more expensive option than dial-up and is perhaps more suitable for those intending to use the Internet extensively for a number of functions.

1. Decide what you want to achieve

Is your web site to be:

- A way of attracting new customers?
- A public relations statement?
- A means of providing a service?
- An experiment?

Ask what benefits you expect from a web site bearing in mind how much time, money, technical and human resource you are going to invest in it. Ask too how you will measure success. You will need to analyse information about who visits your site and what pages they look at.

2. Choose how to host your web site

Renting space on a computer run by an Internet Access Provider has become an established method of setting up on the Web. Most Internet Access Providers offer some free disk space to start up and experiment with as part of their package. This often provides a cheap and low-risk option. When you identify your Internet Access Provider, remember to ask questions concerning developments for your site, usage reports and commercial transactions.

External design consultants will also usually host your site but they will expect you to buy their design services.

Many large organizations host their web site on their own server. This requires a significant investment in hardware and software as well as considerable technical knowledge and skill.

3. Consider whether site design should be outsourced or kept in-house

Outsourcing design to a specialist should result in a professional site. Find out what work they have already accomplished and how successful it was. Think about whether you want to update and maintain the site yourself or hand that work over too. Outsourcing is not necessarily a cheap option and involves a considerable amount of time and effort in explaining your business to the outsider.

In-house development may also be costly depending on whether you bring in specialist staff, or spend time and money on the training and development of your own. If you are building an extensive site in-house, you may need to bring in an experienced web master ("webmestre"). A *web master* is responsible for the design, development and maintenance of a site in both the technical and content aspects. This requires a rare combination of IT, information, design and interpersonal skills.

4. Register your domain name

Your domain name is one of the first things by which people identify you. Choose a domain name that reflects your usual business or trading name. It needs to be registered before you can use it, although your first choice may have already been taken. Your Internet Access Provider will register your domain name for you for a nominal extra charge. Domain names are registered with the following organizations:

- The UK: Nominet (http://www.nic.uk).

- The USA: Internic (http://www.internic.net).

- France: AFNIC—Association Francaise pour le Nommage Internet en Cooperation (http://www.nic.fr)

Figure 6: AFNIC's Home Page

5. Think about the layout of your site

When constructing your site you need to think about:

- Design—how will you convey the image you wish to project?

- Navigation around the site—how many mouse-clicks will it take to find something of interest?

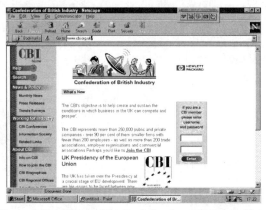

Figure 7: Home Page of the Confederation of British Industry

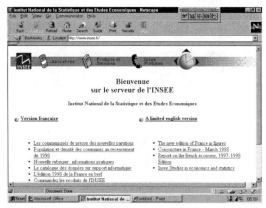

Figure 8: Home Page of the Institut National de la Statistique et des Etudes Economiques

Look at the web sites of other organizations, decide what you like and don't like and ask the opinions of potential users to get on the right track. Their view of a helpful layout may differ from yours.

6. Consider the content of the site

How will you try to get visitors to delve deeper into the site?

- Posting up answers to frequently asked questions on your products or services?

- Providing value-added snippets of information?

- Keeping the site fresh and up-to-date?

A moderate use of colour and graphics can greatly enhance the attractiveness of your site. But their over-use can make your site time-consuming to use. Some web sites offer the alternative of a text-only version, just as others wishing to attract an international clientele, offer alternative language versions. If you want to use video and sound, remember that some users may not have the facilities to take advantage of them.

Although the cost of disc space is very low, information overload for Web users is already a problem. Think of how *you* like to read and absorb new information, perhaps with plenty of white space on the page/screen, in clear, concise and simple-to-understand language. Keep things brief and to-the-point with no long, rambling sentences. Don't be like some web site producers who think that quantity not quality is the key.

7. Plan related hyperlinks and gateways

Hyperlinks will form the foundation of your site with links from one document to another. It is also useful to point users to other sites which might be of interest to them. These will usually be sites that give more information on a particular topic or cover a complementary activity to which you may want to refer. (See the example of Management Link in the previous section.)

8. Plan to get the customer involved

Enable your web site visitors to: offer comments, suggestions or criticisms; take part in product design or testing; get involved in interactive sessions for product or service improvement.

Remember that anything more demanding than straightforward e-mail replies requires fairly sophisticated design and pro-gramming.

9. Consider security issues

Unless you protect it, information that you put on the Web is for public consumption by a worldwide market. It is virtually impossible to follow and police what might happen to your information once it is downloaded to any of the 60+ million computers linked up, notwithstanding international laws on copyright.

If there are sections of your web site that you would wish to secure for some categories of user or customer only, then form a closed user group to which only password-holders are allowed access.

If you wish your web site to link to extremely sensitive information to which access must be even more strictly controlled, for example your customer database, then it is becoming standard practice to protect such information from abuse with a firewall ("mur coupe-feu"). A *firewall* is another computer through which all access traffic is routed and vetted. Anything that does not meet access criteria can be shut out.

10. Promote the site

Unless people know your address — your URL — they will find you in one of a number of ways:

- They will visit your site as a result of a hypertext link from another
- They will use one of the search engines to find you
- Word of mouth recommendation
- They will have seen some of your advertising
- It will be by chance.

It is important that the Search Engines pick up your site. Your Home Page is the principal page that search engines will use for indexing your site and therefore it needs to contain the important concepts and terms that people may use to find you. These may be apparent to the user or hidden away where only the search engines will find them.

Your web site will also need promotion through more traditional media such as business cards, marketing literature, company reports or press or media campaigns. Remember though that the Web is about marketing, so be wary about using one marketing medium to market another. The real trick to a successful web site is not how much you promote it but in the value that visitors / customers can derive from it. It will then promote itself.

In the mid 1990s, President Clinton declared that the Internet was going to turn into 'a global free-trade zone' which would provide a safe environment for people to do business. This was against the background of various forecasts, one of which put Internet turnover at some $1 trillion by the year 2010. Other forecasts have been less ambitious, but most agree that by the year 2001, the Internet will be handling up to $300 billion in gross turnover world-wide, with over $200 billion in the USA, and over $60 billion in Europe (Forrester Research).

Many business people, however, remain sceptical about buying and selling over the Internet, because:

- The Internet can still be a confusing arena for all but the informed and the patient. It can take time to find the information, or results, that you want. Some web sites contain time-consuming graphics to come through, and some have links that don't work because the 'site is still under development'. Over-congested networks can cause delays and, on occasions, overload can lead to breakdown.

- Early experimentation showed that consumers were reluctant to shop on the Internet. They could not try the goods out by seeing, touching, or tasting, and they missed the social aspect of actually 'being there'.

- Consumers have been hesitant to give their credit card number over the Web. The problem is one of knowing that the seller really is who they say they are, and that your credit card number is not disappearing into a black hole, or into the hands of a fraudster. Trading on the Web depends on the verification and authentication of buyer and seller.

- Not all items are suitable for selling on the Internet. It is far easier to sell information products and services than hard goods. This is due—in part—to the nature of distribution. At the moment, the Web is benefiting those industries which are information-rich like books, music and software, which don't rely on the sense of touch and feel, and which are closest to mail-order.

This picture, however, is changing rapidly because:

• The Web is becoming more professional with the presence of household names and with marketers waking up to the idea that marketing must be tailored to specific groups as in other media. More and more people are using the Internet and are becoming more comfortable with it. Consumers will get better at knowing which sites they want to visit and what they will find when they get there. Web sites are beginning to add value beyond what consumers can find in the terrestrial shopping world.

Figure 9: The Amazon Internet Bookshop claims to be the biggest bookshop in the world. This screen offers advice to those using the site for the first time, especially those with worries about paying over the Web.

• Telecommunications are improving and costs are falling as the Internet infrastructure develops. Internet2, with data transmission potential 1,000 times faster than at present, is already being trialled at American Universities.

• Financial institutions world-wide have invested heavily in electronic payment systems. Most major credit card companies in Europe and the USA, including VISA and MasterCard are working with software houses to finalise secure payment systems. The infrastructure for such trading is still expensive but prices will fall as more companies take it up and the banks recoup their investment.

- The Internet can offer greater efficiencies on traditional means of trading by offering a buying medium unconstrained by the barriers of time or place. If you can specify your own requirements for product modification, agree them, and negotiate over price and delivery all from your own back-yard, 24 hours a day, seven days a week, it is much quicker and cheaper for you and for the manufacturer.

Paying electronically

Progress towards full electronic commerce has been slowed by hackers who have broken the systems that promised confidentiality and security. Although these cases have been few and far between, they have nonetheless been rewarded by widespread publicity often out of all proportion to the actual seriousness of what happened.

E-cash

Many potential consumer transactions involve small and anonymous purchases, for example a newspaper or magazine, for which you would not normally use a credit card. For these small purchases, some innovative companies have been working with banks and software houses to devise a currency for the Internet—digital money—as safe and secure as the real thing.

An e-cash account works quite simply. Customers open an account with an e-bank, such as First Virtual, DigiCash, or CyberCash, store their e-cash ("monnaie électronique") on their hard disk or in the bank's computer and use a pass code to authorise payment of goods.

There are comparatively few takers as yet and most of those are the individuals and shops involved in the controlled trials. Perhaps people expect low-cost information to be free—especially on the Web—or they do not like to pay-as-you-go, even for small amounts. Other possible reasons for the slow take-up of e-cash is the failure to publicise such schemes, and consumers' continuing reluctance to shop online.

Credit Card Payments and Encryption

Encryption ("cryptage") is perhaps the most promising way of making credit card payments secure. It is certainly the one which has attracted the most publicity, and investment. Encryption is the term used for scrambling messages so that only the intended recipient can decode and read them.

Visa and MasterCard have collaborated on an encryption technology, Secure Electronic Transaction (SET), that promises to make credit card payments safer than they are in the real world. SET, it is claimed, offers virtually uncrackable encryption. It requires both sender and recipient to have software supplied by the card issuer to prove to each other that they are who they claim to be. SET then verifies that the retailer is qualified to take credit cards and shields the card numbers from the retailer, keeping them coded all the way to the bank, thus providing the security and authentication that buyer and seller require of each other.

An icon representing a golden key or golden padlock should appear in the bottom left of your browser screen. When this symbol is solid—not broken—it indicates that any credit card information supplied will be encrypted. Only the authorised merchant or bank will have the key to unlock the figures at the other end.

Figure 10: The icon representing an open padlock in a site that does not support encryption.

It is estimated that some 80% of European banks will offer a full Internet banking service by the year 2000, although electronic trading still needs the boost of public trust and confidence to carry it beyond the pioneer stage into widespread practice.

A Strategy for Buying and Selling on the Web

With a growing number of organizations demonstrating different ways and means of making money on the Web, and with banks on the point of assuring safe and secure payment transactions, how do we go about selling, and buying, on the Web?

- Find out about your customers' preferences for payment along with their buying habits. Find out whether or not they are gearing up for trading on the Web.
- Determine whether or not your products or services are suitable for electronic transactions and mail-order. If not, remember that many firms are winning business from

business@harrap.eng

unexpected quarters because their site offers a shop-window to customers who would normally not come across their products.

- Find out whether you can afford the infrastructure necessary for electronic trading. This is particularly important where individual sales are of low value. Keep an eye on these costs as they are likely to drop.

- Look at other sites. The end of the 1990s is witnessing a new wave of initiatives heralding the beginnings of electronic commerce. Innovative organizations are exploring new kinds of interactivity with customers, making sites which were fresh two years ago, now seem cumbersome and dated.

- If you decide to go down the trading route think about the tactics you will need to create a shopping community. Think about how you can reassure your customers that electronic transactions are safe. If there is any doubt, then perhaps you should think twice, or provide customers with a warning that it is better to pay via traditional methods.

- Talk to your bank and your Internet Service Provider about their plans for electronic trading and how they can help you. Without their support and advice, it is probably better to stick to a shop-window, whether selling or buying.

The laws and codes of practice laying down what you can and cannot do in the real world apply just as much to the Internet, even though they may be difficult to interpret and enforce. In particular, a company setting up a web site should examine legislation applying to misleading advertising, sellers' obligations, buyers' rights and the ownership of information. Depending on the sophistication of your site, the services of a lawyer may be appropriate.

Advertising and Selling

An organization putting information on the Web for marketing and advertising purposes has a duty to respect standard advertising practice, and ensure that the content of their information is accurate and up-to-date. This is because it is in their interests to make the Web a place where consumers can shop in confidence.

As a general rule, Web advertisements are subject to the laws and regulations of the country where the site is accessed. This can lead to liability under local law. Virgin Atlantic Airways was fined under United States advertising regulations for offering out-of-date price information on its Web site. In 1996, a US court held one Italian company to be infringing a US trademark, simply by offering access to its Web site to Americans.

The codes and standards of the Advertising Standards Authority (ASA) in the United Kingdom, and of the Bureau de Vérification de Publicité (BVP) in France, apply equally to the Web and to traditional media. They are not legally binding but most organizations which breach such codes are willing to toe the line when challenged. Further sanctions exist in the form of legislation, in the UK, with the *Control of Misleading Advertisements Regulations 1988*, which enables the Office of Fair Trading to take action against anyone publishing a misleading advertisement. As more and more organizations use the Web to advertise, the issue of regulations continues to be debated.

Consumer Protection

In the European Union, buyers are protected under the Brussels convention in dealings with companies based in other countries of the EU. Although the onus of proof is on the customer, a European Union citizen can take action in any EU country against a company situated in any other member state. Currently, anyone buying within the EU from a country outside it has no real consumer protection.

The European Distance Selling Directive, adopted by the European Commission in February 1997, is likely to come into effect before the year 2000. It will require all Web vendors to ensure that their terms and conditions for trading are easily accessible on screen. These terms and conditions will have to state under which country's legal jurisdiction the sale is made. Other information which must be provided will include:

- the seller's name and address

- detailed information about the product

- arrangements for delivery and payment

- time of delivery and what happens if delivery is late

- who bears the risk if the product is lost or damaged.

For some products – excluding information-rich products such as software or electronic magazines – the customer will have the right to withdraw from any sales contract within one week. If there is a risk of difficulty in meeting stated delivery terms, sellers may be advised to make it clear on the web site that the company is not making an offer to supply goods, but rather an invitation to the customer to make an offer to purchase.

Taxation

Tax laws are based on geography – where the company is located, or doing business, and on the products and services being sold. But the Internet is changing one's conception of geography – it transcends space and time – and one's notion of a product or service – no longer something you can always touch and feel.

Tax laws are also based on a distinction between goods and services. But if the Internet is also the medium for delivering the product, such as downloading a film, music or a book, then distinctions between goods and services are not so easy to apply.

The problem intensifies with cross-border trade and differing applications of purchase or value added tax.

At present, however, both EU and US officials believe that the Internet should be a customs-free zone. If the World Trade Organization agrees, all levies on electronic transmissions will disappear.

Alternatively a 'bit tax', under which each electronic transmission—fax, phone call, e-mail—is logged and taxed, might be the answer. A bit tax, applying to each digital unit sent over the Internet, irrespective of its content, would mean a shift away from value-added tax to one based purely on the quantity of data transmitted.

Copyright

Technological developments have now far outstripped the capacity of copyright legislation to protect intellectual property. This issue continues to stretch the legislative bodies of the EU and of the US Senate as the focus of copyright embraces document transmission as well as reproduction.

As soon as any intellectual property—be it text, images, graphs, video or music—is available through the Internet, then any monetary value attached to it is at risk. When a customer pays for and receives a document on the Internet, it is only copyright law that stands in the way of instant reproduction or modification. An electronic document can be re-transmitted to hundreds or thousands of others via e-mail or a web site. Copyright transgressions are hard enough to monitor and control in the real world; on the Internet, it is virtually impossible to enforce copyright law without relying on 'good citizenship' to help the aggrieved party.

Although we tend to think of publishing as being about material published in books and magazines, don't take too narrow a view. Anyone who sends an e-mail or puts information on a web site can be considered to be publishing; so, if it's not your information, you should not use it without permission.

Some have said that the Internet will bring about a massive change to copyright legislation, others that the force of copyright itself will influence the nature of business on the Internet. It is not yet certain what the outcome will be.

Privacy of the Individual

While copyright protects others' intellectual property, the Data Protection Act came into force in the UK in 1984 to provide rights to people about whom personal information is held on others' computers (although the Act is being amended to include personal information held *in all forms*, not just that held on computer). The Act requires those who record and use data about individuals to be open about that use and follow practice laid down by the Data Protection Registrar. In 1998, a European Directive on Data Protection reinforced a personal information safeguards throughout the EU. One of the impacts will be to apply data protection principles to information being transferred outside the EU, even within the same organization.

One of the great advantages of the Web is that site owners can track what customers look at, buy or reject. This is possible because when you visit an Internet site, you leave your own Internet address as a calling-card. This is known as address logging, and some view it as an invasion of privacy. It is, however, fundamental to the way the Internet works; a visitor's domain name has to be known by the host site, otherwise it would not know where to direct any information requested. Information can also be collected in other ways, including visitor registration forms, and, more controversially, cookies.

A *cookie* is a piece of information that a web site can send out which can be unknowingly stored on your hard drive. It can pick up information on your Internet habits and activities and be collected by the web site sender at a later date. Some browsers can be configured to alert you to the arrival of a cookie and there are also programs—such as Cookie Crusher and Cookie Crumbler—which will automatically reject all cookies. Some web site owners announce that theirs is a 'cookie-free' site.

A Framework for Global Electronic Commerce

In July 1997 in a proposal called 'A Framework for Global Electronic Commerce', President Clinton outlined the basic rules for international electronic commerce, including making the Internet a duty-free, untaxed zone for electronic buying and selling. The framework—tantamount to a written constitution for the Internet—consists of five principles and nine issues.

Principles

1. The private sector should lead.

2. Governments should avoid undue restrictions on electronic commerce.

3. Where governmental involvement is needed, its aim should be to support and enforce a predictable, minimalist, consistent and simple legal environment for commerce.

4. Governments should recognise the unique qualities of the Internet.

5. Electronic commerce over the Internet should be facilitated on a global basis.

Issues

1. Customs and taxation

2. Electronic payment systems

3. 'Uniform Commercial Code' for electronic commerce

4. Intellectual property protection

5. Privacy

6. Security

7. Telecommunications infrastructure and information technology

8. Content: Advertising and Fraud

9. Technical standards.

The full recommendations are to be found in A Framework for Global Electronic Commerce, The White House, July 1, 1997, at:

> http://www.ecommerce.gov.framewrk.htm

6: DEVELOPING AN INTERNET STRATEGY

Developing a strategy for the Internet means assessing the Internet's weaknesses and opportunities, working out what you want to achieve and how best to tackle it, while appraising your own strengths and weaknesses. Strategic management has more do with how you achieve a vision for the future, than sticking to the present or past.

The Internet – its weaknesses

What we want to achieve will depend very much on the view we have formed of the Internet and on exactly what kind of prospects it holds for us.

The number of new users, the number of new web pages, and spending on products and services all continue to grow at rates in excess of 100% per annum.

For many people, however, the Internet is at worst a non-event, shrouded in mystery, and at best characterized by anarchy and chaos. They point to:

- unregulated anarchy which allows pornography to side by side with respectable information

- information clutter and overload dominated by trivia

- slow response times with delays at popular access points

- much publicized breakdowns because of growing network congestion

- a rate of innovation which seems too rapid for most to keep up with

- a lack of hard evidence that money can be made from the Internet

- a preference for TV – cable or satellite – as a more digestible alternative to the inconsistencies and difficulties of the Web.

The Internet – its opportunities

Such a scenario ignores many influences and signs of progress, such as:

1. The continual growth and use of the Internet in all parts of the world.

2. Continuing technological developments, such as Internet2, offering solutions to business questions.

3. The investment made by major banks and software houses to develop the commercial side of the Web.

4. Early commercial successes that many organizations have enjoyed. The promotion, pump-priming and legislative efforts of national governments and two of the major trading powers – the EU and the US. The entrepreneurial and commercial spirit which will not accept yesterday's way of doing things as valid for tomorrow.

Furthermore, the positive scenario assumes that the Internet will become a reliable platform for conducting business as:

- Consumer purchasing confidence spreads as a result of secure payment systems.

- Adequate and effective protection is given to copyright information.

- Standards emerge from consortia of telecomms, software and trading companies.

- A mix of government subsidy, telecomms investment and consumer payment begins to pipe high performance telecommunications capability into the home and office.

- Private networks, which are more secure and robust, link up to the Internet for those customers willing to pay for premium services.

- Affordable market-based pricing for access and usage emerges.

- The Internet establishes its own identity—or identities—and becomes as integrated in social and business life as the Press and TV.

Models for business

There are currently a number of loose business models in evidence

business@harrap.eng

for the Internet:

1. The *Communications* Model – using the Internet primarily to allow greater flexibility and efficiency through e-mail.

2. The *Advertising* Model – using the organization's web site as a shop window, and paying for advertising banners on other sites and search engines.

3. The *Subscription* Model – offering unlimited access to a service or product, for example, a newspaper, magazine or current awareness updating service in return for payment of an annual sum. This third alternative assumes that people will pay for information on the Web. As yet, they generally seem reluctant to do so, however.

4. The *Niche Marketing* Model – packaging personalized information, news and entertainment services. Here, as a superior alternative to TV, the Web provides an experience for selected groups of people—communities—through its interactive, two-way capability.

5. The *Department Store* Model – setting up as a seller on the Web. This option sees the major obstacles to electronic commerce overcome, and confidence in online buying and selling widespread.

Ten strategic principles

1. Understand how the Internet works and what its potential is by experimenting with it, reading about it and discussing it with others.

2. Consider how the Internet can benefit your customers and keep your business moving forward. This means having a full understanding of your business and what it is trying to achieve.

3. Understand your audience—the profile of your best prospect is the profile of your best customer. Keep an eye on customer buying habits and the level of interactivity they are likely to want. Think about what customers most want to know about your organization and what you most want to know about them. Think about how the Internet can add value to your services and products. This might lie in better information provision, alternative methods of distribution or more customization for individuals and groups.

4. Obtain commitment from senior management and involvement and interest from as many people as possible. You won't get anywhere by making the Internet a sideline that only a few know about and contribute to. Staff need time to feel their way and become familiar with the way the Internet works. Recognise that you will need technical, design and legal expertise. Decide how much resource you can, or are prepared, to put into the Internet.

5. Start small – getting started is more important than getting it perfect straightaway. Go for specific objectives. Look for early wins but not quick fixes. Identify who can help to achieve early success which demonstrates that change is working.

6. Expect your web site to be a cost-centre. Don't just look for sales. Value also those activities which lead indirectly to sales, such as those which generate interest and enquiries from prospective clients.

7. Align and integrate your Internet activities with all the others you perform in the real world for the benefit of customers and staff alike.

8. Think about control policies and procedures which clarify:

• Who may access the Web and who may not, and why.

• What information may be imported from the Web into the organization's systems.

• Who has ownership and responsibility for information on the Web.

9. Monitor the effects of your Internet strategy. Look at the levels of e-mail and Web activity in the organization, the cost-savings in staff-time, direct or indirect income, and customer reaction.

10. Keep your Internet services adaptable, changing and moving forward. This means taking risks, keeping up with new technological developments and exploring new possibilities.

E-MAIL

1. Writing e-mails

- E-mail addresses are made up of two parts, the first being the user's name and the second being the domain name. The two parts are separated by the symbol @ (pronounced "arrobase" in French). It is important to type the exact address – get a single character wrong and the e-mail will not get through.

- Because of the nature of the medium, e-mails are not subject to the formal code of letter-writing that is prevalent in French.

- E-mail is becoming more and more widely used in the French working environment, although it is probably not yet as established a method of business correspondence as it is in English.

- E-mails in French are often written in a slightly less telegraphic style than tends to be the case in English, this being mainly due to the fact that French contains fewer of the abbreviated forms that characterize so much of this type of communication in English. Endings are usually rather informal.

- The same rules of "netiquette" apply as in English, so avoid typing entire words in capital letters as this is equivalent to shouting.

- Note that in the model e-mail below, the headings are in English as most French firms use American-manufactured software.

```
Vincent Guérin, 09:46 08/01/99, Réunion d'équipe          _ □ ×
                        Subject:  Réunion d'équipe

To: Monique Hébrard
From: Vincent Guérin <vguérin@balthazar.com.fr>
Subject: Réunion d'équipe
Cc: Jérôme Lemarchand, Stéphanie Nadeau, Alain Rocard


Monique -

Je propose qu'on se réunisse tous cette semaine (mercredi matin à 9h de préférence)
pour faire le point sur l'état actuel du projet. Il faut discuter des points suivants
avant notre réunion avec nos partenaires de Dublin la semaine prochaine:

(1) Budget
(2) Prévisions de vente 1999-2000
(3) Futurs projets éventuels de coédition
Si vous avez d'autres suggestions, merci de me les faire savoir dès que possible.


Cordialement
Vincent
```

2. Abbreviations and acronyms

Below is a list of French abbreviations which are used in e-mail correspondence and in newsgroups. These abbreviations should only be used when you are sure that the person to whom you are sending the message understands what they mean. Some are familiar in register (labelled *Fam*) and therefore should only be used in casual correspondence with friends or very close colleagues.

Note that because English is the main language of the Internet, English abbreviations (see section in French supplement) are much more well established than French ones.

A+ *Fam*	à plus tard (see you/talk to you etc later)	
actu *Fam*	actualités (news, current affairs)	
alld	allemand (German)	
alp *Fam*	à la prochaine (see you!; until we're next in touch!)	
ama *Fam*	à mon avis (in my opinion)	
amha *Fam*	à mon humble avis (in my humble opinion)	
angl	anglais (English)	
bcp *Fam*	beaucoup (a lot; many)	
BAL	boîte à lettres (mailbox)	
B.D.	base de données (database)	
cad	c'est à dire (that is)	
dc	donc (then, therefore)	
doc.	documents (documents, documentation)	
Doss	dossier (file)	
ds	dans (in)	
envoy.	envoyer (please send)	
err	erreur (error)	
esp	espagnol (Spanish)	
ex.	exemple (example)	
fr	franais (French)	
impr.	impression/imprimer/imprimante (printout; print; printer)	
info *Fam*	information	
K7 *Fam*	cassette	
Ltr	lettre (letter)	
m	même (even; same)	
Mdr *Fam*	mort de rire (hilarious)	
MMS *Fam*	mes meilleurs souvenirs (Best regards)	
nvx	nouveaux (new)	
p	pour (for)	
pb, pbm	problème (problem)	

pr	pour (for)
quoi 2/9 *Fam*	quoi de neuf? (what's new?)
RAS *Fam*	rien à signaler (nothing to report)
stp	s'il te plaît (please)
suiv.	suivant (following)
svp	s'il vous plaît (please)
svt	souvent (often)
urgt	urgent
we	weekend

3. Smileys

Smileys are becoming more and more a feature of e-mail correspondence: again, as with abbreviations, they are probably used more in English than in French, but it is worth illustrating some of the most common ones here. It must be remembered of course that these symbols should only ever appear in the context of casual correspondence.

:-)	Happy; I'm making a joke
:-))	Very happy
:-D	Laughing out loud
:-(	Unhappy
:-((	Very unhappy
:'-(	Crying
:-II	Angry
:-C	Extremely unhappy
:-O	Very surprised; shocked
:-@	Shouting
;-)	Winking
:-I	Frowning
(:-)	Bald
:-)>	Man with a beard
:-)X	Man with a bow-tie
<I-)	Chinaman
3:-)	Cow
8-)	Person wearing glasses
I-)	Sleeping
:-i	Smoking
:-?	Smoking a pipe
:-/	Sceptical
CI:-)	Man wearing a bowler hat
d:-)	Person wearing a cap
[:-)	Person wearing headphones
I-O	Yawning
:-*	Kiss